The *COMPLETE* Effect and HLSL Guide

Sebastien St-Laurent

PUBLISHED BY
Paradoxal Press
9981 Avondale Rd. NE
Redmond, WA 98052
Unites States of America
http://www.ParadoxalPress.com
info@ParadoxalPress.com

Educational facilities, companies, and organizations interested in multiple copies or licensing of this book should contact the publisher for quantity discount information. Training manuals, CD-ROMs, and portions of this book can be tailored for specific needs.

ISBN-10: 0-9766132-1-2
ISBN-13: 978-0-9766132-1-3

Library of Congress Control Number: 2005902999

Printed in the United States of America

President, Paradoxal Press:	Sebastien St-Laurent
Copy Editor:	Dawn Snyder
Technical Reviewer:	Wolfgang Engel
Interior Layout:	Sebastien St-Laurent
Cover Designer:	Sebastien St-Laurent
Indexer:	Dawn Snyder
Proofreader	
Fiction Acquisition:	Nicole St-Laurent

To my wife, Nicole, for all her love and support while writing this book.

To my friends, co-workers and family for their understanding and support.

To my mother, Lina, another victim of cancer. I will miss dearly!

Acknowledgments

First and foremost, I want to thank my wife Nicole for all of her support throughout this project. Writing a book can be a major undertaking, self-publishing it is of another order of magnitude. Without her help and love, I would never have completed this one or might have lost my sanity doing so. I love you!

Wolfgang Engel and Steve Lacey also deserve special mention for their efforts as technical editors for this book. Their help proved invaluable in making sure I was in line and ensuring this book was the best possible book it could be. I also want to send my thanks to the kind people at NVIDIA, ATI Technologies and Microsoft for their technical information, which helped greatly with this production.

About the Author

Sebastien St-Laurent has been programming games professionally for several years, working on titles for the Xbox, PlayStation 2, GameCube, and PC. He started in the video game industry while studying computer engineering at Sherbrooke University in Sherbrooke, Quebec. By interning in a small company called Future Endeavors during his college years, he got into the industry and stood out in the line of graphics engineering.

After graduating from college, he moved to California to work full-time with Z-Axis as lead Xbox engineer, where he worked on several titles including the Dave Mirra Freestyle BMX series. Currently, he is a graphics engineer at the Microsoft Corporation, where he is working within the Microsoft Game Studios.

Having already published a book "*Shaders for Game Programmers and Artists*"; he is now a renowned authority in computer graphics and video game development.

Introduction

After completing my first book, *Shaders for Game Programmers and Artists*, in the spring of 2004 I immediately started thinking about what my next book would be about. Although I did take the summer off to relax and send quality time with my wife, I still had several ideas going through my head. Being a graphics engineer, it is obvious that topics such as shaders are at the core of my every day work but wanted to write something a little different from my previous book while remaining in the scope of things I know best.

After some serious thinking and drawing from my experience as a software developer, I started looking at some of the issues that developers are faced when writing 3D graphic applications today. When developing games on the Xbox platform, shader development was straightforward since the platform was fixed and everybody was running the same hardware. However, I came to new realizations when I start working on a larger scale PC game. When developing a game for a platform such as the PC, you want to take advantage of the newest rendering technologies while ensuring support on a wide range of hardware configurations. It makes sense, not everybody can just go out and spend 500$ every six month for the latest and greatest video card.

This wide range of possible configuration itself leads to the multiplication of shaders. It does make sense when you think about it, sure you want to render nice reflective water on the latest hardware, but you still need to be able to function properly on less advanced video card. This multiplication of shaders leads to nightmares for the developers, having to juggle a multitude of shaders. In addition, how can you determine which shader to use based on the user's hardware configuration. To make matters worse, the latest shader technologies are complex and don't lend themselves well to being written by hand in assembly instructions.

With all these difficulties in mind, Microsoft has introduced the High-Level Shader Language (HLSL) and the effect framework. Both aimed at facilitating the task of shader development and management in addition to creating a standardized art pipeline making it easier for artists to model and take advantage of shaders at every step of the artistic process.

However, at this point in time, it seems like many developers are not aware of the power of this technology and this is why I've set out to write this book. My goal is to not only write a book teaching the basics of writing shaders in HLSL and using the effect framework but also offer a complete reference manual covering this small component of DirectX from A to Z.

Who Should Read This Book

The topic of *The Complete Effect and HLSL Guide* is shader development and management, and therefore it is written for any developers who have some interest in being efficient at using shaders within their applications and focus their time and efforts on more important tasks. Because this book is written as both a teaching and reference manual, it is bound to be of interest to everybody from hobbyist programmers to professional developers.

Finally, with the approach taken throughout this book, *The Complete Effect and HLSL Guide* can also be a valuable asset in the classroom where real-time graphics have taken an even more important place in the computer science curriculum.

What We Will and Won't Cover

The topic of *The Complete Effect and HLSL Guide* is shader development and management, and it is all I will focus on. Since the intent of this book is being both a teaching guide as well as a reference manual, I will be thorough into covering most topics of the HLSL language and the effect framework but will not focus on specific shaders and rendering techniques. The following list summarizes some of the topics covered throughout this book:

- Introduction to both the HLSL shading language as well as the effect framework which are both part of the latest DirectX SDK.
- In depth coverage of the HLSL language syntax, grammar and its use.
- Coverage of all the main components of the effect framework in addition to putting all the pieces of the puzzle together allowing you to develop a shader management framework.

Support

A website is maintained at **http://www.ParadoxalPress.com** that will be used to provide support for this book. This site will be updated regularly to post corrections and updated information as needed. Be sure to check it regularly.

And if you have any questions of feedback or questions in regards to this book, feel free to contact me, Sebastien St-Laurent at <u>sebastien.st.laurent@gmail.com</u>.

Table Of Contents

Chaptrer 1
Shaders and the HLSL Language

Chapter 2
The HLSL Shading Language

Chapter 3
Functions,Nothing but Functions

Chapter 4
Shader Examples

Chapter 5
The Effect File Format

Chapter 6
Semantics and Annotations

Chapter 7
Shader Optimizations and Shortcuts

Chapter 8
Effect Framework Overview

Chapter 9
The Effect

Chapter 10
Sharing Parameters

Chapter 11
Effect State Manager

Chapter 12
Effect Compiler and Include Manager

Appendix A
Shader Assembly Instruction Reference

Appendix B
HLSL Intrinsic Function Reference

<u>Appendix C</u>
<u>Standard Semantics and Annotations</u>

Appendix D
Effect File and HLSL Grammar

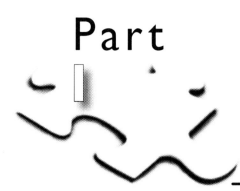

Part

The HLSL Shading Language

Welcome to *The Complete Effect and HLSL Guide*. The title of the book is very much self-explanatory; together we will explore the use of the DirectX effect framework and the HLSL (High-Level Shading Language) shading language throughout the chapters of this book. You will learn how to use and be efficient with the HLSL shader language. In addition, I will teach you how the effect framework, which comes as a part of the DirectX SDK, can be used to facilitate the integration of shaders within your applications. Whether you are developing 3D applications or video games, the increase in shader complexity and the need for backward compatibility make the effect framework a prime choice for the integration and management of shaders.

The goal behind this book is dual. First, it serves as a learning book, teaching you the insights of HLSL and the effect framework. More importantly, however, this book serves as a reference manual, containing all the necessary information not included in the DirectX documentation. So, let's not waste time and get to it!

The first part of the book will focus on the HLSL shader language, teaching you its syntax and use. The second part of this book will focus on the effect framework, explaining how it can simplify the management of shaders for your application. Let's take an in-depth look at the HLSL shading language.

Chapter

Shaders and the HLSL Language

Shader technology has made huge leaps over the last few years. In this chapter, I will go over some of the basic syntax and use of the HLSL shading language. To make the understanding of this technology easier, I have broken up the description of the HLSL syntax over several chapters, each focusing on specific components of the shading language. This chapter will go over the general syntax and overview a few of the fundamentals. The following chapters will go into more details of specific components.

Before I dive into the syntax of HLSL, I will discuss some of the prerequisites for this book and go over a little bit of the history of the HLSL shader language and the effect framework.

Prerequisites

Although this book intends to teach you about HLSL and the effect framework, it has no intention of teaching you the basics of DirectX and Direct3D. Because of this, one of the important prerequisites for this book is that you have a basic understanding of the DirectX API and a basic background in 3D rendering and technologies. All of this is easy to learn even if you are new to 3D graphics!

Beyond the intellectual requirements, here is a basic list of software and hardware needs to use the contents of this book:

- DirectX 9.0 Summer 2004 Update SDK (included on the CD).
- Windows 2000 (with service pack 2) or Windows XP (Home or Professional) operating system.
- Pentium 3 class or better processor.
- At least 256 MB of RAM.
- A high-end 3D graphics card. Although any 3D capable video card would do, I recommend a 2.0 or 3.0 shader model compatible card if you want to try out all the aspects of shader programming.
- And of course, the latest drivers for your video card.

With those prerequisites in mind, you will be able to start exploring and developing the shaders and taking advantage of the effect framework. Now you know what you need to take advantage of this book. Let's go over a little bit of history about shaders and the effect framework.

A Little Bit of History...

Computer graphics and its associated hardware have made significant technological leaps since the introduction of the first consumer level 3D hardware accelerated graphics card, the 3Dfx, in 1995. This card had limited rendering capabilities but finally allowed developers break new grounds and move away from software only solutions. This finally made real-time 3D graphics and games a true reality.

Since then, the following generations of hardware improved significantly on their performance and features. They were still bound, however, by a limited fixed-pipeline architecture, which restricted developers to a constrained set of states that were combined to produce the final output.

The limited functionality of the fixed-pipeline architecture restricted developers in what they could create. This generally resulted in synthetic-looking graphics. At the other end of the spectrum, high-end software-rendering architectures used for movie CG had something that allowed them to go much farther. RenderMan is a shading language developed by Pixar Animation Studios. The purpose was to allow artists and graphic programmers to fully control the rendering result by using a simple, yet powerful programming language. RenderMan allowed creating high quality, photorealistic and non-photorealistic graphics used in many of today's movies, including Toy Story and A Bug's Life.

With the evolution of processor chip making and the increased processing power it brought along came the natural extension of the RenderMan idea to the consumer level graphics hardware. With the release of DirectX 8.0 came the introduction of vertex and pixel shader version 1.0 and 1.1. Although the standard came with limited flexibility and omitted some features such as flow control, it was the first step in giving developers and artists the flexibility needed to produce the stunning and realistic graphics they had always dreamed. Consumer video cards could finally produce graphics that could compete with the renderings produced by Hollywood's movie studios.

During the following few years, graphics hardware and 3D APIs made giant leaps forward in functionality and performance, even shattering Moore's law with respect to technological advancement rate. With the introduction of the DirectX 9.0 SDK and the latest generations of graphics hardware such as the GeForce FX series from NVIDIA and Radeon 9800 series from ATI Technologies, came Vertex and Pixel shader version 2.0 and 2.x. The shader version 3.x was soon to follow.

Note

> The term Moore's Law came from an observation made in 1965 by Gordon Moore, co-founder of Intel, which the number of transistors per square inch had doubled every year since the introduction of the integrated circuit. He also predicted that this trend would continue for at least a few decades, which turned out true so far. Also, since the transistor density relates with the performance of integrated circuits, Moore's Law is often cited as a prediction of future hardware performance increases.

This new shader model brings flexibility never before available to real-time graphic application developers. At the same time, however, most shaders were developed in a low-level language similar to assembly language on a computer. This also meant that as a shader developer, you had to manage registers, variable allocations and optimization in the same way as developers had to do it when programming assembly language on computers. The complexity of the 2.0 and 3.0 shader models added to the headache of developers since different video cards can have different amounts of registers and variables, and might even perform differently with similar instructions.

In an effort to simplify the task and give more optimization freedom to the hardware developers, the Microsoft Corporation introduced the High-Level Shading Language (HLSL) to DirectX version 9.0. This language, similar to a high-level language such as C or C++, allows developers to focus on the task the shader wishes to perform rather than logistics such as determining which registers to use and which combination of instructions is best for a specific card or shader version.

Before I go into what the HLSL language can do for you and how you can use it, let's go over some of the functionality that is given by the different shader versions. Let's face it; before you can write shader, you need to know what the hardware is capable of in the first place. Having a high-level language doesn't make the restrictions of a specific piece of hardware go away but rather hides it from you.

Vertex and Pixel Shader Pipelines and Capabilities

Vertex and pixel shader model 2.0 bring many new significant improvements to the language since the first introduction of version 1.0 and 1.1 with DirectX 8.0. Because of the recent release of DirectX 9.0 and the release of vertex and pixel shader 2.0 compliant video cards, this book will focus mostly on using shaders based on this technology.

Note

Although that at the time of this writing, 3.0 shader model cards are only starting to surface, their use is still limited. Although I will explain some of the specifics of 3.0 hardware, I have decided to stick with 2.0 shaders and below for most examples within this book.

Since I assume you already have a basic knowledge of 3D and basic shaders, let's start by going over the significant changes introduced by the second generation of shader languages over their legacy counterparts.

Vertex Shader 2.0 and 2.x includes the following improvements over their 1.x counterpart:

- Support for integer and boolean data types and proper setup instructions.
- Increased number of temporary and constant registers.
- Maximum instruction count allowable for a program has increased. Giving developers more flexibility (the minimum required by the standard has gone from 128 to 256 but each hardware implementation can support more).
- Many new macro instructions allowing complex operations such as sine/cosine, absolute and power.
- Support for flow control instruction such as loops and conditionals.

The following list outlines Pixel Shader 2.0 and 2.x improvements from the 1.x model:

- Support for extended 32-bit precision floating-point calculations.
- Support for arbitrary swizzling and masking of register components.
- Increase in the number of available constant and temporary registers.
- Significant increase of the minimum instruction card allowed by the standard from 8 to 64 arithmetic and 32 texture instructions. Pixel shader 2.x allows even more instructions by default and allows the hardware to go beyond the standard's minimum requirements.
- Support for integer and boolean constants, loop counters and predicate registers.
- Support for dynamic flow control including looping and branching.
- Gradient instructions allowing a shader to discover the derivate of any input register.

With this rich set of improvements, developers are now free to set their creativity loose and create stunning effects. At this point, it is probably good to do an overview of their architecture to give you a better understanding of how the information flows throughout the graphics hardware.

When rendering 3D graphics, geometric information is passed to the graphics hardware through the use of a rendering API such as Direct3D. Once this information is received by the hardware, it invokes the vertex shader for every vertex in your mesh. Figure 1.1 includes the functional diagram for a vertex shader 2.0 implementation as dictated by the specifications.

As you can see from Figure 1.1, vertices come in from a stream that is supplied by the developer through the 3D rendering API. The stream contains all the information needed to properly render the geometry such as positions, colors and texture coordinates. As the information comes in, it is put into the proper input registers, $v0$ to $v15$, for use by the vertex shader program. The vertex shader program then has access to many other registers to complete its task. Constant registers are read-only registers which must be set ahead of time and are used to carry static information to the shader. Under the vertex shader 2.0 standard, constant registers are vectors and can be floating-point numbers, integer values or boolean values. Take note that registers within the vertex shader, are all stored as a 4 component vector where you can process each component in parallel or individually by using swizzling and masking.

On the right side of Figure 1.1, are the *Temporary Registers,* which are used to store intermediate results generated by the vertex shader. Obviously, because of their temporary nature, you can both write and read from those registers. Take note of the registers named $a0$ and aL, which are counter registers for indexed addressing and for keeping track of loops. Also keep in mind that because HLSL is a high-level shading language, you will not need to take care of register allocation. It will happen transparently as the shader is compiled to its final form.

With access to the *Input Registers*, *Temporary Registers* and *Constant Registers*, the vertex shader program is now free to process the incoming vertices and manipulate them in whichever way the developer sees fit. Once the processing is complete, it must pass the results to the final *Output Registers*. The most important one is $oPos$, which needs to contain the final screen space projected position for the vertex. The other registers carry information such as colors and the final texture coordinates.

Once the vertex shader has done its job, the information is then passed along to the rasterizer. This part of the hardware takes care of deciding the screen pixel coverage of each polygon. It also takes care of other rendering tasks such vertex information interpolation and occlusion which helps reduce the overall work needed by the hardware. Once the rasterizer has determined the pixel coverage, the pixel shader is invoked for each screen pixel drawn. Figure 1.2 includes the functional diagram for the pixel shader architecture.

As you can see from the diagram in Figure 1.2, the hardware sends the pixels it calculates through the input *Color* and *Texture Registers*. Those values are based on the perspective interpolation of the values defined through the vertex shader. Registers $v0$ and $v1$ are meant to be the interpolated diffuse and specular lighting components. The registers $t0$ to tN carry interpolated texture lookup coordinates. Finally, the registers $s0$ to sN point to the textures which the pixel shader will sample

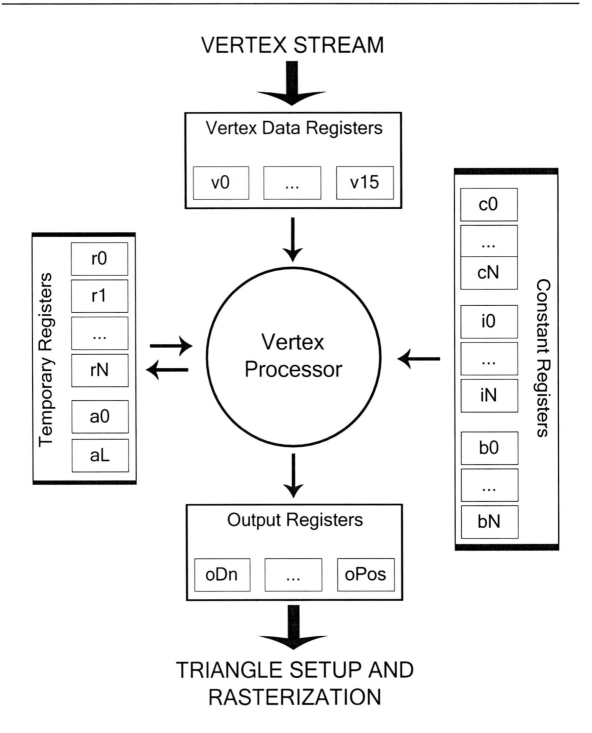

Figure 1.1: Functional diagram for the vertex shader hardware architecture.

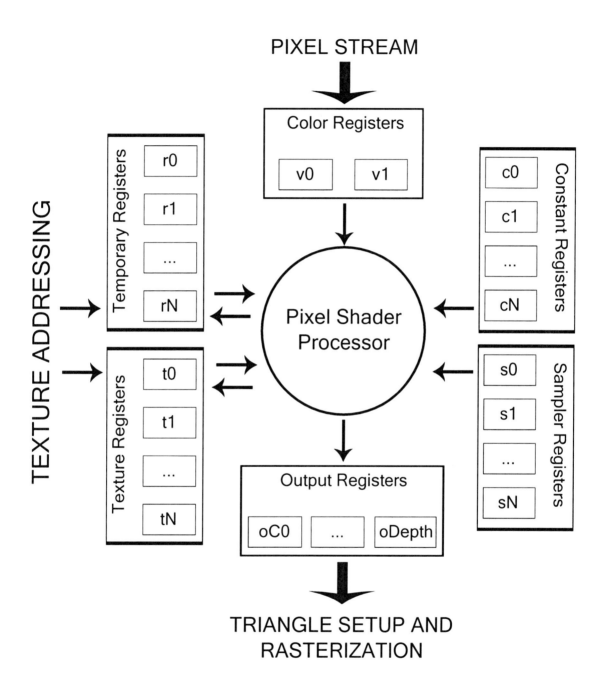

Figure 1.2: Functional diagram for the pixel shader hardware architecture.

during the processing of the pixel. Although those registers have clear semantics, they can be used to carry any information from the vertex shader onto the pixel shader.

The *Constant Registers*, c0 to cN, can only be read and are setup ahead of time by the developer with values useful to the shader. Finally, the *Temporary Registers*, r0 to rN, are read/write and keep track of intermediate results during the processing of the pixel. When using HLSL, all register usage and allocation is done automatically and is transparent to the user.

Most registers in pixel shaders, with exception to some addressing registers and loop counters, are vectors comprised of four floating-point values. The advantage of the vector architecture is that it allows processing of multiple values at the same time. By default, all floating-point values are processed as 32-bit precision floating-point numbers. The pixel shader specification allows processing of 16-bit precision values, which can be enabled by special instructions. On certain hardware implementations, the use of 16-bit floating-point arithmetic can be significantly faster.

Once the pixel has gone through the pixel shader, the output information is then used to blend the final result onto your frame buffer which is then presented on your computer screen.

Keep in mind that this is a simplified survey of the rendering architecture and much more happens behind the scenes. This architecture may also vary slightly from one hardware implementation to another; however, the standard does guarantee that for two different implementations with the same capabilities, the final output must be the same.

The High-Level Shading Language

Because of the increased complexity of the 2.0 and 3.0 shader models, it became increasingly tedious for developers to be efficient at developing shaders. The shader instruction set becoming more closely related to instruction sets found on general processors, it made sense to consider developing a high-level language to simplify and abstract the development of shader. This is where the High-Level Shading Language (HLSL) comes in to play. This language was developed by the Microsoft Corporation as a way to abstract shaders and let developers focus on the more important task of shader design rather than the fine grain details of register allocation and instruction optimization.

As with any high-level language, HLSL is defined by a set of syntax rules, reserved words and operands. In this section, I will go over its general syntax briefly. Do not worry, as I will go into the specific details of some of the components and give specific examples in later chapters.

Reserved Words

As with any programming language, it is comprised of identifiers and keywords. HLSL is no exception to this rule and this also implies that there is a set of keywords, defined for the purpose of the language with special meaning and thus cannot be used by your code. The first important category language elements are the keywords. They are defined as reserved identifiers used to represent constant values to simply control the behavior of your code. Table 1-1 below summarizes all the HLSL keywords along with a brief description of its meaning.

Table 1-1 HLSL Keywords

Keyword	Definition
asm	This keyword is case insensitive and is used to allow the manual insertion of shader assembly instruction inside a shader. The syntax for this instruction is as follow: `asm{ /* assembly instructions */ }`
asm_fragment	Reserved for future use.
bool	This keyword is used to identify data of boolean type. See Chapter 2 for more information on data types.
column_major	This keyword is used in conjunction with matrices to indicate that the data is presented in a column major form.
compile	This keyword is used when declaring vertex or pixel fragments (or shaders), indicating with which profile to compile the fragment.. This keyword is to be used when assigning a shader directly to the vertex or pixel shader effect state.
compile_frgment	This keyword is used when declaring vertex or pixel fragments (or shaders), indicating with which profile to compile the fragment.
const	This keyword is used to define a constant variable.
discard	This keyword is used within a fragment shader to cancel rendering of the current pixel.
decl	This keyword is case insensitive and is used in addition to the `asm` keyword to define constant register values for assembly defined shaders.
do	This keyword is in combination with the `while` keyword to define conditional do-while loops.
double	This keyword is to identify data of the double precision floating-point type. See Chapter 2 for more information on data types.
else	This keyword is used in combination with the `if` keyword to define conditional if-else statements.
extern	This keyword is used within variable declarations to indicate that this variable can be accessed from outside the effect. See Chapter 2 for more information on data types.
false	This keyword is the false constant value for the boolean data type. See Chapter 2 for more information on data types.

Table 1-1 HLSL Keywords

Keyword	Definition
float	This keyword is to identify data of the single precision floating-point type. See Chapter 2 for more information on data types.
for	This keyword is used to define loop statements.
half	This keyword is to identify data of the half precision floating-point type. See Chapter 2 for more information on data types.
if	This keyword is used to define if-else conditional statements.
in	This keyword is used to specify that a function parameter is for input only. See Chapter 3 for more information on functions.
inline	This keyword is used to hint to the compiler that a function is to be inlined. See Chapter 3 for more information on functions.
inout	This keyword is used to specify that a function parameter is for both input and output. See Chapter 3 for more information on functions.
int	This keyword is used to define data of the integer type. See Chapter 2 for more information on data types.
matrix	This keyword is used to identify data of the matrix type. See Chapter 2 for more information on data types.
out	This keyword is used to specify that a function parameter is for output only. See Chapter 3 for more information on functions.
pass	This keyword is case insensitive and is used to define multiple passes within multipass effect. Note that this keyword relates more closely to effect files and will be discussed in Part II of this book.
pixelfragment	This keyword is used to define a pixel fragment (or shader).
return	This keyword is used to return values from a function. See Chapter 3 for more information on functions.
register	This keyword is used to pre-reserve registers for use as constants.
row_major	This keyword is used in conjunction with matrices to indicate that the data is presented in a row major form.
sampler	This keyword is to represent the sampler data type. Samplers are used to represent a combination of texture and texturing attributes (such as filtering). See Chapter 2 for more information on data types.
sampler1D	This keyword is similar to the sampler keyword but is used to represent a sampler to a 1D texture. See Chapter 2 for more information on data types.

Table 1-1 HLSL Keywords

Keyword	Definition
sampler2D	This keyword is similar to the sampler keyword but is used to represent a sampler to a 2D texture. See Chapter 2 for more information on data types.
sampler3D	This keyword is similar to the sampler keyword but is used to represent a sampler to a 3D texture. See Chapter 2 for more information on data types.
samplerCUBE	This keyword is similar to the sampler keyword but is used to represent a sampler to a cubemap texture. See Chapter 2 for more information on data types.
sampler_state	This keyword is used to define a sampler by defining a block of information representing the state of a sampler.
shared	This keyword is used to indicate that a global variable can be shared across multiple effects. See Chapter 2 for more information on data types.
stateblock	This keyword is used to declare variables of the type `stateblock`, used to contain a set of effect states. Note that this keyword is generally used for effect files. See Part II of this book for more information on effect files
stateblock_state	This keyword is used to define a state block containing a set of effect states.
static	This keyword is used to define static variables. See Chapter 2 for more information on data types and variables.
string	This keyword is used to define data of string type. See Chapter 2 for more information on data types.
struct	This keyword is used to define structures. See Chapter 2 for more information on data types.
technique	This keyword is case insensitive and is used to define different techniques to accomplish an effect. Note that this keyword relates more closely to effect files and will be discussed in Part II of this book.
texture	This keyword is to represent the texture data type. See Chapter 2 for more information on data types.
texture1D	This keyword is similar to the `texture` keyword but is used to represent a 1D texture. See Chapter 2 for more information on data types.
texture2D	This keyword is similar to the `texture` keyword but is used to represent a 2D texture. See Chapter 2 for more information on data types.
texture3D	This keyword is similar to the `texture` keyword but is used to represent a 3D texture. See Chapter 2 for more information on data types.

Table 1-1 HLSL Keywords

Keyword	Definition
textureCUBE	This keyword is similar to the `texture` keyword but is used to represent a cubemap texture. See Chapter 2 for more information on data types.
true	This keyword is the true constant value for the boolean data type. See Chapter 2 for more information on data types.
typedef	This keyword is used to declare a new data type. See Chapter 2 for more information on data types.
uniform	This keyword is used to declare a variable as uniform, meaning all shader runs will see the same initial value to the variable. See Chapter 2 for more information on data types.
vector	This keyword is to represent the vector data type. See Chapter 2 for more information on data types.
vertexfragment	This keyword is used to define a vertex fragment (or shader).
void	This keyword is used to represent a void (or empty) data type. See Chapter 2 for more information on data types.
volatile	This keyword is used as a hint to the compiler to indicate that a variable will change often. See Chapter 2 for more information on data types.
while	This keyword is used to define a conditional do-while loop.

This may seem like a lot to absorb, and it may seem confusing, especially if you are new to HLSL. Do not worry; this book is a learning book as well as a reference book. The information in Table 1-1 is mostly for reference, and you will see how it can be used as we explore the syntax of the HLSL language as well as give examples. At this point in time, I want to outline all the major syntax and grammar components of the language. I will go into more details as we move forward.

In addition to the keywords in Table 1-1, there is a set of reserved keywords in HLSL that have no use currently. These keywords are essentially reserved for future use and have been listed in Table 1-2.

Table 1-2 HLSL Reserved Words

auto	break	case	catch
default	delete dynamic_cast	dynamic_cast	enum
explicit	end	goto	long
mutable	namespace	new	operator
private	protected	public	reinterpret_cast
short	signed	sizeof	static_cast
switch	template	this	throw
try	typename	union	unsigned
using	virtual		

Pre-Processor directives

In addition to reserved keywords, the HLSL language also defined a set of preprocessor directives to control the compilation of a program. The list of basic preprocessor directives supported includes the following: *#define*, *#endif*, *#else*, *#endif*, *#error*, *#if*, *#ifdef*, *#ifndef*, *#include*, *#line*, *#pragma* and *#undef*. A summary description of these directives is included in Table 1-3 below:

Table 1-3 Pre-Processor Directives

Directive	Definition
#define	This directive is used to declare a new compiler macro.
#if, #elseif, #endif, #ifdef, #ifndef	This set of directives is used to define a copiler conditional directive.
#error	This directive is used to force the compiler to emit an error and is generally used in conjunction with the conditional directives.
#include	This directive is used to include an external file into the compilation process.
#line	This directive is substituted with the current line number at which the directive is included within the source file.
#pragma	This directive is used to enable and control certain compiler behaviors. They will be discussed later in more details.

Take note that the *#include* directive will only function when the HLSL compiler is supplied with an *ID3DXInclude* interface. See Chapter 12 for more information on the include manager interface.

 *Note*

> Take note that the `#include` directive will only function when the HLSL compiler is supplied with an `ID3DXInclude` interface. See Chapter 12 for more information on the include manager interface.

The `#pragma` directive defines a set of specific sub-directives specific to the HLSL language. The `pack_matrix` directive can be used as follows:

```
#pragma pack_matrix (row_major) // or column_major
```

This directive tells the compiler how matrices defined within the HLSL file should be interpreted (either row or column major). I will discuss this in more detail in Chapter 2 when I will discuss the different data types defined by HLSL.

The second `#pragma` subdirective of interest is the `warning` directive. It helps control the output of warning messages by the HLSL compiler. The syntax of this directive is as follows:

```
#pragma warning( type : warning-number )
```

The *type* parameter defines how to threat the warnings specified in *warning-number*. The second parameter is a space-separated list of warning numbers that you want affected. Below is the list of the possible *type* parameters:

- **once**: Will only display the specified warnings once and ignore from that point on.
- **default**: Restored the treatment of the specified warnings to the default behavior.
- **disable**: Ignores all occurrences of the specified warnings.
- **error**: Treat the specified warnings as if they were compilation errors.

The final subdirective to the `#pragma` preprocessor directive is `def`. This instruction serves to give the compiler some hints as to what some of the registers should contain on a specific compilation profile. Keep in mind that this is an optimization hint to the compiler, and the final decision as to how registers are used is always up to the compiler.

 *Note*

> Currently, only the constant registers (`c#`) are supported by the `#pragma def` instruction.

A compilation profile defines a combination of vertex or pixel shader along with a hardware version to target. A complete list of the current profiles is available in Table 1-4.

Table 1-4 HLSL Compilation Profiles

Profile	Definition
vs_1_1	Vertex Shader version 1.1
vs_2_0	Vertex Shader version 2.0
vs_2_x	This profile represents the extended Vertex Shader version 2.0, which has extra capabilities which include predication, dynamic flow control and a number of temporary registers greater than 12.
vs_3_0	Vertex Shader version 3.0
ps_1_1	Pixel Shader version 1.1
ps_1_2	Pixel Shader version 1.2
ps_1_3	Pixel Shader version 1.3
ps_1_4	Pixel Shader version 1.4
ps_2_0	Pixel Shader version 2.0
ps_2_x	This profile represents the extended Pixel Shader version 2.0, which has extra capabilities which include predication, dynamic flow control and a number of temporary registers greater than 12.
ps_3_0	Pixel Shader version 3.0

 Note

Although not exposed within the HLSL language, Direct3D exposes two variants to the pixel 2.0 profile. The *ps_2_a* and *ps_2_b* profiles are similar to the *ps_2_0* profile but offers some extra functionality as follows:

• Number of temporary registers is greater or equal to 22 (32 for *ps_2_b*).
• Arbitrary source swizzle. (only *ps_2_a*)
• Gradient instructions: dsx, dsy. (only *ps_2_a*)
• Predication. (only *ps_2_a*)
• No dependent texture read limit. (only *ps_2_a*)
• No limit for the number of texture instructions.

Also keep in mind that the 2.a and 2.b profiles do not offer backward compatibility between each other and were offered as an intermediate way of exposing new functionality until the 3.0 shader model was available.

Understanding the HLSL Syntax

Now that we have gone over what the reserved words and some of the preprocessor directives for the HLSL syntax are, we can start going over the syntax itself. Syntaxes for computer languages are generally presented in Backus-Naur Form (BNF) which is an easy to understand form.

Grammars defined as BNF are really easy to follow as they have a form which is straightforward and easy to decipher. I will go over it right away since I will use it a few times later on in the following chapters. Generally, each line of the grammar represents a rule. Each rule defines a result and of what it is comprised. For example:

If-statement: `KW_IF KW_LPAREN expression KW_RPAREN statement`

In this grammar rule, we define an *if* conditional statement. This statement is defined as the *if* keyword followed by an expression enclosed within parenthesis followed by a statement. The definition of *expression* and *statement* is being defined in following rules. In addition to the basic rules, a few important operators can be used within the rules that you should know.

- **a | b**: The pipe character can used to define an *or* condition within a rule.
- **(a)**: Parenthesis can be used to enclose segments of the rule into a block.
- **[a]**: A set of rules within square braces means the segment is optional.
- **a +**: The use of the plus character indicates one or more repetitions of the segment.
- **a ***: The use of the star character indicates any number of repetitions of the segment.

With the information above, you should be able to read through grammar rules pretty easily. Before I show the HLSL grammar syntax, a few lexical conventions will beexplored.

Lexical Conventions

Although the syntax of a language defines how everything ties together and, for example, what defines a function or a statement, it only defines that an expression may be a combination of operators and identifiers. This means that the language syntax does not define the grammar of the language (i.e., what is an identifier). The next few paragraphs detailsome of the basic lexical conventions used by the HLSL compiler.

Whitespaces

White spaces within the HLSL language are defined as being any one of the following:

- Space.
- Tab.

- End of line.
- C style comments (/* */).
- C++ style comments (//).
- Assembly style comments (;) within an `asm` block.

Numbers

Numbers within HLSL can either be floating-point or integer numbers. Floating-point numbers are represented as follows:

```
Float: (fractional-constant [exponent-part] [floating-suffix]) |
       (digit-sequence exponent-part [floating-suffix])

Fractional-constant: ( [digit-sequence] . digit-sequence ) |
                     ( digit-sequence . )

Exponent-part: ( e [sign] digit-sequence ) | ( E [sign] digit-sequence )

Sign: + | -

Digit-sequence: digit | ( digit-sequence digit )

Floating-suffix: h | H | f | F
```

Integer numbers follow a similar syntax:

```
Integer: integer-constant [integer-suffix]

Integer-constant: digit-sequence | ( 0 digit-sequence ) |
                  (0 x digit-sequence)

Digit-sequence: digit | ( digit-sequence digit )

Integer-suffix: u | U | l | L
```

Characters

The HLSL language allows strings and characters to be defined. Strings being composed of characters, let's start by looking at the definition of character:

- 'c' (character)
- '\t', '\n', … (escape characters)
- '\###' (octal escape sequence)

- '\x##' (hexadecimal escape sequence)

 Note

Take note that escape characters cannot be used within preprocessor directives.

Strings themselves are enclosed within quotes and can contain any valid combination of characters as previously defined.

Identifiers

Identifiers represent language elements such as function names or variables. With exception to reserved keywords outlined earlier, identifiers are defined as any combination of letters and digits as long as the first character is a letter.

Operators

The HLSL language defines a set of operators used within expressions. Table 1-5 enumerates all the standard operators along with their meaning. If you are familiar with C and C++, most of the operators should seem straightforward to you.

Table 1-5 HLSL Operators

Operator	Definition
++	Unary increment
--	Unary decrement
&&	And
||	Or
==	Equal
::	Scope (for structures and classes)
<<	Left binary shift
<<=	Self assigning left binary shift. This means that $a <<= b$ is equivalent to $a = a << b$.
>>	Right binary shift
>>=	Self assigning right binary shift. This means that $a >>= b$ is equivalent to $a = a >> b$.

Table 1-5 HLSL Operators

Operator	Definition
...	Ellipsis operator (used for variable parameter functions)
<=	Lesser than or equal to
>=	Greater than or equal to
!=	Not equal
*=	Self assigning multiplication. This means that a *= b is equivalent to $a = a * b$.
/=	Self assigning division. This means that a /= b is equivalent to $a = a / b$.
+=	Self assigning addition. This means that a += b is equivalent to $a = a + b$.
-=	Self assigning subtraction. This means that a -= b is equivalent to $a = a - b$.
%=	Self assigning modulo. This means that a %= b is equivalent to $a = a \% b$.
&=	Self assigning and. This means that a &= b is equivalent to $a = a \& b$.
|=	Self assigning or. This means that a |= b is equivalent to $a = a \mid b$.
^=	Self assigning power of. This means that a ^= b is equivalent to $a = a \wedge b$.
->	Indirection operator, used to access structure members.

Language Syntax

The syntax for the HLSL language is pretty straightforward. Although it may look complex, you will get the hang of it as you use the language. In addition, you should not worry too much about the syntax itself at this point in time as we'll explore specific components of the language in the next few chapters. Since the actual syntax is quite long, I have decided to include it in Appendix D. You can also refer to the DirectX SDK documentation for more complete details.

Looking at the top of the listing, you can see that an HLSL file is defined as a `program`. Each program is either empty or is composed of a set of `decls` (declarations). Declarations are a little more complicated. The first two lines serve to define that a declaration is a combination of one of many `decl` (declaration). From there, a declaration is defined either as an empty statement, a type declaration, a variable declaration, a structure declaration, a function declaration or a technique declaration. The grammar defines the different types of declarations and so on.

Summary and what's next?

In this chapter, I have briefly overviewed the history of DirectX and how the shader technology has progressed over the past few years. With the increased complexity of the new shader models 2.0 and 3.0, developers needed to be able to take advantage of the new capabilities of the language but at the same time able to be efficient at the task. Since the capabilities of the new shader pipelines resembled more and more of the instruction sets of modern processors, it made sense to develop a high-level language, allowing developers to focus on the task of creating shaders without having to worry about little details such as register allocations.

Because of this need, Microsoft has developed and released the HLSL shading language as part of the DirectX SDK, finally allowing developers to leverage the latest shader innovations and bring even more realism to their graphics. In this chapter, I have gone over some of the basic concepts behind the grammar of the HLSL language. Although this may have seemed like a lot to absorb in a single chapter, you need not to worry, as I'll go into more details on some of the specifics over the next few chapters.

In the next chapter, I will start discussing the concepts of variables, expressions and data types exposed by the HLSL shading language. Let's get going…

Chapter

2

The HLSL Shading Language

In this chapter I will go over most of the basic concepts of the HLSL language, including the rich set of available data types, how to define variables, and how shader code is written. You may wonder about functions and their use in shaders. Although they play an integral part in writing shaders using HLSL, I have decided to detail this topic in its own chapter. In Chapter 3, I will go into more details on how functions are defined and which pre-built functions the HLSL language offers developers.

Before moving forward, I want to mention that you may have noticed in the previous chapter that some of the HLSL syntax contained concepts such as techniques, render states and passes. Although they are part of the HLSL syntax, they are in reality used within effect files, a superset of HLSL. I will cover these topics in more detail in the second part of this book.

Enough with the chitchat, let's get to the meat of the topic and discuss one of the more important components of any high-level language, the data types.

Data Types

Data types are at the core of any programming language. Without them you would not be able to define variables or exchange information between functions. How can you store data if you do not have the means to represent it? As with any high-level language, HLSL defines a set of predefined data types, which can be broken down into the following categories:

- Scalar Types
- Vector Types
- Matrix Types
- Object Types

As well as the above list of predefined types, the HLSL language also allows the definition of user-defined composite types such as arrays and structures. Before I actually jump into the specifics of the data types within the HLSL language, a few little details should be mentioned in regards to the way data is represented on most 3D hardware. When dealing with numbers, the primitive of choice is floating point numbers which can either be 16 or 32-bits depending on the architecture. With that in mind, the hardware could operate on one value at a time, but this would not be the most efficient approach. Instead the hardware works on units of four numbers (or vectors) and can apply operations to all four components at the same time. This brings in certain considerations with regard to how non-vector data will be stored on your hardware.I will discuss this a little later.

In addition to floating-point values, newer hardware has built-in support for *integer* and *boolean* values, but their use is generally limited to branching, looping and conditional instructions. Over the next few pages, I will go over all the specific data types and explain how to use them.

Scalar Types

Scalar types are defined by the HLSL standard as singular atomic values. They are the most basic types and are used to compose all the more complex ones such as vectors, matrices and structures. Table 2-1 enumerates all the scalar types exposed and their meaning.

Table 2-1 HLSL Scalar Types

Scalar Type	Possible values
bool	true or false
int	32-bit signed integer
half	16-bit floating-point number
float	32-bit floating-point number
double	64-bit floating-point number

Take note that not all shader targets have native support for *integer*, *half* or *double* values. If your shader is compiled for a target that does not support a specific format, it will be emulated through use of the *float* type. Results may not be as accurate as using the true native type. Unless you are certain that your target platform supports a specific type, it is better to stick with standard floating-point numbers for the sake of consistency and portability.

Note

Compiler profiles have only been briefly discussed in the previous chapters but serve to tell the HLSL compiler for which shader architecture to generate its code. The values of compiler profiles closely map to the vertex and pixel shader versions available but with a few exceptions for which the instruction set is unchanged.

Vector and Matrix Types

Vectors and matrices are a standardized way in HLSL to represent one-dimensional and two-dimensional arrays of data composed from scalar types. They are generally used for the representation of 3D data such as normals and transformation matrices.

The vector type is defined by the HLSL standard as a one-dimensional array comprised of one particular scalar type. By default, a vector is an array composed of four floating-point values. As shown in Table 2-2, you can also manually define arbitrary vectors.

Table 2-2 HLSL Vector Types

Vector Type	Values
vector	A vector of four float components.
vector< type, size>	A vector containing *size* components of the specified *type*.

Also, for convenience, the HLSL language predefines a set of standard vector types which can be used for quick convenience. Below is a list of all the predefined vector types:

```
typedef vector <float, 4> VECTOR;
typedef vector <bool, #> bool#;
typedef vector <int, #> int#;
typedef vector <half, #> half#;
typedef vector <float, #> float#;
typedef vector <double, #> double#;
```

You may remember that I mentioned how the graphics hardware is based on vectors. As you can see, the vector data type just discussed closely maps to the hardware, and the compiler will map your data to hardware vectors. When you use vectors smaller than four entries, the compiler will try and compact the data by stuffing other variables in the remaining components.

Now that I've discussed vectors, you may wonder how you can access the individual components of the vector. Individual vector components may be accessed in many different ways. The following list shows different possible access modes for array components. Take note that for arrays of size greater than four, the extra components can only be accessed by index.

- **By component**: vector.x, vector.y, vector.z, vector.w
- **By color**: vector.r, vector.g, vector.b, vector.a
- **By index**: vector[0], vector[1], vector[2], vector[3]

Now let's discuss matrix data types. Matrix types are defined by the HLSL standard as two-dimensional arrays comprised of one particular scalar type. By default, a matrix is a four-by-four array comprised of floating-point values. As shown in Table 2-3, arbitrary matrices can also be manually defined.

Table 2-3 HLSL Matrix Types

Matrix Type	Values
matrix	A four-by-four matrix of floats
matrix<type,rows,cols>	A matrix of *rows* rows and *cols* columns with the specified type

Also, for convenience, the HLSL language predefines a set of standard matrix types.

```
typedef matrix <float, 4, 4> MATRIX;
typedef matrix <bool, #, #> bool#x#;
typedef matrix <int, #, #> int#x#;
typedef matrix <half, #, #> half#x#;
typedef matrix <float, #, #> float#x#;
typedef matrix <double, #, #> double#x#;
```

Similar to vectors, matrices will be stored in the hardware by using a set of consecutive vectors in memory, each representing a distinct row of matrix data. You can address individual row-vectors of matrices by using an array style addressing. For example, you can address a single row of a matrix by using an index such as *Matrix[3]*, which will return a vector of the correct size. You may also address individual components of a matrix through an indexed row access followed by a standard vector access, such as *Matrix[2].x* or *Matrix[3][2]*.

Individual components of a matrix can also be accessed on a per-component basis using one of the following two notations.

One-based:

```
_11    _12    _13    _14
_21    _22    _23    _24
_31    _32    _33    _34
_41    _42    _43    _44
```

Zero-based:

```
_m00    _m01    _m02    _m03
_m10    _m11    _m12    _m13
_m20    _m21    _m22    _m23
_m30    _m31    _m32    _m33
```

You may remember the `#pragma pack` directive discussed in Chapter 1. This directive can be used to control how matrix data is represented within a shader by using `row_major` or `col_major`. By default, matrix packing is set to column-major. This means each column of the matrix is stored in a constant register. On the other hand, a row-major matrix packs each row of the matrix in a constant register.

In general, column-major matrices are more efficient than row-major matrices because they conform more closely to the data that Direct3D expects and will generally lead to shaders using fewer instructions.

 *Note*

> Note that the matrix packing pragma will only affect matrices in global variables or passed as function parameters. Matrices defined within the body of a shader will ignore this parameter and always be treated as row-major.

Component Access and Swizzle

As mentioned above, individual float components of vector and matrix types can be addressed much like accessing a structure member. The table below summarizes vector and matrix access.

```
_11, x, r    _12,y,g    _13,z,b    _14,w,a
_21          _22        _23        _24
_31          _32        _33        _34
_41          _42        _43        _44
```

You can also define vectors containing specific components, commonly called swizzles, by using a subscript formed by concatenating two to four of these names together. Here are valid examples:

```
bgr, yyzw, _12_22_32_42
```

The same can also be done with matrices.

```
tempMatrix._m00_m11 = worldMatrix._m00_m11;
tempMatrix._11_22_33 = worldMatrix._24_23_22;
temp = fMatrix._m00_m11;
temp = fMatrix._11_22;
```

Note that all sizzles must come from the same subscript set, (*xyzw*, *rgba*, or *_11* to *_44*). Sets cannot be mixed. The same component may be repeated more than once. If a component is repeated, the swizzle is invalid as the target of an assignment.

 *Note*

> Not all hardware profiles support the complete set of swizzling operations. On 1.x pixel shaders, some swizzle operations are not supported. The HLSL compiler will compensate for this by emulating the operation, but it does come with a performance penalty.

Object Types

The HLSL language also defines a wide range of object data types. These types are generally used to represent handles to nonnumeric data or composite types. Two common examples of such types are textures and structures. Below is a list of the object types defined:

- Samplers
- Textures
- Structures
- Vertex and pixel shaders
- Strings

The topic of structures will be discussed in further detail in the section on user-defined types.

Strings are simply ASCII defined strings and serve little purpose beyond their use within annotations. I will not detail this type at the moment, but I will now take some time to discuss the topic of samplers, shaders, and textures.

Samplers and Textures

The HLSL shader language defines these two data types as a representation of the information used within your shaders to access texture information. A texture is essentially a handle to a physical pixel data available on the hardware. A sampler on the other hand represents the combination of a set of texture sampling parameters such as the wrapping mode or mipmapping properties.

Vertex and Pixel Shaders

The HLSL shader language defines two data types which can be used to contain both vertex and pixel shaders. Those types are defined as *vertexshader* and *pixelshader*. Shader types can be directly assigned shader code if the shader is defined in assembly form using the *asm* keyword:

```
vertexshader vs =
  asm
  {
    vs_2_0
    dcl_position v0
    mov oPos, v0
  };
```

If you are using high-level instructions, you will define your shaders within functions, which can then be compiled and assigned to a shader variable. Below is an example of the high-level approach for a pixel shader:

```
pixelshader ps = compile ps_2_0 psmain();
```

Structures and User Defined Types

In addition to allowing a rich set of predefined variable types as you have seen earlier in this chapter, the HLSL language allows you to create new types. These types will generally be a structure, which is an object type composed of a set of other types (built-in or user-defined) or the declaration of a new type name-based on an existing type.

The keyword *struct* is used to define structure types. Structures are defined as composite types used to group common data into a single entity. Structures are defined through the following syntax:

```
struct [ID] { members }
```

Below is an example of the creation of a new structure:

```
struct Circle
{
    float4 Position;
    float  Radius;
};
```

In addition to structures, the HLSL language allows you to define new types by using the *typedef* keyword to declare a new name for an existing type. Below is the syntax for new type definitions.

```
typedef [const] type id [array_suffix] [, id ...] ;
```

Array suffixes can follow the *ID*, allowing the definition of arrays as new types. When a type has been declared, it can be referenced by using its *ID*. Note that an *array_suffix* consists of one or more *literal_integer_expression*, representing the dimension of the array.

Type Casts

Typecasts are known in programming jargon as the ability to convert one type to another. HLSL supports many built-in type conversions. Table 2-4 summarizes the possible conversions between the built-in data types.

Table 2-4 Type Conversions in HLSL

Type Conversion	Validity
Scalar-to-scalar	Such conversions are always valid. When casting from bool type to an integer or floating-point type, *false* is considered to be zero, and *true* is considered to be one. When casting from an integer or floating-point type to bool, a zero value is considered to be *false* When casting from a floating-point type to an integer type, the value is rounded down to the nearest integer.
Scalar-to-vector	Such conversions are always valid. This cast works by copying the scalar to fill the vector.
Scalar-to-matrix	Such conversions are always valid. This cast works by copying the scalar to fill the matrix.
Scalar-to-object	Such conversions are never valid.
Scalar-to-structure	Valid if all elements of the structure are numeric. This cast works by copying the scalar to fill the structure.
Vector-to-scalar	Such conversion is always valid. The conversion selects the first component of the vector to fill the scalar.
Vector-to-vector	The destination vector must not be larger than the source vector. The cast works by keeping the left-most values and truncating the rest.
Vector-to-matrix	For this conversion to be valid, the size of the vector must be equal to the size of the matrix.

Table 2-4 Type Conversions in HLSL

Type Conversion	Validity
Vector-to-object	Such conversions are never valid.
Vector-to-structure	Such conversion is valid only if the structure is not larger than the vector and all components of the structure are numeric
Matrix-to-scalar	This conversion is always valid. The scalar is filled with the upper-left component of the matrix.
Matrix-to-vector	This conversion is valid only if the size of the matrix equals the size of the vector.
Matrix-to-matrix	For this type conversion to be valid, the destination matrix must not be larger than the source matrix in both dimensions. The cast works by keeping the upper-left values and truncating the rest.
Matrix-to-object	This type conversion is never valid.
Matrix-to-structure	For this conversion to be valid, the size of the structure must be equal to the size of the matrix, and the components of the structure must all be of a numeric type.
Object-to-scalar	This type conversion is never valid.
Object-to-vector	This type conversion is never valid.
Object-to-matrix	This type conversion is never valid.
Object-to-object	This type of conversion is only valid if both object types are of the same type
Object-to-structure	For this type conversion to be valid, the structure must not contain more than one member. The type of that member must be identical with the type of the object.
Structure-to-scalar	For this conversion to be valid, the structure must contain at least one member. This member must be numeric.
Structure-to-vector	For this conversion to be valid, the structure must be at least the size of the vector. The first components must be numeric, up to the size of the vector.
Structure-to-matrix	For this conversion to be valid, the structure must be at least the size of the matrix. The first components must be numeric, up to the size of the matrix.
Structure-to-structure	For this conversion to be valid, the destination structure must not be larger than the source structure. A valid cast must exist between all respective source and destination components.

Defining Variables

The HLSL language allows you to define variables containing constants, inputs, outputs and temporary values. By the standard, variables are defined through the following syntax.

```
[static uniform volatile extern shared] [const] type id [array_suffix]
[:semantics] [= initializers] [annotations] [, id …];
```

As you can see from the syntax definition, variables can be prefixed with various keywords which change the way the compiler treats the variable. Table 2-5 reviews the different prefixes and their effect.

Table 2-5 Variable Prefixes

Prefix	Definition
static	For global variables, this prefix signals that the value is internal and cannot be exposed to other shaders externally. For local variables, this indicates that its value will persist from call to call. Initialization of static variables is done only once. If no initialization value is given, zero will be assumed.
uniform	Global variable declarations with the `uniform` prefix indicates that they are uniform inputs to the shader. All non-static global variables are considered to be uniform.
extern	Global variable declarations with the `extern` prefix indicates that they are external inputs to the shader. All non-static global variables are considered to be external.
volatile	The `volatile` keyword is a compiler hint to indicate that the value of this variable is to change often.
shared	The `shared` keyword used on a global variable is a compiler hint to indicate that the value of this variable will be shared among several effects.
const	Variables declared as const cannot be modified from their initialization values.

One thing to notice from the syntax for variable declarations is the *semantics* part. Semantics have no explicit meaning within the HLSL language but are used to define a mapping within your shader variables and meaning of the variable for the effect framework.

The semantics for variables are generally used for vertex and pixel shader function inputs, mapping them to a specific meaning such as a vertex position or texture coordinate. For example, the `COLOR0` semantic is used to tell the compiler that the specific variable is the first diffuse color which, on most shader versions, will get put into the `d0` register.

Global variables can also have annotations as shown in the above syntax. Annotations are of the form *{ member_list }*, where *member_list* represents a list of member declarations, each of them being initialized to a literal value. Annotations are only a method of communicating metadata about a parameter to an effect and cannot be referenced from inside the program.

Semantics as well as annotations will be discussed in greater details in Chapter 6.

Statements and Expressions

As with any high-level language, HLSL also contains statements and expressions. Although theses elements are part of functions, which are covered in the next chapter, I want to go over theses elements right away since they serve as the main building blocks for shaders.

Statements

Statements are used to control the flow of execution of your programs. The HLSL language defines multiple types of statements for your use. Below is a list of the categories of statements defined by the HLSL grammar.

- An expression
- A statement block
- Return statement
- Flow control statement

Going through each element of the list in order, the first item in line is expressions. I will be discussing them later in this section. The second type is a statement block.

In simple terms, a statement block is list of statements enclosed within a set of curly braces. Its use is to enclose groups of statements together and also defines a sub-scope, which means that any variables defined in a statement block only exist within that block.

```
{ [statements] }
```

The following item on our list is a return statement. Return statements are used within a function to return a result to its caller. This is the syntax for the return statement:

```
return [expression];
```

As you can see from the syntax above, a return expression is defined as the return keyword followed by an expression. Keep in mind that for the shader code to compile, the type of the expression will need to match the return type defined by the function.

Finally, the last item on our list is flow control expressions. They are used to control how the execution of a program proceeds:

```
if ( expression ) statement [else statement]

do statement while ( expression )

while (expression) do statement

for ( [expression | variable_decleration ] ; [expression] ; [expression])
statement
```

As you can see from the syntax above, these flow control statements closely resemble their equivalents in C or C++. There are some performance considerations to using flow control statements within your shaders that you will need to consider.

Flow-Control Performance Considerations

Most current vertex and pixel shader hardware are designed to run a shader linearly, executing each instruction once. The HLSL supports flow control, including static branching, predicated instructions, static looping, dynamic branching, and dynamic looping. Because of the limitations of some shader implementations, the use of flow control instructions has some important performance considerations.

For example, the 1.1 vertex shader architecture has no dynamic branching support, so using *if* statements will result in assembly language shader code that implements both sides of the *if*. The code is executed linearly, but only the output results from first portion of the *if* statement to use is taken as a result. Here is an example in code that was compiled for *vs_1_1*:

```
if (Value > 0)
    Position = Value1;
else
    Position = Value2;
```

This will result in the following assembly code:

```
// Calculate linear interpolate (lerp) value in r0.w
mov r1.w, c2.x
slt r0.w, c3.x, r1.w

// Lerp between value1 and value2 based on compare result
mov r7, -c1
add r2, r7, c0
mad oPos, r0.w, r2, c1
```

From the above code you can see that the use of an *if* statement within 1.1 vertex shader model will result in both expressions being calculated with an interpolation to decide on the right result. With real dynamic flow control, this expression would only need two instructions, but in this case would require five instructions.

In addition to *if* statements, some hardware allows for either static or dynamic looping, but most require linear execution.

Although HLSL support flow control instructions for all shader models except for the 1.x pixel shaders, true flow control is only supported on the hardware with 3.0 vertex and pixel shaders through a set of 18 flow control assembly instructions. This implies that any non-3.0 shader will have its flow control transformed into code, which will execute both sides of conditionals and unroll loops. Since hardware flow control is still in its infancy within graphics hardware, its performance is still marginal. Care must be taken to ensure proper execution. I will discuss performance considerations of branching more extensively in Chapter 7.

Most types of flow control can be either static or dynamic. With static flow control, the expression used in the statement is actually constant and can be determined ahead of time. For example, static branching allows for blocks of code to be switched on or off based on a *boolean* shader constant. This is a convenient method for enabling or disabling code paths based on the type of object currently being rendered. Between rendering calls you can decide which features you want to support with the current shader then set the *boolean* flags needed to get that behavior.

On the other side, dynamic branching is what most developers are familiar. With dynamic branching, the comparison condition resides in a variable, which means that the comparison is done at runtime. The performance cost is the cost of the branch plus the cost of the instructions on the side of the branch taken. Dynamic branching is currently available for vertex shaders on certain hardware supporting dynamic flow control.

Expressions

Now that I have discussed statements, let's go over expressions. Expressions are defined as literals, variables, or some combination of literals and variables composed using operators. Available operators and their meaning are described below in Table 2-6.

Table 2-6 Expression Operators

Operator	Usage	Definition	Associativity
()	(value)	Sub expression	Left to right
()	id(arg)	Function call	Left to right
()	type(arg)	Type constructor	Left to right
[]	array[int]	Array subscript	Left to right
.	structure.id	Member selection	Left to right
.	value.swizzle	Component swizzle	Left to right
++	variable++	Postfix increment (per-component)	Left to right
--	variable--	Postfix decrement (per-component)	Left to right
++	++variable	Prefix increment (per-component)	Right to left
--	--variable	Prefix decrement (per-component)	Right to left
!	!value	Logical not (per-component)	Right to left
-	-value	Unary minus (per-component)	Right to left
+	+value	nary plus (per-component)	Right to left
()	(type) value	Typecast	Right to left
*	value * value	Multiplication (per-component)	Left to right
/	value / value	Division (per-component)	Left to right
%	value % value	Modulus (per-component)	Left to right
+	value + value	Addition (per-component)	Left to right
-	value - value	Subtraction (per-component)	Left to right
<	value < value	Less than (per-component)	Left to right
>	value > value	Greater than (per-component)	Left to right
<=	value <= value	Less than or equal to (per-component)	Left to right
>=	value >= value	Greater than or equal to (per-component)	Left to right
==	value == value	Equality (per-component)	Left to right
!=	value != value	Inequality (per-component)	Left to right
&&	value && value	Logical AND (per-component)	Left to right
||	value||value	Logical OR (per-component)	Left to right
?:	float?value:value	Conditional	Right to left

Table 2-6 Expression Operators

Operator	Usage	Definition	Associativity
=	variable=value	Assignment (per-component)	Right to left
*=	variable*=value	Multiplication assignment (per-component)	Right to left
/=	variable/=value	Division assignment (per-component)	Right to left
%=	variable%=value	Modulus assignment (per-component)	Right to left
+=	variable+=value	Addition assignment (per-component)	Right to left
-=	variable-=value	Subtraction assignment (per-component)	Right to left
,	value,value	Comma	Left to right

Unlike the C language, short-circuit evaluation of the `&&`, `||`, and `?:` expressions will never short-circuit because of the way they are evaluated by the hardware. You may also have noticed that many of the operators are labeled as being "per-component" (including comparison operators). This suggests that, for each component of the input value (which are 4D vectors), the operation is performed independently. The result is placed in the matching component of the output vector.

Summary and what's next?

In this chapter, I have gone over some of the basic concepts behind the HLSL language. At this point, you should have a good understanding of the data types exposed by the language, how to declare variables and how to construct statements and expressions. As you have seen, the constructs in the HLSL language are really similar to the ones found in C and C++.

The major caveat when writing shaders in a high-level language is that you always have to keep in mind the capabilities of the hardware. This is particularly true when dealing with flow control instructions. Since earlier generations of shader hardware had no support for any form of flow control, this has some performance considerations.

Moving forward, in the next chapter, I will complete our discussion of the HLSL language by discussing functions. In this chapter, I will discuss how you can use the rich library of pre-built functions within the HLSL language and construct your own functions. Let's not waste time and get right to it…

Chapter

3

Functions, Nothing but Functions

In the previous chapter, we covered the major components of the HLSL syntax. The only thing missing at this point is an explanation of how functions are defined and can be used to declare and enhance your shaders. Functions are an important part of any high-level language and will play a big part in the creation of shaders. HLSL is no exception. The syntax of the HLSL language allows for two types of functions. Built-in (or intrinsic) functions expose a library of predefined functionality for use in your shader and exposing some of the special instructions available on certain shader architectures.

User-defined functions are created by you. These user-defined functions can be used either to define a shader as a whole or simply to componentize functionality you wish to reuse often.

Over the next few sections, I will discuss both types of functions and conclude with a discussion of how you can use functions to define shaders. Let's start with the rich library of built-in functions offered by the HLSL shader language.

Built-in Functions

The High-Level Shader Language contains a wide variety of built-in, or intrinsic, functions. Those functions will be useful when developing your shaders. They offer a wide variety of functionality ranging from mathematical operations to texture sampling. Table 3-1 quickly overviews all the functions available within the HLSL shader language.

Table 3-1 HLSL Built-In Functions

Function	Use
abs	Calculate the absolute value of the input.
acos	Return the arccosine of the input.
all	Test for non-zero values.
any	Test for any non-zero values in the input.

Table 3-1 HLSL Built-In Functions

Function	Use
asin	Return the arcsine of the input.
atan	Return the arctangent of the input.
atan2	Return the arctangent of y/x.
ceil	Return the smallest integer which is greater than or equal to the input.
clamp	Return the input clamped to the range *[min, max]*.
clip	Discard pixel if any component of the input is less than zero.
cos	Return the cosine of the input.
cosh	Return the hyperbolic cosine of the input.
cross	Return the cross product of two 3-D input vectors.
ddx	Return the partial derivative in the screen space x coordinate.
ddy	Return the partial derivative in the screen space y coordinate.
degrees	Return the conversion of the input values from radians to degrees.
determinant	Return the determinant of the input matrix.
distance	Return the distance between two input points.
dot	Return the dot product of the two input vectors.
exp	Return the base-e exponential of the input value.
exp2	Return the base-2 exponential of the input value.
faceforward	Determines if a polygon is front facing.
floor	Return the greatest integer which is less than or equal to x.
fmod	Return the floating-point remainder *f* of *a / b*.
frac	Calculate fractional part f of the input value.
frexp	Return the mantissa and exponent of the input.
fwidth	Return abs(ddx(x))+abs(ddy(x)).
isfinite	Return *true* if the input is finite, *false* otherwise.
isinf	Return *true* if the input value is equal to *+INF* or *-INF*.
isnan	Return *true* if the input value is equal to *NAN* or *QNAN*.
ldexp	Reverse operation to *frexp* and returns $x*2^{exp}$.
len / length	Return the length of the input vector.
lerp	Return interpolates between two input vectors.
lit	Return a lighting vector (ambient, diffuse, specular, 1).

Table 3-1 HLSL Built-In Functions

Function	Use
log	Return the base-e logarithm of the input.
log10	Return the base-10 logarithm of the input.
log2	Return the base-2 logarithm of input.
max	Return the greater of two input values.
min	Return the lesser of two input values.
modf	Split the value x into fractional and integer parts.
mul	Perform matrix multiplication between input matrices.
normalize	Return the normalized vector, also defined as `x / length(x)`.
pow	Return the input value raised to the specified power.
radians	Return conversion of the input value x from degrees to radians.
reflect	Return the reflection vector given the entering ray direction `i` and the surface normal `n`.
refract	Return the refraction vector `v`, given the entering ray direction `i`, the surface normal `n`, and the relative index of refraction `eta`.
round	Round the input to the nearest integer.
rsqrt	Return the reciprocal square root of the input value.
saturate	Clamp input to the range [0, 1].
sign	Compute the sign of the input.
sin	Compute the sine of the input.
sincos	Return the sine and cosine of the input.
sinh	Compute the hyperbolic sine of the input.
smoothstep	Compute a smooth Hermite interpolation of the input values.
sqrt	Return the square root of the input value.
step	Returns `(x >= a) ? 1 : 0`.
tan	Compute the tangent of the input.
tanh	Compute the hyperbolic tangent of the input.
transpose	Return the transpose of the input matrix.
tex1D*	Perform a 1D texture lookup.
tex2D*	Perform a 2D texture lookup.
tex3D*	Perform a 3D texture lookup.
texCUBE*	Perform a cubemap texture lookup.

To be a little practical, let me show you an example of how these functions can be used. Let's say that you have a pixel you wish to texture and illuminate with a directional light. You will need to determine the lighting contribution, fetch the texture and then combine the two together. First, to determine the contribution of a directional light, you will need to compute the dot product of the pixel normal and the light's direction. This is easily accomplished using the *dot* function as follows:

```
LightIntensity = dot( LightDirection, PixelNormal);
```

One little problem that can arise because of this operation is that a pixel facing away from the light will have a negative intensity. To avoid this, ensure that the intensity is between zero and one. Guess what? We are in luck; this is exactly what the saturate function is for, andhere is how you would use it:

```
LightIntensity = saturate( dot( LightDirection, PixelNormal ) );
```

Before we can apply the lighting to our object, we will need to get its pixel color from a texture. Assuming we already have the proper texture coordinates and that we will be using a simple 2D texture, you can accomplish this with the following code:

```
PixelColor = tex2D( ObjectTexture, TextureCoord );
```

The last step is to combine the lighting with the pixel color. For this, we need the color of the light with its intensity combined with the pixel color. This is straight forward, but take care to notice how the vectored nature of the shader architecture takes care of all the color components at once:

```
FinalColor = ( LightColor * LightIntensity ) * PixelColor;
```

This example is really simple but it shows how much you can accomplish with only three lines of code. Before we move on, the use of built-in functions. Each of these functions has varying parameters depending on their functionality. In addition, because of hardware support, not all of these functions are available on all versions of vertex and pixel shaders.

For a complete reference on the built-in HLSL functions, please refer to Appendix A, which contains a complete reference on them. This reference contains a full definition of the functions along with supported shader version, description of its use and even performance considerations when using each of them.

User-defined functions

As well as the wide selection of intrinsic (or built-in) functions offered by the HLSL language, you can define your own custom functions in a similar way to the C language. Below is the syntax used to declare a function:

```
[static inline target] [const] return_type id ( [parameter_list] )
{ [statement] };
```

The following is the syntax used to define custom function prototypes:

```
[static inline target] [const] return_type id ( [parameter_list] );
```

As you can see, a function can be prefixed by a set of modifiers allowing you to change the compiler's behavior in regards to the function. Table 3-2 outlines the possible user-defined function prefixes and their meaning.

Table 3-2 User-Defined Function Prefixes

Prefix	Definition
static	This prefix indicates the function will exist only within the scope of the current shader program and may not be shared. This keyword is mostly irrelevant in the context of this book.
inline	This prefix shows the function's instructions are to be copied within the calling code instead of issuing an actual function call. Take note that this is simply a compiler hint and does not guarantee this behavior. Also note that this is the current default behavior for the HLSL compiler.
target	This prefix indicates for which pixel/vertex shader version the code is intended. This allows the compiler to make the best decisions when building the code.
const	This prefix indicates for which pixel/vertex shader version the code is intended. This allows the compiler to make the best decisions when building the code.

Take in consideration that all functions are inlined by default and thus may not be called recursively. This is because of the way functions are processed, compiled and executed by the vertex and pixel shader hardware. Shader hardware can only execute code in a linear fashion and cannot jump to other locations within the code. This means that functions are always inlined within the calling code. A consequence of recursion is that the code path becomes unpredictable and thus is disallowed.

Parameters defined in the *parameter_list* also follow a particular syntax defining how they are declared:

```
[uniform in out inout] type id [: semantic] [= default]
```

As you can see, parameters can also be prefixed by modifiers and by special keywords, allowing control of the compiler's behavior. Table 3-3 describes the allowed parameter prefixes with their meaning.

Table 3-3 Function Parameter Prefixes

Prefix	Definition
in	This prefix is the default behavior and shows that the parameter is intended to be read only by the function.
out	This prefix is intended to indicate that the parameter is a result value, and any changes made to its value will be sent back to the caller.
inout	This prefix combines both the behavior of *in* and *out*.
uniform	This prefix is synonymous to *in* but also points out that the value comes from constant data from within the shader

When a `semantic` value is associated with parameter, it serves to indicate to the compiler the source of the input. For example, a *TEXCOORD0* semantic value will tell the compiler that it should substitute this variable with the first set of texture coordinates. Note that semantics for parameters are only meaningful for the top-level function of a shader, that is the entry point to either a vertex or pixel shader.

The only topic I have not yet covered with regard to functions is the *return_type* parameter, which is used to define the type of data the function can return. For a function that does not return data or returns data only through `out` parameters, this type should be defined as `void`, or nothing.

When a function must return a value, the type of data returned can be by any of the basic data types defined in HLSL. It can also be a structure, which allows the return of several values combined together. Below is an example of the use of a return structure:

```
struct VS_OUTPUT
{
    float4  vPosition       : POSITION;
    float4  vDiffuse        : COLOR;
};

VS_OUTPUT VertexShader_Tutorial (float4 inPos : POSITION )
{
    VS_OUTPUT Result;

    // Do something...
    return Result;
}
```

From within the body of a function, to return a value you will need to make use of the `return` keyword followed by a value (or variable) of the same type as defined in the function declaration.

One thing you may wonder at this point is the use of the *out* prefix for parameters. In fact, you can substitute the use of a return type with the use of an *out* parameter. The code below illustrates our previous example with the use of an *out* parameter:

```
struct VS_OUTPUT
{
    float4   vPosition          : POSITION;
    float4   vDiffuse           : COLOR;
};

void VertexShader_Tutorial (float4 inPos : POSITION,
                            out VS_OUTPUT outReturn )
{
    VS_OUTPUT Result;

    // Do something…
    outReturn = Result;
}
```

As you can see, creating functions in HLSL is easy and resembles the approach taken in other high-level language. Before we move to more complex function and shader examples, let's look at how you can use functions to define shaders.

Creating Shaders from Functions

The main purpose of being able to create user-defined functions is the ability to define shaders from them.

Although the declaration of a shader is mostly useful within the context of the effect framework, I wanted to take a little time to give you an overview of what to expect. It serves as a good example of user function declaration.

```
Shader = compile shaderProfile FunctionName();
```

In this syntax, the *shaderProfile* element can be either one of the vertex or pixel shader profiles as defined in Chapter 1. You can also see that the *FunctionName* element is the HLSL function, which will be compiled into your shader. This makes the process of defining shaders easy as you can create your shader code as a function and use the above syntax to declare your actual compiled shaders.

To make this example more complete, I've include a sample to illustrate a simple lighting pixel shader function and how it is compiled.

```
float4 lighting(in float3 normal, in float3 light,
                in float3 halfvector, in float4 color)
{
     float4 color;
     color = dot(normal,light) * color;
     color += dot(light,halfvector) * color;
     return color;
}

float4 myShader (in float2 tex:TEXCOORD0,
                in float3 normal:TEXCOORD1,
                in float3 light:TEXCOORD2,
                in float3 halfvector:TEXCOORD3,
                in float4 color:COLOR0)
{
    // Compute the lighting color
    Float4 lightColor = light(normal,light,halfvector,color);

    // Fetch the texture color
    Float4 txrColor = tex2D(texture_sampler,tex);

    // Modulate the final color
    Return lightColor * txrColor;
}
```

Summary and what's next?

In this chapter, I have overviewed the last missing HLSL concept called functions. The language itself offers a rich library of over 70 built-in functions to create shaders. Probably the more important is the fact that you can create your own functions whether they are used to define shaders or to componentize your functionality for re-use. The reality is that functions are probably one of the most important components of HLSL, and you will use them every time you wish to define a shader.

Now that we have all the major components, are we ready to start looking into the effect framework? Not just yet! In the next chapter I will define a few basic shaders. Not only will they serve as practical examples of what can be done with the HLSL shader language but also as our example code that will be used throughout the rest of this book.

Chapter 4

Shader Examples

In the previous chapters, I detailed the ins-and-outs of the HLSL shader language. The one thing I had not bothered demonstrating is how to actually write shaders. Although this is not a book on how to write shaders, it was fitting to give a few examples of basic shaders. These shaders will come in handy later as I start using the effect framework and to illustrate core concepts.

Keep in mind that to create complete shaders, you not only need the shader code but a set of render states and variables which need to be setup based on proper semantics. Since we have not made it to the topic of building complete effects yet, I will only concentrate on the vertex and pixel fragment codes at this point. I will expand on these later in this book.

The Bare Minimum Shader

To have something rendering on the screen, a bare minimum task needs to be accomplished. First, you will need to take the incoming vertex positions (which are in world space) and convert them to screen space. This is performed by using the world-view-projection matrix, containing all the necessary transformations to take an object from its local space and bringing it into projected space corresponding to your screen coordinates. For now, we'll assume that this combined transformation matrix is contained in a variable named *view_proj_matrix*.

The first thing we need to do is define the structure used to pass the vertex information from our vertex shader onto our pixel shader. You can define this in a structure called *VS_OUTPUT*, or any name you wish. All we need at this point is the position of the vertex.

```
struct VS_OUTPUT
{
    float4 Pos:      POSITION;
};
```

You may notice the *POSITON* semantics attached to the *Pos* variable; this tells the effect system how this value should be passed to the pixel shader. Semantics will be discussed in a later chapter. The only thing missing at this point is the vertex shader code. This code will take the incoming vertex position and transform it with the *view_proj_matrix*, which can be done by using the *mul* built-in function. Putting this code in a function called *vs_main* would yield the following output:

```
VS_OUTPUT vs_main( float4 inPos: POSITION )
{
    VS_OUTPUT Out;

    // Output a transformed and projected vertex position
    Out.Pos = mul(view_proj_matrix, inPos);

    return Out;
}
```

Take note that the input parameter *inPos* is also followed by the semantics declaration *POSITION*. This tells the vertex shader how to map the geometry stream information to this input parameter. This brings us to the second component of a bare minimum shader. Now that you know where the vertices will be on-screen, you need to define what they should look like. The easiest way is to use a single constant color. Within a pixel shader, the return value of the shader is usually defined as a *float4* which will be used as the screen color for this pixel in the form of red, green, blue and alpha. Putting the appropriate code in a function named *ps_main*, yielded the following:

```
float4 ps_main( void ) : COLOR0
{
    //  Output constant color
    float4 color;
    color[0] = color[3] = 1.0; // Red and Alpha on
    color[1] = color[2] = 0.0; // Green and Blue off
    return color;
}
```

The pixel shader code is simple enough, and you can notice the *COLOR0* semantic on the return of the function, telling our compiler that this function returns the color to be applied to this particular pixel. It's nothing too complicated, nor is it intended to be in this chapter. This code, as-is, is not very useful. As I mentioned above, we'll use this code as the basis to develop full-blown shaders and effects later in the book.

Making it Colorful

Now that we have the code for basic rendering, how about adding a little more color by applying a texture to the geometry? For the shader to be able to use a texture, it will need a global variable of type *sampler*. We'll explain later how you can use semantics and the effect framework to set up textures. For now, this is how the texture would be set up:

```
sampler Texture0;
```

Before you can use the texture, you need to know where to sample the textures in the first place. To do this, your pixel will need some texture coordinates. Texture coordinates will come in to your vertex shader (from your geometry data), processed and passed on to the pixel shader. Texture coordinates are passed in parameters, which used the *TEXCOORDx* semantics. This tells the hardware how to exchange the data between the vertex and pixel shaders. Here is the resulting vertex shader code with all our adjustments.

```
struct VS_OUTPUT
{
   float4 Pos:      POSITION;
   float2 Txr1:     TEXCOORD0;
};

VS_OUTPUT vs_main(
      float4 inPos: POSITION,
      float2 Txr1: TEXCOORD0
)
{
   VS_OUTPUT Out;

   // Output our transformed and projected vertex
   // position and texture coordinate
   Out.Pos = mul(view_proj_matrix, inPos);
   Out.Txr1 = Txr1;

   return Out;
}
```

The pixel shader is easy to define. With the sampler variable already created, you will need to sample the texture by using the *tex2D* built-in function. The final pixel shader code with all the changes is shown below.

```
sampler Texture0;
float4 ps_main(
      float4 inDiffuse: COLOR0,
      float2 inTxr1: TEXCOORD0
) : COLOR0
{
   // Output the color taken from our texture
   return tex2D(Texture0,inTxr1);
}
```

Shining Some Light

Although rendering objects with a basic texture might be enough, it definitely fails to be realistic. In the quest to create realistic scenes, one of the steps usually taken is to apply lighting to objects.

The real world is filled with lights, from the sun to light bulbs. Without light, there wouldn't be much to see in the first place!

Although lighting can be a complex topic of its own, in the realm of 3D graphics, lights are generally simplified to a few basic types.

- **Ambient lighting**: a gross approximation of the total level of lighting in a scene coming from a multitude of discreet lights. This serves as a good guess significantly reduce the number of lights to consider within a particular scene. Ambient lighting generally manifests itself as a constant colored light, affecting the object uniformly.
- **Diffuse lighting**: Materials presenting a microscopic rough surface has the effect of reflecting incoming light uniformly in all directions. This has the result of causing the perceived lighting to be the same from any viewing angle.
- **Specular lighting**: When the surface of a material is smooth and presents little roughness, light reflects off the surface in a non-uniform way. This means that for specular lighting, the light intensity will not only depend on the light to surface angle but also on the viewing angle.

In addition to the influence that light can have on an object surface, you also need to consider how lights can be classified themselves. Although light generally emits from a surface, such as a light bulb or the sun, we can usually consider light as either being directional or coming from a point source.

Directional lights are the simplest form of lighting available. They do not have a position and simply assume that all light rays are parallel to one another and heading in the same direction. What kind of light behaves like this? Well in reality, none. A directional light only has the purpose of estimating the case where a uniform source of light is sufficiently far away and that you can estimate it by assuming that all rays of light are parallel to one another.

The best example of this would be sunlight. Considering the sun can be treated as a point light and that it is located million of miles away from earth, rays that hit the surface of the earth are almost parallel and considered directional light. This concept is shown in Figure 4.1.

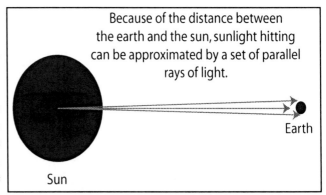

Because of the distance between the earth and the sun, sunlight hitting can be approximated by a set of parallel rays of light.

Sun

Earth

Figure 4.1: Light rays from the sun can be considered parallel because of the sun to earth distance.

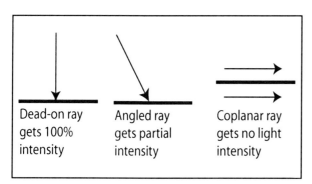

Figure 4.2: The intensity of light on a surface relates to the angle between the light direction and the surface normal.

Another consequence of the fact that a directional light has no position means that it does not attenuate over distance. The only factors to consider in the end are the direction and color of the light rays. One question that may come to mind is how this light influences the surface. As Figure 4.2 shows, you only need to consider the angle inbetween the light rays and the surface normal.

Knowing this, you can simply find out the intensity of the light on a particular point of the surface by taking the dot product inbetween the light direction and surface normal and factoring in the light color. This would yield the following shader code:

```
Color = Light_Color * saturate(dot( Light_Direction, inNormal ));
```

Note that in the above code that we use the *saturate* function. This function allows us to ensure a positive result as a face away from the light would get a negative lighting value. You could have also used the `clamp` function, but to clamp between zero and one, the `saturate` function will yield more efficient code.

Most of the light in a scene comes in the form of a light bulb, torch or similar lighting element. When you think about it, most of those sources are small, finite and located at a discreet position within your scene. For simplification, you may consider all of them as being a source of light contained as a single discreet point in your scene, therefore a point light.

With such lights, rays will emerge in a radial fashion as illustrated in Figure 4.3. This means that any object in any position relative to the light will get affected in the same way. Since the intensity of light on a surface is determined by the relationship between the light rays and the surface normal, the only extra step to take is to discover the direction of the rays of light in the first place. Determining

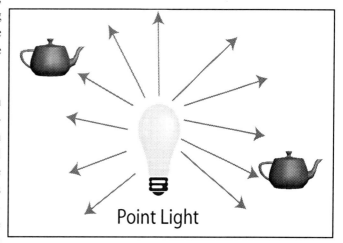

Figure 4.3: How rays of light emerge from a Point Light.

the vector from the source of light to the 3D position of the surface point you are considering can easily do this. Finding out the angle based attenuation for a point light yields the following code:

```
// Compute the normalized light direction vector and use it to determine
// the angular light attenuation.
float3 Light_Direction = normalize( inPos - Light_Position );
float AngleAttn = saturate(dot( inNormal, Light_Direction ));
```

Another consideration with point lights is that the light attenuates based on distance. The first step is to determine the distance from the surface to the light. This can be easily done with the following shader code:

```
float Distance = length( inPos - Light_Position );
```

Generally, point light will attenuate proportionally to the square of the distance from the light. To allow flexibility within your scene, however, you would adjust the light based on the inverse of the distance, distance and distance squared. Thiscode illustrates how it can be done:

```
// Compute distance based attenuation. This is defined as:
// Attenuation = 1 / ( LA.x + LA.y*Dist + LA.z*Dist*Dist )
float DistAttn = saturate(1 / ( LightAttenuation.x +
                                LightAttenuation.y * Dist +
                                LightAttenuation.z * Dist * Dist ));
```

Integrating the pieces of code developed earlier for a point light with the vertex shader gives you the following vertex shader code:

```
struct VS_OUTPUT
{
    float4 Pos:         POSITION;
    float2 TexCoord:    TEXCOORD0;
    float2 Color:       COLOR0;
};

float4 Light_PointDiffuse(float3 VertPos, float3 VertNorm, float3 LightPos,
                          float4 LightColor, float4 LightAttenuation)
{
    // Determine the distance from the light to the vertex and the direction
    float3 LightDir = LightPos - VertPos;
    float  Dist = length(LightDir);
    LightDir = LightDir / Dist;

    // Compute distance based attenuation. This is defined as:
    // Attenuation = 1 / ( LA.x + LA.y*Dist + LA.z*Dist*Dist )
    float DistAttn = saturate(1 / ( LightAttenuation.x +
                                    LightAttenuation.y * Dist +
                                    LightAttenuation.z * Dist * Dist ));
```

```
        // Compute surface/light angle based attenuation defined as dot(N,L)
        // Note: This must be clamped as it may become negative.
        float AngleAttn = saturate(dot(VertNorm, LightDir) );

        // Compute final lighting
        return LightColor * DistAttn * AngleAttn;
    }

VS_OUTPUT vs_main(float4 inPos: POSITION, float3 inNormal: NORMAL,
                  float2 inTxr: TEXCOORD0)
{
    VS_OUTPUT Out;

    // Compute the projected position and send out the texture coordinates
    Out.Pos = mul(view_proj_matrix, inPos);
    Out.TexCoord = inTxr;

    float4 Color;

    // Compute light contribution
    Color = Light_PointDiffuse(inPos, inNormal, Light1_Position,
                                Light1_Color, Light1_Attenuation);

    // Output Final Color
    Out.Color = Color;

    return Out;
}
```

The function *Light_PointDiffuse* is used to factor out the lighting code so you may write shaders using multiple lights. We'll do this in later chapters.

Now that we have a diffuse point light shader, we need to consider the specular portion to the lighting equation. The major difference with specular lighting is that the lighting intensity is not only influenced by the surface to light angle but also by the light to viewer angle.

A common way in which this is implemented is with what is called the half vector. This vector is essentially the halfway vector in-between the view vector and the incident light vector.

The view vector is determined by taking a view position and transforming it into object space. In this case we'll assume a vector at (0,0,10). This object-space view vector can then be combined to the vertex position. The following code illustrates how this is done:

```
EyeVector = -normalize(mul(inv_view_matrix,float4(0,0,10,1))+inPos);
```

With this *EyeVector*, you can determine the half vector by combining it with the incident light vector and then normalizing the result. Since both vectors are normalized to start with, the result is equivalent to averaging them with *(A+B)/2*. The following code shows how you can do this:

```
HalfVect = normalize(LightDir-EyeVector);
```

Once you have the half vector, the angle-based light intensity can simply be determined by computing the dot product between the half vector and the surface normal and raising the result to the power of m. Raising the result to a certain power controls the specular exponent of the light. The higher the value, the smaller and sharper the lighting highlight will be. For this example shader, we'll assume a specular power of 32, but this can be adjusted as needed.

Combining all these elements into a function called *LightPoint_Specular* gives the following vertex shader code:

```
struct VS_OUTPUT
{
    float4 Pos:        POSITION;
    float2 TexCoord:   TEXCOORD0;
    float2 Color:      COLOR0;
};

float4 Light_PointSpecular(float3 VertPos, float3 VertNorm, float3 LightPos,
                           float4 LightColor, float4 LightAttenuation,
                           float3 EyeDir)
{
    // Determine the distance from the light to the vertex and the direction
    float3 LightDir = LightPos - VertPos;
    float  Dist = length(LightDir);
    LightDir = LightDir / Dist;

    // Compute half vector
    float3 HalfVect = normalize(LightDir-EyeDir);

    // Compute distance based attenuation. This is defined as:
    // Attenuation = 1 / ( LA.x + LA.y*Dist + LA.z*Dist*Dist )
    float DistAttn = saturate(1 / ( LightAttenuation.x +
                                    LightAttenuation.y * Dist +
                                    LightAttenuation.z * Dist * Dist ));

    float SpecularAttn =  pow( saturate(dot(VertNorm, HalfVect)),32);

    // Compute final lighting
    return LightColor * DistAttn * SpecularAttn;
}

VS_OUTPUT vs_main(float4 inPos: POSITION, float3 inNormal: NORMAL,
                  float2 inTxr: TEXCOORD0)
{

    VS_OUTPUT Out;
```

```
    // Compute the projected position and send out the texture coordinates
    Out.Pos = mul(view_proj_matrix, inPos);
    Out.TexCoord = inTxr;

    // Output the ambient color
    float4 Color = Light_Ambient;

    // Determine the eye vector
    float3 EyeVector = -normalize(mul(inv_view_matrix,float4(0,0,10,1))+inPos);

    // Compute light contribution
    Color = Light_PointSpecular(inPos, inNormal, Light1_Position,
                                Light1_Color, Light1_Attenuation,
                                EyeVector);

    // Output Final Color
    Out.Color = Color;

    return Out;
}
```

When considering lighting, most people think that lighting an object per-vertex is enough. This is generally true for highly tessellated objects but fails on complex shapes and low detail ones. The reason behind this is the way interpolation of colors between vertices happens.

When you light your object per-vertex, the lighting color is calculated once for each vertex and then linearly interpolated across the polygon. The reality, however, is that the lighting values are dependent on the incident light angle, the surface normal and the viewer position (for specular lighting). The interpolation of color resulting from the per-vertex lighting calculations does not give the same results as interpolating each component individually, especially on large polygons.

Imagine the following case where you have one flat surface being lit by a single point light. With per-vertex lighting, the color will be determined for each vertex then interpolated. With per-pixel lighting, you will interpolate each component needed for lighting then calculate on a per-pixel basis. Figure 4.4 shows you an example of the difference between vertex and pixel based lighting for a simple flat surface.

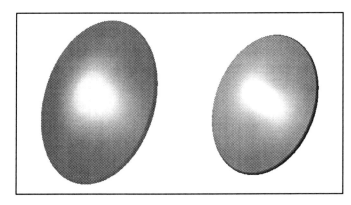

Figure 4.4: Vertex and pixel-based lighting for a simple flat surface lit by a single point light.

When dealing with high polygon counts, per-vertex lighting does well because each individual polygon covers little of the screen, and each pixel suffers from little interpolation error. When dealing with lower detail geometry, however, pixel- based lighting is the way to go for correct lighting!

Another added advantage of per-pixel lighting is the ability to add detail, which doesn't exist in the original mesh. By using bump maps and normal maps, you can add bumpiness to your geometry on a per-pixel level, which doesn't exist on the geometry but which creates the illusion of such detail by using appropriate lighting.

Starting with diffuse lighting, you will need to decide what lighting components can be interpolated to be sent to the pixel shader and which ones need to be processed per-pixel. From the end to the beginning, what defines diffuse lighting is the dot product in-between the surface normal and the light vector.

This dot product defines the intensity of the lighting, but the results of such an operation cannot be interpolated properly. Because of this, the dot product will need to be processed for each pixel and moved to the pixel shader.

The two components of this dot product are the surface normal and light vector. Vectors will interpolate correctly when put in on a per-vertex basis. This means you can calculate them ahead of time for each vertex and pass them on to the pixel shader, which will take care of computing the final dot product.

 *Note*

> Although normals can be interpolated linearly, such interpolation can yield vectors that are not normalized. To correct this, it is a good idea to renormalize the vector by using the built-in HLSL *normalize* function for normals, which are interpolated in the transition from a vertex to a pixel shader.

For this to happen, you will need to add those two components to the vertex shader output structure. They can be passed to the pixel shader using the *TEXCOORD1* and *TEXCOORD2* semantics. Applying the modifications will yield the following output structure:

```
struct VS_OUTPUT
{
    float4 Pos:        POSITION;
    float2 TexCoord:   TEXCOORD0;
    float3 Normal:     TEXCOORD1;
    float3 LightDir:   TEXCOORD2;
};
```

You will also need to change the vertex shader to pass those values to the output structure. Since you will be dealing with a single light, it will be easier at this point to remove the lighting function and copy the relevant code in the *vs_main* function. Keep in mind that we will be dealing with multiple lights later on in this book.

One thing you may have noticed that was not mentioned is the distance based attenuation. Although the interpolation of this component is not perfect, lights have a sufficient range of action, and small differences in distance will not to make a significant difference in the result, and hence does not need to be computed per-pixel.

Since this attenuation factor is a single scalar value, the easiest way to pass it to the pixel shader without wasting another register is to simply make the *LightDir* vector a *float4* and put this result in the *W* component of this vector. Applying all those changes should give you the following vertex shader:

```
struct VS_OUTPUT
{
    float4 Pos:        POSITION;
    float2 TexCoord:   TEXCOORD0;
    float3 Normal:     TEXCOORD1;
    float4 LightDir:   TEXCOORD2;
};

VS_OUTPUT vs_main(float4 inPos: POSITION, float3 inNormal: NORMAL,
                  float2 inTxr: TEXCOORD0)
{
    VS_OUTPUT Out;

    // Compute the projected position and send out the texture coordinates
    Out.Pos = mul(view_proj_matrix, inPos);
    Out.TexCoord = inTxr;

    // Move the normal to the pixel shader
    Out.Normal = inNormal;

    // Compute and move the light direction to the pixel shader
    float4 LightDir;
    LightDir.xyz = Light1_Position - inPos;
    float Dist = length(LightDir.xyz);
    LightDir.xyz = LightDir.xyz / Dist;

    // Compute the distance based attenuation. Distance can be interpolated
    // fairly well so we will precompute it on a per-vertex basis.
    LightDir.w = saturate(1 / ( Light1_Attenuation.x +
                                Light1_Attenuation.y * Dist +
                                Light1_Attenuation.z * Dist * Dist ));

    // Output the light direction
    Out.LightDir = LightDir;
    return Out;
}
```

On the pixel shader end, the task is simply a matter of taking the incoming vectors and computing the dot product and the final lighting color. For the convenience, the lighting code can be put in a function called `Light_PointDiffuse` as was done earlier in the per-vertex lighting shader. In essence, the lighting computation code is the same as the vertex shader version.

You will also need to add the input parameters to the pixel shader main function, `ps_main`, so the interpolated normal and light direction can be read. With all those adjustments, you should end up with the following pixel shader:

```
float4 Light-PointDiffuse(float4 LightDir,
                          float3 Normal,
                          float4 LightColor)
{
    // Compute suface/light angle based attenuation defined as dot(N,L)
    float AngleAttn = saturate(dot(Normal, LightDir.xyz) );

    // Compute final lighting (Color * Distance Attenuation *
    // Angle Attenuation)
    return LightColor * LightDir.w * AngleAttn;
}

float4 ps_main(float3 inNormal:TEXCOORD1,
               float4 inLightDir:TEXCOORD2) : COLOR
{
    // Compute the lighting contribution for this single light
    return Light_PointDiffuse(inLightDir,inNormal,Light1_Color);
}
```

Not too hard yet, huh? Now it is time to tackle the specular per-pixel lighting shader... The basic process is the same as what was done with the diffuse lighting shader. The core of this shader is the dot product between the light vector and the half vector. As with the diffuse lighting shader, this computation will need to be done on the pixel shader.

This means that both the light vector and the half vector will need to be calculated in the vertex shader and passed to the pixel shader. In the same way you have done with the diffuse lighting shader, you will need to add the proper variables to the output structure. With the changes, the output structure should look as follows:

```
struct VS_OUTPUT
{
    float4 Pos:        POSITION;
    float2 TexCoord:   TEXCOORD0;
    float3 Normal:     TEXCOORD1;
    float4 LightDir:   TEXCOORD2;
    float3 HalfVect:   TEXCOORD3;
};
```

Within the vertex shader code, you will need to calculate the normal, light vector, half vector and distance-based attenuation. This is simply a matter taking the specular lighting shader code developed in the previous chapter and applying a few changes. Once you have done this, you should have the following code:

```
struct VS_OUTPUT
{
    float4 Pos:        POSITION;
    float2 TexCoord:   TEXCOORD0;
    float3 Normal:     TEXCOORD1;
    float4 LightDir:   TEXCOORD2;
    float3 HalfVect:   TEXCOORD3;
};

VS_OUTPUT vs_main(float4 inPos: POSITION, float3 inNormal: NORMAL,
                  float2 inTxr: TEXCOORD0)
{
    VS_OUTPUT Out;

    // Compute the projected position and send out the texture coordinates
    Out.Pos = mul(view_proj_matrix, inPos);
    Out.TexCoord = inTxr;

    // Determine the distance from the light to the vertex and the direction
    float4 LightDir;
    LightDir.xyz = Light1_Position - inPos;
    float  Dist = length(LightDir.xyz);
    LightDir.xyz = LightDir.xyz / Dist;

    // Compute the per-vertex distance based attenuation
    LightDir.w = saturate(1 / ( Light1_Attenuation.x +
                                Light1_Attenuation.y * Dist +
                                Light1_Attenuation.z * Dist * Dist ));

    // Determine the eye vector and the half vector
    float3 EyeVector = -normalize(mul(inv_view_matrix,float4(0,0,10,1))+inPos);
    Out.HalfVect = normalize(LightDir-EyeVector);

    // Output normal and light direction
    Out.Normal = inNormal;
    Out.LightDir = LightDir;

    return Out;
}
```

On the pixel shader front, it is simply a matter of creating a function called *Light_PointSpecular*, which will take the input vectors and compute the dot product. With this, you can then consider the lighting color and the distance attenuation. The following pixel shader code implements all these changes:

```
float4 Light_PointSpecular(float3 Normal, float3 HalfVect, float4 LightDir,
                           float4 LightColor)
{
    // Compute suface/light angle based attenuation defined as dot(N,L)
    // Note : This must be clamped as it may become negative.
    float SpecularAttn =  pow( saturate(dot(Normal, HalfVect)),32);

    // Compute final lighting
    return LightColor * LightDir.w * SpecularAttn;
}

float4 ps_main(float3 inNormal:TEXCOORD1, float4 LightDir:TEXCOORD2,
               float3 HalfVect:TEXCOORD3) : COLOR
{
    // Simply route the vertex color to the output
    return Light_PointSpecular(inNormal,HalfVect,LightDir,Light1_Color);
}
```

Bumpy Surfaces

Now that you can light each pixel of your object individually, we'llexplore the topic of normal mapping. Since you are rendering each pixel individually, what prevents you from adding extra information to each pixel, which can add some extra details to the geometry?

The reality is that real objects are not just bound by polygons and that details go much deeper. Imagine a brick wall… Even though you can represent this wall with a simple planar polygon and textures, bricks have much more 3D detail not represented by such geometry. Figure 4.5 shows this in more detail…

All this extra detail could be represented by geometry but would create tremendous amounts of polygons thatwould be almost impossible to manage (at least with today's hardware). Another solution to the problem is to consider the impact of the added detail visually. Since the extra geometry details are small, they do not affect the shape of the object itself but mostly will have an impact on how an object gets lit.

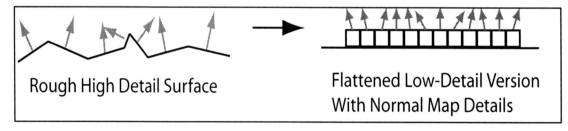

Figure 4.5: Small extra detail compared to the flat polygon representation.

Now that you are rendering each pixel individually nothing prevents you from modifying the normal for each pixel so that it takes account of the added details for this portion of the object. This is where normal mapping comes in to play.

When you are dealing with normal maps, each pixel refers to the current surface normal which is usually either in object space or world space. However, since you are texturing your object with a texture or bump map, which isn't necessarily built for this object, there is no way for the bump map or normal map to specify a new normal without any knowledge of the surface of the object. One solution is to ensure that your texture has a relationship with your object and that the normal map refers to the normals in object-space. This is impractical, however, as it prevents texture reuse and requires special texture authoring for each bumped object in your scene. The fact that the bump texture has knowledge of the surface of the objects will also prohibit you from animating or deforming the surface, restricting your use of normal maps even further.

A more practical approach is to create a new uniform coordinate system, which would be the same for every pixel on your object and from your normal texture can be built. To accomplish this, you need to consider that if your object was not bumped, the normal for each point on the surface would be perpendicular to the surface itself.

When applying a normal map to a surface, you are in essence modifying the normal along the two vectors which go along the *U* and *V* texture coordinates. Putting all this together yields a three vector coordinate system which can be calculated on a per-pixel basis. Figure 4.6 illustrates this coordinate system.

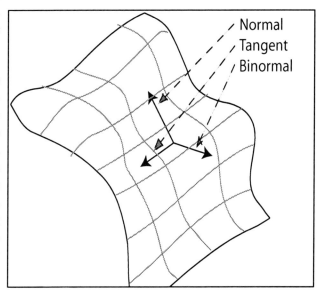

As you can see from Figure 4.6, the vectors along the *U* and *V* texture coordinates are respectively called tangent and binormal. Those vectors are defined as the 3D spatial direction in which the *U* and *V* texture coordinates are headed for a particular point on the surface. How to generate those vectors is outside the scope of this book, but be assured the *D3DXMESH* interface within DirectX gives you functionality to create tangent space vectors.

When doing lighting with tangent space, all you need to do is build a tangent space matrix from the surface normal, tangent

Figure 4.6: How the tangent space coordinate system is generated.

and binormal vector. This matrix can then be used to transform any of the lighting components into this coordinate system by multiplying it by the tangent space matrix.

Once this operation has been completed, all your lighting components will be interpolated relative to the local tangent space for each pixel. The following piece of code shows how you can make a tangent space matrix and use it to convert a vector from object space to tangent space:

```
// Build the tangent space matrix
float3x3 TangentSpace;
TangentSpace[0] = inTangent;
TangentSpace[1] = inBinormal;
TangentSpace[2] = inNormal;

// Transform a vector from object space to tangent space
LightDir = mul(TangentSpace,LightDir);
```

When working in tangent space, all lighting vectors become relative to the interpolated surface normal for this pixel. This means that when doing operations such as bump mapping, you can now store the values a simple relative values since you are working with a coordinate system which represents the same thing no matter what point on the surface you are dealing with. In the case of a normal map, the texture uses a three-color component, which represents the actual normal of the surface in tangent space.

With this knowledge, it is now time to take our per-pixel diffuse/specular shader and use a normal map to enhance the lighting on the object. The changes required to the vertex shader are simple. The first step is to introduce the tangent space matrix code developed in the previous section. Then, you will need to transform both the half-vector and light vector into tangent space before passing them to the pixel shader.

Keep in mind that because you are working in tangent space, the orientation of the surface normal is implicit, and its deviations will be read from the normal map. Because of this, it does not need to be passed to the pixel shader, and you can remove this from the output structure.

With this set of adjustments, you should obtain the following vertex shader code:

```
struct VS_OUTPUT
{
    float4 Pos:        POSITION;
    float2 TexCoord:   TEXCOORD0;
    float4 LightDir:   TEXCOORD1;
    float3 HalfVect:   TEXCOORD2;
};

VS_OUTPUT vs_main(float4 inPos: POSITION, float3 inNormal: NORMAL,
                  float3 inTangent:TANGENT, float3 inBinormal:BINORMAL,
                  float2 inTxr: TEXCOORD0)
```

```
    {
        VS_OUTPUT Out;

        // Compute the projected position and send out the texture coordinates
        Out.Pos = mul(view_proj_matrix, inPos);
        Out.TexCoord = inTxr;

        // Determine the distance from the light to the vertex and the direction
        float4 LightDir;
        LightDir.xyz = mul(inv_view_matrix,float3(80,00,-80)) - inPos;
        float  Dist = length(LightDir.xyz);
        LightDir.xyz = LightDir.xyz / Dist;

        // Compute the per-vertex distance based attenuation
        LightDir.w = saturate(1 / ( Light1_Attenuation.x +
                                    Light1_Attenuation.y * Dist +
                                    Light1_Attenuation.z * Dist * Dist ));

        // Determine the eye vector
        float3 EyeVector = -normalize(mul(inv_view_matrix,float4(0,0,10,1))+inPos);

        // Transform to tangent space and output
        // half vector and light direction
        float3x3 TangentSpace;
        TangentSpace[0] = inTangent;
        TangentSpace[1] = inBinormal;
        TangentSpace[2] = inNormal;
        Out.HalfVect = mul(TangentSpace,normalize(LightDir.xyz+EyeVector));
        Out.LightDir = float4(mul(TangentSpace,LightDir.xyz),LightDir.w);

        return Out;
    }
```

On the pixel shader's end, the only change needed is in relation to the surface normal. Since all the lighting components are passed to the pixel shader in tangent space, this means that they are already relative to the interpolated vertex surface normal, which is implicit through the definition of tangent space. The actual normal on any point of the surface will then come from the normal map.

To do this, you will need to sample the normal map texture and convert it from an unsigned value to a signed one. This value will then be the pixel specific normal and can be substituted to the vertex interpolated normal from the previous shader implementations.

The final pixel shader code for this bumped lighting shader is as follows:

```
float4 Light_Point(float3 Normal, float3 HalfVect, float4 LightDir,
                   float4 LightColor)
{
    // Compute both specular and diffuse factors
    float SpecularAttn =  pow( clamp(0, 1,dot(Normal, HalfVect)),16);
```

```
    float DiffuseAttn = saturate(dot(Normal, LightDir));

    // Compute final lighting
    return LightColor * LightDir.w * (SpecularAttn+DiffuseAttn);
}

float4 ps_main(float2 inTxr:TEXCOORD0,float4 LightDir:TEXCOORD1,
               float3 HalfVect:TEXCOORD2) : COLOR
{
    // Read bump and influence the normal
    float3 normal = tex2D(Bump,inTxr) * 2 - 1;

    // Simply route the vertex color to the output
    return tex2D(Texture0,inTxr)*
           (0.15+Light_Point(normal,HalfVect,LightDir,Light1_Color));
}
```

Summary and what's next?

In this chapter I have showed you a few basic shaders, which will be used throughout the book to help with the construction of shaders. Remember, this book isn't intended to teach you how to build shaders, and I assumed you had some understanding of shaders and lighting throughout this chapter. The important piece of information for you to understand is how you can use the effect system to manage your shaders.

This is exactly what I will start discussing over the next chapters. Now that I've gone over the HLSL shader language, it is time to discuss the effect system and how you can use it to you advantage. So, get ready! It is now time for the main course.

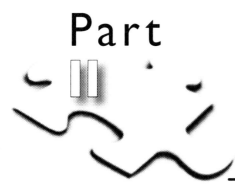

Part II

Moving From HLSL to Effect Files

In the first section of this book, I focused only on the HLSL shading language and how you can take advantage of it to write shaders. Although a shader language allows the creation of an actual shader, there is more to the use of shaders than just the shader code.

For example, you may want to construct several shaders to create the same effect so that a wide range of users with various video cards can all share a similar experience. In addition, DirectX exposes several rendering states that may be set through your application but are often in direct relationship to the actual shader you wish to use.

This is where effect files come into play. As well as allowing you to define vertex and pixel shader code, they enable you to create several various techniques for a single effect in addition to allowing you to specify specific render states about the effect.

Over the next few chapters I will discuss the format of effect files and how you can use them to construct complex effects. In addition, I will also discuss a few related topics such as the use and function of the standard semantics and annotations and how you can take advantage of some optimization features built into the effect framework.

Chapter 5

The Effect File Format

So far, you should have a good understanding of how the HLSL shader language works and how you can use it to write shaders. As you may have noticed, however, I have not yet discussed how to use these shaders in a real context. There is more involved in creating effects than just the shader code by itself. I will now go through the process with you in greater detail.

When rendering geometry, you will need not only to consider which shader to use but also how to configure the hardware to render the geometry they way you want it; this is generally done by using render states and texture stage states.

There is also a wide variety of rendering hardware out there, and not all of them have the same capabilities. For example, you could develop all of your shaders to take advantage of the 2.0 shader model, leaving all older video cards in the dark, as they cannot take advantage of the features you are using. The effect framework, through the use of effect files, allows for the creation of multiple techniques for a single effect, which can be used independently of each other as your application sees fit. It thus allows you to create variations of your effect, which can function on a wide variety of hardware configurations.

In this chapter I will go over the extension to the HLSL language, which becomes an effect file and explain all of its different components. Lets start by discussing the file format itself.

The Anatomy of an Effect File

The HLSL shader language as overviewed in the first part of this book does not describe an actual file format but how individual shaders are written. An effect file (or .FX file) is an extension around the HLSL specification, allowing you not only to specify shaders but also define how those shaders are used by the hardware through the specification of relevant rendering states.

If you remember in Chapter 1, I discussed the grammar to the HLSL language. I had not mentioned beforethat this grammar not only defines the shading language but also describes the complete grammar for an effect file. Although I will not go over the grammar again, I will discuss some of the components which are core to an effect file. The complete grammar has been included in Appendix D for reference.

An effect file not only serves to define shaders but also the context in which they are used. The container for this context is called a technique. Here is the language grammar for a technique:

```
TechniqueDecl : T_KW_TECHNIQUE IdOpt AnnotationOpt TechniqueBody
TechniqueBody : TechniqueBegin TechniqueEnd
TechniqueBody : TechniqueBegin PassDecls TechniqueEnd
TechniqueBegin : '{'
TechniqueEnd : '}'
```

As you can see from the grammar above, a technique is described by the `technique` keyword followed by an identifier for the technique and an optional annotation. What is more interesting is the content of the technique. As you can see, the technique declaration essentially contains a *PassDecls* which represents one of many render passes to the technique.

 *Note*

Annotation blocks and semantics will be described in greater details in Chapter 6.

Not all effects can be realized by rendering your geometry once. For example, a complex lighting effect which can easily be done in a single pass on a 2.0 shader card may require multiple passes to be rendered on a 1.x card. The use of the *PassDecls* within the grammar allows for a technique to define multiple rendering passes for a single effect. The grammar for rendering passes is described below:

```
PassDecls : PassDecl
PassDecls : PassDecls PassDecl
PassDecl : T_KW_PASS IdOpt AnnotationOpt StateBlock
```

In a fashion similar to a technique, a rendering pass is defined by the `Pass` keyword followed by an optional annotation block. The content of a pass is defined by a *StateBlock* which represents a grouping of render states to be used by the effect.

A *StateBlock* is a simple list of states which has the following grammar:

```
StateBlock : StateBlockBegin StateBlockEnd
StateBlock : StateBlockBegin States StateBlockEnd
StateBlockBegin : '{'
StateBlockEnd : '}'

States : State
States : States State
```

```
State : Id StateIndex StateExprBegin StateExpr StateExprEnd
```

From the above grammar, you can see that a state block is a sequence of one or multiple states. States themselves are analogous to fixed pipeline render states used within DirectX with the exception that the vertex and pixel shaders may also be specified as a state. The following section will go over the topic of effect states and describe their use.

Effect States

Render states within an effect file essentially controls the hardware and sets it up for rendering. Their content is somewhat similar to the familiar DirectX fixed pipeline render states but also exposes some new states more relevant to the setup of shaders. The basic syntax for an effect state is as follows:

```
state [ [index] ] = expression;
```

As I have just mentioned, the state is similar to the traditional fixed function pipeline states; a complete list of states is provided in the following sections. The *index* component is an optional integer index which can be used to identify a particular state within an array of effect states (such as texture stage states). And finally, the *expression* portion of the state assignment contains a simple expression (as defined by the effect file grammar), which must match the type needed by the particular effect state.

 Note

> Although there is no requirement that the HLSL/effect grammar be case sensitive, certain applications will enforce case sensitivity. Because of this, you should stick to using the proper cases for the state names and certain constant values to ensure maximum compatibility.

Effect states can be broken up into the following categories:

- Light States
- Material States
- Render States
- Pixel Pipe States
- Vertex Pipe States
- Shader States
- Shader Constant States
- Texture States

- Texture Stage States
- Transform States

Because the states in each category can be numerous, I have broken down the description of each into several sections which I will go over one by one. Let's start by taking a look at the light states.

Light States

To ensure the best performance when applying an effect, all components of a light or a material should be specified in the effect file. States that you fail to declare are set to some default value because there is no way for Direct3D to set light states individually. All available light states along with their description are listed in Table 5-1 below.

Table 5-1 Light States

State	Type	Values
LightAmbient[n]	float4	The ambient color for the specified light. See the `Ambient` member of `D3DLIGHT9` in the DirectX SDK documentation for more details.
LightAttenuation0[n]	float	The first attenuation parameter for the specified light. See the `Attenuation0` member of `D3DLIGHT9` in the DirectX SDK documentation for more details.
LightAttenuation1[n]	float	The second attenuation parameter for the specified light. See the `Attenuation1` member of `D3DLIGHT9` in the DirectX SDK documentation for more details.
LightAttenuation2[n]	float	The third attenuation parameter for the specified light. See the `Attenuation2` member of `D3DLIGHT9` in the DirectX SDK documentation for more details.
LightDiffuse[n]	float4	The diffuse lighting color for the specified light. See the `Diffuse` member of `D3DLIGHT9` in the DirectX SDK documentation for more details.
LightDirection[n]	float3	The direction vector for the specified directional light. See the `Direction` member of `D3DLIGHT9` in the DirectX SDK documentation for more details.
LightEnable[n]	bool	This value must be either `True` or `False` and controls whether the specified light is active or not. See the `bEnable` argument of `IDirect3DDevice9::LightEnable` in the DirectX SDK documentation for more details.

Table 5-1 Light States

State	Type	Values
LightFalloff[n]	float	The intensity of the specified spotlight between the inner and outer cone. See the `Falloff` member of `D3DLIGHT9` in the DirectX SDK documentation for more details.
LightPhi[n]	float	The angle of the outer cone of the specified spotlight. See the `Phi` member of `D3DLIGHT9` in the DirectX SDK documentation for more details.
LightPosition[n]	float3	The position of the selected point or spotlight. See the `Position` member of `D3DLIGHT9` in the DirectX SDK documentation for more details.
LightRange[n]	float	The maximum distance the light has an effect. See the `Range` member of `D3DLIGHT9` in the DirectX SDK documentation for more details.
LightSpecular[n]	float4	The specular lighting component for the specified light. See the `Specular` member of `D3DLIGHT9` in the DirectX SDK documentation for more details.
LightTheta[n]	float	The angle of the inner cone for the specified spotlight. See the `Theta` member of `D3DLIGHT9` in the DirectX SDK documentation for more details.
LightType[n]	dword	The type of light for the specified light. Values are the same as the array of `D3DLIGHTTYPE` without the `D3DLIGHT_` prefix.

Remember to set all states for a light that you intend to use especially when dealing with fixed pipeline shaders, as the default values might not give you the expected results. Now, let's move on and discuss material related render states.

Material States

Material states control specific material attributes as defined within the `D3DMATERIAL9` structure. Keep in mind that, as with the light states, if you fail to declare any state, they will be set to some default value because there is no way for Direct3D to set material states individually. The list of material states is available in the Table 5-2 below.

Table 5-2 Material States

State	Type	Values
MaterialAmbient	float4	Same value as the `Ambient` member of `D3DMATERIAL9`. Refer to the DirectX SDK documentation for more details.
MaterialDiffuse	float4	Same value as the `Diffuse` member of `D3DMATERIAL9`. Refer to the DirectX SDK documentation for more details.
MaterialEmissive	float4	Same value as the `Emissive` member of `D3DMATERIAL9`. Refer to the DirectX SDK documentation for more details.
MaterialPower	float	Same value as the `Power` member of `D3DMATERIAL9`. Refer to the DirectX SDK documentation for more details.
MaterialSpecular	float4	Same value as the `Specular` member of `D3DMATERIAL9`. Refer to the DirectX SDK documentation for more details.

The material states directly correspond to the `D3DMATERIAL9` structure. Refer to the DirectX documentation for more details on how to use this structure to control material properties. With material states covered, let's move on to the pixel pipeline render states.

Pixel Pipe Render States

The pixel pipeline render states within an effect file have names similar to the fixed function pipeline states, which are accessible through the Direct3D API. The set of available pixel pipe render states is listed in Table 5-3 below.

Table 5-3 Pixel Pipe States

State	Type	Values
AlphaBlendEnable	bool	This value must be either `True` or `False` and controls if the alpha blending is to be enabled. The values are the same as `D3DRS_ALPHABLENDENABLE` in `D3DRENDERSTATETYPE`.

Table 5-3 Pixel Pipe States

State	Type	Values
AlphaFunc	dword	This render state controls the function used when doing alpha test. This value is the same as *D3DCMPFUNC* without the *D3DCMP_* prefix. See *D3DRS_ALPHAFUNC* in the DirectX documentation for more details.
AlphaRef	dword	This render state controls the reference value used for alpha testing. The value is the same as *D3DRS_ALPHAREF*.
AlphaTestEnable	dword	This value must be either *True* or *False* and controls if the hardware will do alpha testing. See *D3DRS_ALPHATESTENABLE* in the DirectX documentation for more details.
BlendOp	dword	This render state controls the operation used for alpha blending and contains the same values as *D3DBLENDOP* without the *D3DBLENDOP_* prefix.
ColorWriteEnable	dword	This render state controls which color components are written out to the frame buffer and must be a bitwise combination of *RED|GREEN|BLUE|ALPHA*. See *D3DRS_COLORWRITEENABLE* in the DirectX documentation for more details.
DepthBias	float	This render state controls the z-buffering bias used when rendering and contains the same values as *D3DRS_DEPTHBIAS*.
DestBlend	dword	This render state controls the destination parameter for alpha blending and contains the same values as *D3DBLEND* without the *D3DBLEND_* prefix.
DitherEnable	bool	This render state must be either *True* or *False* and controls whether the hardware can use dithering to generate its output color. The values are the same as *D3DRS_DITHERENABLE*.
FillMode	dword	This render state defines how geometry must be filled by the hardware and must contain the same values as *D3DFILLMODE* without the *D3DFILL_* prefix.

Table 5-3 Pixel Pipe States

State	Type	Values
LastPixel	dword	This render state must be either *True* or *False* and controls the rasterizing process of triangles. See *D3DRS_LASTPIXEL* in the DirectX documentation for more details.
ShadeMode	dword	This render state controls the method used by the hardware to fill triangles and contains the same values as *D3DSHADEMODE* without the *D3DSHADE_* prefix.
SlopeScaleDepthBias	float	This render state controls the depth bias used by the hardware when rendering shadow maps and must contain the same values as *D3DRS_SLOPESCALEDEPTHBIAS*.
SrcBlend	dword	This render state controls the source component used for alpha blending and must contain the same values as *D3DBLEND* without the *D3DBLEND_* prefix.
StencilEnable	bool	This render state must be either *True* or *False* and indicates if the stencil buffer is to be used and contains the same values as *D3DRS_STENCILENABLE*.
StencilFail	dword	This render state controls stencil buffer operations and contains the same values as *D3DSTENCILCAPS* without the *D3DSTENCILCAP_* prefix. See *D3DRS_STENCILFAIL* in the DirectX documentation for more details.
StencilFunc	dword	This render state controls stencil buffer operations and contains the same values as *D3DCMPFUNC* without the *D3DCMP_* prefix. See *D3DRS_STENCILFUNC* in the DirectX documentation for more details.
StencilMask	dword	This render state controls stencil buffer operations and contains the same values as *D3DRS_STENCILMASK* in the DirectX documentation for more details.

Table 5-3 Pixel Pipe States

State	Type	Values
StencilPass	dword	This render state controls stencil buffer operations and contains the same values as `D3DSTENCILCAPS` without the `D3DSTENCILCAP_` prefix. See `D3DRS_STENCILPASS` in the DirectX documentation for more details.
StencilRef	int	This render state controls the reference value for stencil buffer operations and must contain the same values as `D3DRS_STENCILREF`.
StencilWriteMask	dword	This render state controls stencil buffer operations and contains the same values as `D3DRS_STENCILWRITEMASK`.
StencilZFail	dword	This render state controls stencil buffer operations and contains the same values as `D3DSTENCILCAPS` without the `D3DSTENCILCAP_` prefix. See `D3DRS_STENCILZFAIL` in the DirectX documentation for more details.
TextureFactor	dword	This render state is used to set the constant texture factor color and must be of the type `D3DCOLOR`. See `D3DRS_TEXTUREFACTOR` in the DirectX documentation for more details.
Wrap0 - Wrap15	dword	These render states control the texture wrapping parameters for the specified texture. The values are the same as the values used by `D3DRS_WRAP0`. Valid values are: `COORD0` (which corresponds to `D3DWRAPCOORD_0`), `COORD1` (which corresponds to `D3DWRAPCOORD_1`), `COORD2` (which corresponds to `D3DWRAPCOORD_2`), `COORD3` (which corresponds to `D3DWRAPCOORD_3`), `U` (which corresponds to `D3DWRAP_U`), `V` (which corresponds to `D3DWRAP_V`), `W` (which corresponds to `D3DWRAP_W`)
ZEnable	dword	This render state tells the hardware if it should use z-buffering and must contain the same values as `D3DZBUFFERTYPE` without the `D3DZB_` prefix.

Table 5-3 Pixel Pipe States

State	Type	Values
ZFunc	dword	This render state controls which function is used to test against the Z-Buffer and must contain the same values as *D3DCMPFUNC* without the *D3DCMP_* prefix. See *D3DRS_ZFUNC* in the DirectX documentation for more details.
ZWriteEnable	bool	This render state must be either *True* or *False* and controls whether the hardware should update the depth within the Z-Buffer. See *D3DRS_ZWRITEENABLE* in the DirectX documentation for more details.

That's it for pixel pipeline render states. It now makes sense to look at the normal counterpart of pixel states, vertex pipeline render states.

Vertex Pipe Render States

On the flip side of pixel pipeline render states are the vertex pipeline render states. These states control the behavior of the hardware with regard to the processing of vertices and are mostly equivalent to the fixed pipeline render states exposed by the DirectX SDK. All available vertex pipe states are listed below in Table 5-4.

Table 5-4 Vertex Pipe States

State	Type	Values
Ambient	float4	This render state controls the ambient lighting color applied to vertices and contains the same values as *D3DRS_AMBIENT*.
AmbientMaterialSource	dword	This render state defines the material source for the per-vertex ambient color and contains the same values as *D3DMATERIALCOLORSOURCE* without the *D3DMCS_* prefix. See *D3DRS_AMBIENTMATERIALSOURCE* in the DirectX documentation for more details.
Clipping	bool	This render state must either *True* or *False* and defines if the polygons need to be clipped to the view frustum. See *D3DRS_CLIPPING* in the DirectX documentation for more details.

Table 5-4 Vertex Pipe States

State	Type	Values
ClipPlaneEnable	dword	This render state must contain a bitwise combination of the *D3DCLIPPLANE0* - *D3DCLIPPLANE5* macros which will control the use of the specified user clip planes. See *D3DCLIPPLANEn* and *D3DRS_CLIPPLANEENABLE* in the DirectX documentation for more details.
ColorVertex	bool	This render state must be either *True* or *False* and controls if vertex color is applied. See *D3DRS_COLORVERTEX* in the DirectX documentation for more details.
CullMode	dword	This render state controls the culling mode of the rendered triangles and must contain the same values as *D3DCULL* without the *D3DCULL_* prefix.
DiffuseMaterialSource	dword	This render state controls the material source for the vertex diffuse color and contains the same values as *D3DMATERIALCOLORSOURCE* without the *D3DMCS_* prefix. See *D3DRS_DIFFUSEMATERIALSOURCE* in the DirectX documentation for more details.
EmissiveMaterialSource	dword	This render state controls the material emissive source for the vertex and contains the same values as *D3DMATERIALCOLORSOURCE* without the *D3DMCS_* prefix. See *D3DRS_EMISSIVEMATERIALSOURCE* in the DirectX documentation for more details.
FogColor	dword	This render state controls the color used for fogging and must contain the same values as *D3DCOLOR*. See *D3DRS_FOGCOLOR* in the DirectX documentation for more details.
FogDensity	float	This render state controls the density of fogging and contains the same values as *D3DRS_FOGDENSITY*.
FogEnable	bool	This render state must be either *True* or *False* and controls whether fogging is enabled. See *D3DRS_FOGENABLE* in the DirectX documentation for more details.
FogEnd	float	This render state controls the fog end distance and contains the same values as *D3DRS_FOGEND*.
FogStart	float	This render state controls the fog start distance and contains the same values as *D3DRS_FOGSTART*.

Table 5-4 Vertex Pipe States

State	Type	Values
FogTableMode	dword	This render state controls which table mode to use for fogging and contains the same values as *D3DFOGMODE*. See *D3DRS_FOGTABLEMODE* in the DirectX documentation for more details.
FogVertexMode	dword	This render state controls which vertex fogging mode to use and contains the same values as *D3DFOGMODE* without the *D3DFOG_* prefix. See *D3DRS_FOGVERTEXMODE* in the DirectX documentation for more details.
IndexedVertexBlendEnable	bool	This render state must be either *True* or *False* and controls whether to use vertex blending. See *D3DRS_INDEXEDVERTEXBLENDENABLE* in the DirectX documentation for more details.
Lighting	bool	This render state must be either *True* or *False* and controls whether lighting is enabled for the rendered vertices. See *D3DRS_LIGHTING* in the DirectX documentation for more details.
LocalViewer	bool	This render state must be either *True* or *False* and enables camera relative specular highlights. See *D3DRS_LOCALVIEWER* in the DirectX documentation for more details.
MultiSampleAntialias	bool	This render state must be either *True* or *False* and controls how triangles are rendered when using an antialiased render target. See *D3DRS_MULTISAMPLEANTIALIAS* in the DirectX documentation for more details.
MultiSampleMask	dword	This render state contains a set a bits controlling the anti-aliasing process and must contain the same values as *D3DRS_MULTISAMPLEMASK*.
NormalizeNormals	bool	This render state must be either *True* or *False* and controls whether any normals passed to the fixed pipeline will be automatically normalized. See *D3DRS_NORMALIZENORMALS* in the DirectX documentation for more details.
PatchSegments	float	This render state is used to control if n-Patches are enabled and should contain the same values as *nSegments* in *IDirect3DDevice9::SetNPatchMode*.

Table 5-4 Vertex Pipe States

State	Type	Values
PointScale_A	float	This render state is a control parameter for point sprites. See `D3DRS_POINTSCALE_A` in the DirectX documentation for more details.
PointScale_B	float	This render state is a control parameter for point sprites. See `D3DRS_POINTSCALE_B` in the DirectX documentation for more details.
PointScale_C	float	This render state is a control parameter for point sprites. See `D3DRS_POINTSCALE_C` in the DirectX documentation for more details.
PointScaleEnable	bool	This render state controls whether point sprites are enabled and must be either `True` or `False`. See `D3DRS_POINTSCALEENABLE` in the DirectX documentation for more details.
PointSize	float	This render state controls the size of a point sprite and must contain the same values as `D3DRS_POINTSIZE`.
PointSize_Min	float	This render state controls the minimum size of a point sprite and must contain the same values as `D3DRS_POINTSIZE_MIN`.
PointSize_Max	float	This render state controls the maximum size of a point sprite and must contain the same values as `D3DRS_POINTSIZE_MAX`.
PointSpriteEnable	bool	This render state must contain either `True` or `False` and is used to enable point sprites. See `D3DRS_POINTSPRITEENABLE` in the DirectX documentation for more details.
RangeFogEnable	bool	This render state must be either `True` or `False` and is used to activate range based fog. See `D3DRS_RANGEFOGENABLE` in the DirectX documentation for more details.
SpecularEnable	bool	This render state must be either `True` or `False` and controls whether specular lighting should be applied to the vertices. See `D3DRS_SPECULARENABLE` in the DirectX documentation for more details.
SpecularMaterialSource	dword	Same values as `D3DMATERIALCOLORSOURCE` without the `D3DMCS_` prefix. See `D3DRS_SPECULARMATERIALSOURCE`.

Table 5-4 Vertex Pipe States

State	Type	Values
TweenFactor	float	This render state is used to control vertex blending and must contain the same values as `D3DRS_TWEENFACTOR`.
VertexBlend	dword	This render state is used to control vertex blending and must contain the same values as `D3DVERTEXBLENDFLAGS` without the `D3DVBF_` prefix. See `D3DRS_VERTEXBLEND` in the DirectX documentation for more details.

As you can see, both the vertex and pixel pipeline render states can control many of the aspects of rendering geometry. However, at this point we have not touched the topic of texturing. The following section will cover the sampler stages that control how textures are sampled and applied to your geometry.

Sampler/Sampler Stage States

Texturing is at the core of rendering with modern hardware, but to do so correctly, you need to define some attributesto tell the hardware how the textures must be processed. This leads us to the sampler states, comprised of two components: *Sampler States* and *Sampler Stage States*.

The first state of interest when dealing with texturing is the *Sampler* state. This state controls the sampling of a texture and can contain either *NULL* or a sampler state blockindicating how to sample the texture.

The second component of interest is the sampler stage states, which are used to sample textures. Sampler state determines filtering types and texture addressing modes and contains numerous sub-states. These sampler stage states are listed below in Table 5-5.

Table 5-5 Sampler Stage States

State	Type	Values
AddressU[16]	dword	This sampler stage state controls the texture wrapping along the *U* axis and contains the same values as *D3DTEXTUREADDRESS* without the *D3DTADDRESS_* prefix. See *D3DSAMP_ADDRESSU* in the DirectX documentation for more details.
AddressV[16]	dword	This sampler stage state controls the texture wrapping along the *V* axis and contains the same values as *D3DTEXTUREADDRESS* without the *D3DTADDRESS_* prefix. See *D3DSAMP_ADDRESSV* in the DirectX documentation for more details.
AddressW[16]	dword	This sampler stage state controls the texture wrapping along the *W* axis and contains the same values as *D3DTEXTUREADDRESS* without the *D3DTADDRESS_* prefix. See *D3DSAMP_ADDRESSW* in the DirectX documentation for more details.
BorderColor[16]	float4	This sampler stage state is a *D3DCOLOR* which controls the texture border color when clamping. See *D3DSAMP_BORDERCOLOR* in the DirectX documentation for more details.
MagFilter[16]	dword	This sampler stage state controls the mip-mapping and contains the same values as *D3DTEXTUREFILTERTYPE* without the *D3DTEXF_* prefix. See *D3DSAMP_MAGFILTER* in the DirectX documentation for more details.
MaxAnisotropy[16]	dword	This sampler stage state controls anisotropic filtering and contains the same values as *D3DSAMP_MAXANISOTROPY* without the *D3DSAMP_* prefix.
MaxMipLevel[16]	int	This sampler stage state controls the mip-mapping level and contains the same values as *D3DSAMP_MAXMIPLEVEL* without the *D3DSAMP_* prefix.
MinFilter[16]	dword	This sampler stage state controls the mip-mapping and contains the same values as *D3DSAMP_MINFILTER* without the *D3DSAMP_* prefix.
MipFilter[16]	dword	This sampler stage state controls the mip-mapping and contains the same values as *D3DSAMP_MIPFILTER* without the *D3DSAMP_* prefix.

Table 5-5 Sampler Stage States

State	Type	Values
MipMapLodBias[16]	float	This sampler stage state controls the mip-mapping bias and contains the same values as `D3DSAMP_MIPMAPLODBIAS` without the `D3DSAMP_` prefix.
SRGBTexture	float	This sampler stage state controls the SRGB gamma correction value and contains the same value as `D3DSAMP_SRGBTEXTURE` without the `D3DSAMP_` prefix.

Since textures are an important component of rendering, the use of the sampler states will be a critical part of setting up any effect. Even more important than the use of textures is the use of vertex and pixel shaders with their own set of related states. This is exactly what I will cover in the next section.

Shader/Shader Constant States

Shaders are a very important part of effects and rendering. They can also be set-up through the effect file system. You will need to be able to set-up individual shaders and also control shader constants used by the shaders.

The first item on our plate is setting-up individual shaders; the approach is the same as with every other render state covered so far in this chapter and uses the following syntax:

```
PixelShader = <shader of pixelShader type>;
VertexShader = <shader of vertexShader type>;
```

The shaders can be either *NULL*, a block of shader assembly, a shader compile target or a pixel/vertex shader parameter. Using this render state is equivalent to using the `IDirectX9::SetVertexShader` and `IDirectX9::SetPixelShader` API calls.

Once you have a shader setup, you may need to set constants for the shader. Although in the case of a HLSL based shader, you do not need to define constants explicitly since the HLSL code can use variables defined within the effect file, the same is not true for assembly defined shaders. With the HLSL shader, the effect compiler will see which variables the shader uses and assign them to constant registers as needed, for assembly shaders, you must do this manually through the proper shader constant effect states.

The render states allowing you to set-up shader constants are listed below in Table 5-6.

Table 5-6 Shader Constant States

State	Type	Values
PixelShaderConstant	float[m[n]]	This pixel shader constant takes in an m-by-n array of floats; m and n are optional.
PixelShaderConstant1	float4	This pixel shader constant takes in one 4-D float.
PixelShaderConstant2	float4x2	This pixel shader constant takes in two 4-D floats.
PixelShaderConstant3	float4x3	This pixel shader constant takes in three 4-D floats.
PixelShaderConstant4	float4x4	This pixel shader constant takes in four 4-D floats.
PixelShaderConstantB	bool[m[n]]	This pixel shader constant takes in an m-by-n array of bools; m and n are optional.
PixelShaderConstantI	int[m[n]]	This pixel shader constant takes in an m-b-n array of ints; m and n are optional.
PixelShaderConstantF	float[m[n]]	This pixel shader constant takes in an m-by-n array of floats; m and n are optional.
VertexShaderConstant	float[m[n]]	This vertex shader constant takes in an m-by-n array of floats; m and n are optional.
VertexShaderConstant1	float4	This vertex shader constant takes in one 4-D float.
VertexShaderConstant2	float4x2	This vertex shader constant takes in two 4-D floats.
VertexShaderConstant3	float4x3	This vertex shader constant takes in three 4-D floats.
VertexShaderConstant4	float4x4	This vertex shader constant takes in four 4-D floats.
VertexShaderConstantB	bool[m[n]]	This vertex shader constant takes in an m-by-n array of bools; m and n are optional.
VertexShaderConstantI	int[m[n]]	This vertex shader constant takes in an m-by-n array of ints; m and n are optional.
VertexShaderConstantF	float[m[n]]	This vertex shader constant takes in an m-by-n array of floats; m and n are optional.

In addition to shader states and sampler states, texture states control the textures to use and also the fixed pipeline texturing process. This will becovered in the next section.

Texture/Texture Stage States

Texture states are an important component of any texture as it sets up the hardware by telling it which textures to use and how to use them. When using HLSL shaders, you may set those implicitly by using texture variables within your HLSL shader; thus leaving the register allocation decision to the compiler. When using the fixed pipeline, however, you will need to set those explicitly and use the following syntax:

```
Texture[n] = <object of Texture type>;
```

The texture object within the above syntax must be either *NULL* or a texture object. This will setup the specified texture onto the supplied texture stage. In addition to specifying a texture, you will need to tell the fixed pipeline hardware how to use it. This is done by using the texture stage render states specified in Table 5-7 below.

Table 5-7 Texture Stage States

State	Type	Values
AlphaOp[8]	dword	This texture stage state controls the alpha blending operation and must be the same as *D3DTEXTUREOP* without the *D3DTOP_* prefix. See *D3DTSS_ALPHAOP* in the DirectX documentation for more details.
AlphaArg0[8]	dword	This texture stage state controls the alpha blending operation and must be the same as *D3DTA* without the *D3DTA_* prefix. See *D3DTSS_ALPHAARG0* in the DirectX documentation for more details.
AlphaArg1[8]	dword	This texture stage state controls the alpha blending operation and must be the same as *D3DTA* without the *D3DTA_* prefix. See *D3DTSS_ALPHAARG1* in the DirectX documentation for more details.
AlphaArg2[8]	dword	This texture stage state controls the alpha blending operation and must be the same as *D3DTA* without the *D3DTA_* prefix. See *D3DTSS_ALPHAARG2* in the DirectX documentation for more details.
ColorArg0[8]	dword	This texture stage state controls the color blending operation and must be the same as *D3DTA* without the *D3DTA_* prefix. See *D3DTSS_COLORARG0* in the DirectX documentation for more details.

Table 5-7 Texture Stage States

State	Type	Values
ColorArg1[8]	dword	This texture stage state controls the color blending operation and must be the same as *D3DTA* without the *D3DTA_* prefix. See *D3DTSS_COLORARG1* in the DirectX documentation for more details.
ColorArg2[8]	dword	This texture stage state controls the color blending operation and must be the same as *D3DTA* without the *D3DTA_* prefix. See *D3DTSS_COLORARG2* in the DirectX documentation for more details.
ColorOp[8]	dword	This texture stage state controls the color blending operation and must be the same as *D3DTEXTUREOP* without the *D3DTOP_* prefix. See *D3DTSS_COLOROP* in the DirectX documentation for more details.
BumpEnvLScale[8]	float	This texture stage state controls the bumpmapping operations and must be the same values as *D3DTSS_BUMPENVLSCALE* without the *D3DTSS_TCI* prefix.
BumpEnvLOffset[8]	float	This texture stage state controls the bumpmapping operations and must be the same values as *D3DTSS_BUMPENVLOFFSET* without the *D3DTSS_TCI* prefix.
BumpEnvMat00[8]	float	This texture stage state controls the bumpmapping operations and must be the same values as *D3DTSS_BUMPENVMAT00*.
BumpEnvMat01[8]	float	This texture stage state controls the bumpmapping operations and must be the same values as *D3DTSS_BUMPENVMAT01*.
BumpEnvMat10[8]	float	This texture stage state controls the bumpmapping operations and must be the same values as *D3DTSS_BUMPENVMAT10*.
BumpEnvMat11[8]	float	This texture stage state controls the bumpmapping operations and must be the same values as *D3DTSS_BUMPENVMAT11*.
ResultArg[8]	dword	This texture stage state controls what is done with the result of a texture stage and must be the same as *D3DTA* without the *D3DTA_* prefix. See *D3DTSS_RESULTARG* in the DirectX documentation for more details.

Table 5-7 Texture Stage States

State	Type	Values
TexCoordIndex[8]	dword	This texture stage state controls the source of texture coordinates and must be the same values as `D3DTSS_TEXCOORDINDEX` without the `D3DTSS_TCI` prefix.
TextureTransform-Flags[8]	dword	This texture stage state controls the texture coordinate transformation operations and must be the same values as `D3DTEXTURETRANSFORMFLAGS` values without the `D3DTTFF_` prefix. See `D3DTSS_TEXTURETRANSFORMFLAGS` in the DirectX documentation for more details.

That is it for texture stage states. Next and last on our list of effect states is transform states.

Transform States

The transform states are used to initialize transformation matrices by the rendering pipeline. In a way similar to the texture states, you only need to explicitly set the transform states for fixed pipeline operations as you can simply operate on matrix variables within an HLSL shader function. One thing to note is that effects use transposed matrices for efficiency reasons. You may provide transposed matrices to an effect, or an effect will automatically transpose the matrices before using them depending on which API function you use to pass them to Direct3D. The list of available transform states is enumerated blow in Table 5-8.

Table 5-8 Transform States

State	Type	Values
ProjectionTransform	float4x4	This transform state controls the projection matrix and takes in a 4-by-4 matrix of floats. See `D3DTS_PROJECTION` in the DirectX documentation for more details.
TextureTransform[8]	float4x4	This transform state controls the texture transform matrices and takes in a 4-by-4 matrix of floats. See `D3DTRANSFORMSTATETYPE` in the DirectX documentation for more details.
ViewTransform	float4x4	This transform state controls the view matrix and takes in a 4-by-4 matrix of floats. See `D3DTS_VIEW` in the DirectX documentation for more details.

Table 5-8 Transform States

State	Type	Values
WorldTransform	float4x4	This transform state controls the object world transform matrix and takes a 4-by-4 matrix of floats.

That does it for all of the effect states! As you can see, there is a lot to use and choose from to build your effect. After learning about all these effect states, you may now wonder how they are to be used. In the following sections I will go over how you can use effect components including effect states to build effects.

Using Techniques and Passes

Although the effect is the sum of all the shaders and render states that compose it, an equally important part in constructing effects is the techniques and passes used to put everything together. The concept behind effects is that an effect file contains a single effect, which can be executed using one or several techniques. Each of the techniques can in turn have multiple passes, which define how the geometry is to be rendered.

Although I have somewhat covered this in the beginning of this chapter, I wanted to give a simple example of a completed effect. For this example, I will stick with something real simple, a shader which applies no texture but simply does a basic diffuse lighting on an object.

To start off, let's define the shader code, which is basically taken from the code defined in Chapter 4.

```
struct VS_OUTPUT
{
    float4 Pos:       POSITION;
    float2 TexCoord:  TEXCOORD0;
    float2 Color:     COLOR0;
};

float4 Light_PointDiffuse(float3 VertPos, float3 VertNorm, float3 LightPos,
                          float4 LightColor, float4 LightAttenuation)
{
    // Determine the distance from the light to the vertex and the direction
    float3 LightDir = LightPos - VertPos;
    float  Dist = length(LightDir);
    LightDir = LightDir / Dist;

    // Compute distance based attenuation. This is defined as:
    // Attenuation = 1 / ( LA.x + LA.y*Dist + LA.z*Dist*Dist )
    float DistAttn = clamp(0,1, 1 / ( LightAttenuation.x +
```

```
                                        LightAttenuation.y * Dist +
                                        LightAttenuation.z * Dist * Dist ));

    // Compute surface/light angle based attenuation defined as dot(N,L)
    // Note: This must be clamped as it may become negative.
    float AngleAttn = clamp(0, 1, dot(VertNorm, LightDir) );

    // Compute final lighting
    return LightColor * DistAttn * AngleAttn;
}

VS_OUTPUT vs_main(float4 inPos: POSITION, float3 inNormal: NORMAL,
                  float2 inTxr: TEXCOORD0)
{
    VS_OUTPUT Out;

    // Compute the projected position and send out the texture coordinates
    Out.Pos = mul(view_proj_matrix, inPos);
    Out.TexCoord = inTxr;

    float4 Color;

    // Compute light contribution
    Color = Light_PointDiffuse(inPos, inNormal, Light1_Position,
                               Light1_Color, Light1_Attenuation);

    // Output Final Color
    Out.Color = Color;

    return Out;
}

float4 ps_main(float4 inColor:COLOR) : COLOR
{
    // Simply route the vertex color to the output
    return inColor;
}
```

For this shader, I will ignore the variables and focus on only techniques and passes. This particular shader needs a single pass but can be implemented using several techniques. For example, we can instruct the effect that the first available pass will make use of both the pixel and vertex shader. Since we are not using any textures for this example, this is straightforward and accomplished by setting both the *VertexShader* and *PixelShader* states. The effect file code for this is below:

```
technique TVertexAndPixelShader
{
    pass P0
    {
        // shaders
        VertexShader = compile vs_1_1 vs_main();
```

```
            PixelShader  = compile ps_1_1 ps_main();
        }
    }
```

If you look at the pixel shader code that we are using, it simply moves the color from the vertex shader to the output. Because of this, we could easily implement a second technique which accommodates video cards without pixel shader support. This can be accomplished by setting the right texture stage states to output the diffuse color and make sure to set the *PixelShader* state to *NULL*. The code for this technique is below:

```
technique TVertexShaderOnly
{
    pass P0
    {
        // texture stages
        ColorOp[0]   = SELECTARG2;
        ColorArg1[0] = TEXTURE;
        ColorArg2[0] = DIFFUSE;
        AlphaOp[0]   = SELECTARG2;
        AlphaArg1[0] = TEXTURE;
        AlphaArg2[0] = DIFFUSE;
        ColorOp[1]   = DISABLE;
        AlphaOp[1]   = DISABLE;

        // shaders
        VertexShader = compile vs_1_1 vs_main();
        PixelShader  = NULL;
    }
}
```

As you can see, the whole process is straightforward. With this set-up, your application can elect to use any of the techniques that is appropriate. Direct3D will even make this task easier by removing techniques from the list that the current hardware cannot support.

Summary and what's next?

In this chapter I have showed you exactly what an effect file is and explained the states that can be used. With the combination of techniques, passes and the possibility to control almost any of the states offered by Direct3D, the effect framework is a very powerful way of defining rendering effects which are easy to author, edit and even carry from one application to another.

You may remember from the shader code we have discussed so far the use of semantics such as *TEXCOORD0*. In the next chapter, I will discuss the use of annotations and semantics, and most importantly discuss the use of standard annotations and semantics, which define an easy way for applications to communicate with one another.

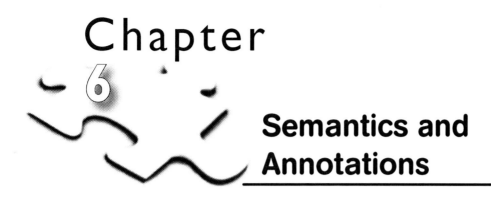

Chapter
6

Semantics and Annotations

So far I have covered the theory behind both the HLSL shading language and the use of an effect file. As you may remember, I had discussed early on in this book that one of the purposes behind the use of effect files is that they not only make the management of effects easier but allow for applications to share a common language so they can share effects.

If you take into consideration what you have learned so far about effects, however, something seems to be missing. How does an application know which variable should contain the projection matrix? One approach would be to impose a certain naming convention to which all applications would adhere. Although this would work in theory, it would become messy and make it difficult to allow for future extensions.

The approach taken by the DirectX team was to allow you to add a set of metadata to your effects to establish the meaning and purpose of variables, shaders and even shader parameters. This metadata is what is called semantics and annotations.

Both serve a specific purpose and will be explored throughout this chapter. In addition, standard semantics and annotations, a pre-defined set of metadata encompassing most common types of variables and actions can be taken within all common effects.

Since semantics and annotations make it possible for an application to understand the intent behind a parameter, it is a topic of great interest to effect developers. It can allow effects designed for run-time purposes to be used interactively within 3D authoring applications and thus improve the efficiency of the whole art pipeline.

Before I get into the specifics of how each semantic and annotation function, I wanted to go over a few examples to give a good overall idea of why they are so useful. For instance, an effect parameter which the application is expected to fill with the current world transformation matrix could use a semantic like this:

```
float4x4 MyWorldMatrix : World;
```

The `World` semantic is a standard semantic which has been defined as a 4x4 floating-point matrix meant to contain the world transformation for the current geometry. As you can see, attaching this standard semantic to an effect parameter makes it possible for an application to understand the intent of this effect parameter regardless of the parameter's name.

 Note

> Although I will be discussing standard semantics and annotations later in this chapter, you can find a complete listing of all the standard semantics and annotations in Appendix C.

Some parameters need additional information to specify their use. This is where annotations come into play. For example, the parameter below uses the diffuse semantic which identifies it as a diffuse lighting color. However, what is the diffuse color of? The annotation can identify the usage as shown here:

```
float4 MyLightDiffuseColor : Diffuse
<
    string Object = "Light";
>;
```

The annotation is attached to a parameter inside of a pair of angle brackets. This annotation has a single string identifying the parameter use as a light. This means the diffuse color parameter is the diffuse color of a light. This annotation used a single string, but annotations can use several strings to identify different types of information such as user interfaces.

As you can see with the few examples above, the use of the proper semantics and annotations can not only make your files easier to understand but can efficiently allow multiple application to understand the same effect file in the same way, regardless of who wrote the application.

Exploring Semantics

Semantics within an effect file are used to specify the direct meaning of a variable or parameter. By using the proper semantic, your application can automatically know which variables to fill and what values to put in them. Within the current definition of the effect language, there are two main types of semantics: shader semantics and parameter semantics.

Shader semantics are used to define the source for the various vertex, whereas pixel shader function parameters are required for the shader to function properly since they bind these inputs to the specified vertex data coming from the DirectX API. On the other hand, variable semantics are used to define the use of various variables defined within an effect file and are optional. Let's now explore both types of semantics.

Shader Semantics

As mentioned, shader semantics bind shader function input and output parameters with pipeline data such as your vertex data. The use of a shader semantic on a shader function parameters is straightforward and follows the syntax below:

```
[Modifiers] ParameterType ParameterName [: Semantic] [= Initializers]
```

Adding a shader semantic is an easy and necessary task so that your shaders can properly exchange information with the hardware. Shader semantics can easily be divided into four categories: vertex shader input, vertex shader output, pixel shader input and pixel shader output. Over the next few pages, I will present the four categories in a set of tables describing the semantics and their meaning. Keep in mind that in the tables below, n is an optional integer between 0 and the number of resources supported for the particular semantic (for example, *PSIZE0*, *COLOR1*, etc).

The first type of shader semantic is vertex input semantics. They serve to define how vertex information from your vertex buffer will be translated into the proper input parameters for your vertex shader function. The vertex shader input semantics are summarized below in Table 6-1.

Table 6-1 Vertex Input Semantics

Semantic	Definition
POSITION[n]	Used to convey the vertex position in object space.
POSITION	Used to convey the transformed vertex position. The *POSITION* semantic tells the runtime that the vertex is transformed and the vertex shader should not be executed.
BLENDWEIGHT[n]	Used to convey the vertex skinning blending weights.
BLENDINDICES[n]	Used to convey the vertex skinning blending indices.
NORMAL[n]	Used to convey the vertex normal vector.
PSIZE[n]	Used to convey the point size of a point sprite.
COLOR[n]	Used to convey vertex diffuse and specular color.
TEXCOORD[n]	Used to convey vertex texture coordinates.
TANGENT[n]	Used to convey vertex tangent vectors.
BINORMAL[n]	Used to convey vertex binormal vectors.
TESSFACTOR[n]	Used to convey the tessellation factor when using N-Patches.

Once you have your vertex shader inputs, you will eventually process the data and send these results to your pixel shader for processing. These outputs from your vertex shader will be sent to your pixel shader by specifying the proper vertex shader output semantic on your output parameters. The list of available vertex shader output semantics is enumerated below in Table 6-2.

Table 6-2 Vertex Output Semantics

Semantic	Definition
POSITION[n]	Used to specify the position of a vertex in homogenous space. You can calculate the position in screen-space by dividing (x,y,z) by w. It is a requirement that every vertex shader write out a parameter with this semantic.
PSIZE	Used to pass the point sprite size to the pixel shader.
FOG	Used to pass the vertex fog intensity to the pixel shader.
COLOR[n]	Used to pass both the diffuse or specular color of a vertex to the pixel shader. All vertex shader prior to 3.0 should clamp any parameter that uses this semantic between 0 and 1, inclusive. The vertex shader 3.0 model has no restriction on the data range.
TEXCOORD[n]	Used to pass texture coordinates to the pixel shader.

Most of the values passed through the vertex shader output semantic will be interpolated and passed per-pixel to the pixel shader based on the type of semantic used. These values will then be consumed by the pixel shader input semantics. The list of available pixel shader input semantics is in Table 6-3 below:

Table 6-3 Pixel Input Semantics

Semantic	Definition
COLOR[n]	Used to bind the diffuse or specular color coming from the vertex shader to a pixel shader input parameter. For shaders before version 3.0, this data ranges between 0 and 1, inclusive. Starting with pixel shader 3.0, there is no restriction on the data range.
TEXCOORD[n]	Used to bind incoming texture coordinates from the vertex shader to the specified pixel shader inputs.
VPOS	Contains the current pixel (x,y) location.
VFACE	Used to indicate the current pixel belongs to a back-facing primitive. A negative value indicates a primitive facing backwards, while a positive value suggests a primitive facing the camera.

With its input parameters properly bound, the pixel shader can now do its work and apply any processing needed to its input pixels. Once its task is complete, it will need to send its output to the hardware for final screen rendering. This is done with the use of the proper pixel shader output semantics listed below in Table 6-4:

Table 6-4 Pixel Output Semantics

Semantic	Definition
COLOR[n]	This semantic is required for pixel shaders and is used to specify the output color of the pixel. Any pixel shader prior to version 3.0 should clamp a parameter that uses this semantic between 0 and 1. For pixel shaders beyond 3.0 shaders, the data range is dependent on the render target format.
DEPTH[n]	This semantic is optional and is used to change the output depth of the pixel. Note that using this type of output may have performance implications as the hardware cannot take advantage of early depth rejection since the depth value may be modified by the shader.

Variable Semantics

With the exception of shader function parameters, you also need a way to specify how other variables of your shaders are to be treated by the effect framework and your application. In the same way as with shader parameters, adding the proper semantics to the variables of your shader can add an actual meaning to each of your effect variables. For example, the effect parameter that the application is expected to fill with the current world transformation matrix could use a semantic like this:

```
float4x4 MyWorldMatrix : World;
```

The `World` semantic is a standard semantic which has been defined as a 4x4 floating-point matrix which contains the world transformation. Attaching this standard semantic to an effect parameter makes it possible for an application to understand the intent of this effect parameter and thus know which values to put into the variables.

A complete listing of all standard semantics is available in Appendix C, but keep in mind that although the standard semantics are meant to cover most of the needs of a 3D application, you can also create your own semantics as needed.

Exploring Annotations

Semantics are used to bind variables and parameters to a meaning used by the application in order to apply the proper value to this variable or parameter. Some parameters require additional information to specify the exact parameter usage, This is where annotations come into play.

The parameter below defines a diffuse light color variable, butwhich light are we talking about? In addition, you can even specify the user interface components used by the application to allow dynamic editing of the value. Take a look at the effect code below with the added annotations:

```
float4 MyTweakableLightDiffuseColor : Diffuse
<
    string Object = "Light";

    string UIWidget = "Color";
    float4 UIMin = float4(0.2, 0.2, 0.2, 1.0);
    float4 UIMax = float4(1.0, 1.0, 1.0, 1.0);
    string UIName = "The diffuse color of the light";
>;
```

As you can see, this example has several annotations. They are attached to a diffuse light color, intended to be interactively adjusted by a user. The annotations define the following:

- *Object*: identifies the purpose of the diffuse color.
- *UIWidget*: identifies the type of control or widget used to control the parameter value.
- *UIMin*: identifies the minimum value for this control.
- *UIMax*: identifies the maximum value for this control.
- *UIName*: is a help string that can be displayed over the control if the user hovers a mouse over the control to cause it to pop up.

Several annotations can be use to control different aspects of variable. In addition of a standard set annotations (enumerated in Appendix C), you can also define your own annotations used within your application to add any type of metadata that you need.

Scripting Annotations

In order to extend the capabilities of annotations a special set of scripting annotations were added to specify a list of render tasks for the application to perform. The complete list of commands is available in Appendix C, but they allow you to do general rendering tasks such as clearing render targets and rendering geometry.

Here's an example of a script which requests that the application clear the render target to blue when the effect is rendered:

```
float4 MyClearColor = float4(0.0, 0.0, 1.0, 0.0);

float Version : StandardsGlobal
<
    string Script = "ClearSetColor = MyClearColor;"
                    "Clear = Color;";
> = 0.8;
```

The float variable named *Version* has the *StandardsGlobal* semantic attached. This semantic specifies that this parameter stores the version number of the standard semantic and annotations specification used in this effect. Each parameter that contains a script must have at least one *Script* or *ScriptSetup* annotation attached. Script commands are executed every time the effect is used for rendering. *ScriptSetup* commands are executed only once as part of initialization of the effect. Execution of each script always begins at the script annotation within the parameter with the *StandardsGlobal* semantic; however, each script can call a script on effect techniques. The example below illustrates this cascading execution within a set of scripts:

```
Texture MyRenderTargetTexture : RenderColorTarget
<
    // Request the application create a 256x256 render target texture for
    // use by the effect
    string ResourceType = "2D";
    float3 Dimensions = float3( 256, 256, 0 );
    int MIPLevels = 1;
>;

float Version : StandardsGlobal
<
    // Script sets the render target, draws the scene using the given
    // technique and pass, and restores the original render target
    String Script = "RenderColorTarget = MyRenderTargetTexture;"
                    "Technique = MyTechnique;"
                    "RenderColorTarget = ;";
> = 0.8;

technique MyTechnique <string Script = "Pass = MyPass;";>
{
    pass MyPass <string Script = "Draw = Scene;";    >
    {
        // Render state and shader assignment
    }
}
```

This scripting annotation does the following:

- Switches the current render target to the specified texture parameter.
- Sets the current technique and executes the contained script. This sets the current pass and requests that the application draw the entire scene using the current technique and pass.
- Sets the render target to *NULL* which restores the render target to the previous surface.

As you can see, the use of scripting annotations comes in handy to automate some tasks especially when dealing with applications that work on a predetermined pipeline where the scripting annotations can be the only way to use specialized features such as render targets. Keep in mind that you can get more details on the scripting annotations by taking a look at Appendix C.

Summary and what's next?

One of the major key points of the effect framework is that effect files are a portable way of defining effects so that they can be used by multiple applications. Just a basic effect language on its own is far from sufficient because although the use of techniques, passes and HLSL shaders define functionality, they do not specify any intent behind the functionality.

Semantics and annotations come to the rescue by adding much needed metadata to the effect file. This metadata serves as additional information specifying the intent behind each parameter and variable of an effect, thus allowing multiple applications to use the same effects and easily exchange information.

Moving forward, in the next chapter, I will discuss various optimization techniques you can use within the effect framework to allow you to make the best out of your shaders and effects.

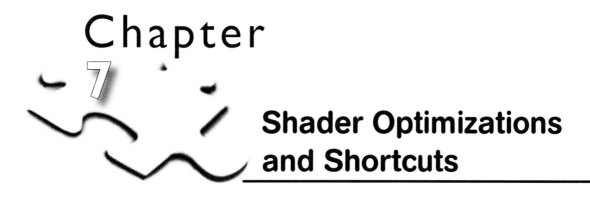

Chapter 7

Shader Optimizations and Shortcuts

Writing shaders that look good on-screen is one aspect to all graphical application developers. Each developer, however, wants to squeeze as much performance from their rendering hardware as it will allow them to put more visual assets on the screen. Optimization purists would argue that no shaders should be written in a high-level language and should be written in assembly. With today's technology, compilers are capable of producing more efficient code, or at least equivalent to what a human can produce through assembly level programming.

This chapter will not focus on how to actually optimize code in assembly form but how you can make the compiler's life easier at letting it do the optimization. I will also cover a few aspects of shaders you need to be aware from a performance perspective.

This chapter is divided into two sections. The first one covers some of the tips and tricks you can use to make shaders efficient by helping out the compiler into generating more optimal code. This section also includes details as to which features of the shader language have more significant performance implications. In the second section of this chapter, I will discuss the topic of preshaders, a new feature of the HLSL language which can give you an even more significant performance boost when you know how to take advantage of it.

Writing Efficient Shaders

Creating visual effects that appeal to the user through the use of shaders may seem like the most important task to a graphical application developer. Great care must also be taken to ensure that your shaders are not only visually appealing, but that they make use of the hardware in an efficient way.

The reality is that you can write the best looking shader out there, but if it uses all the system resources, it may be the only object you could render at an interactive rate. Through some clever optimizations and taking advantage of the HLSL compiler, you can increase your performance where more effects can be displayed simultaneously.

Not All Instructions are Equal

The first aspect to consider is the instruction use of a particular shader. Although you may write your code using intrinsic HLSL instructions, you may want to consider what the function will generate once compiled. A more complete description of how each intrinsic HLSL function is compiled has been included in the appendices and will show some concrete examples of situations you need to be aware of or avoid if necessary.

In addition, the appendices also contain a table explaining the assembly level set of instructions for each vertex and pixel shader profiles along with a description of the performance cost associated with each instruction.

Since this is the core topic of this section, I will not leave you hanging and give a few examples of some known bad case scenarios. An easy way to determine the cost of a particular shader is to use the command line HLSL compiler (fxc.exe) to output all the needed information about the resulting shader.

Take a look at the following vertex shader function:

```
float4 main(float4 inPos:POSITION) : POSITION|
{
  return exp(inPos);
}
```

Do not worry, this shader doesn't do anything special and is intended to be an extreme performance case of a simple intrinsic function to analyze. As you can see, all this shader does is take the input vertex position and return the base-2 exponential as the calculated position.

Does the hardware have an exponential instruction it can use to calculate this? Yes, it does! It is not, however, as simple as you think. Using the command-line compiler, here is the assembly result from this simple shader:

```
def c0, 1.44269502, 0, 0, 0
mul r0, v0, c0.x
exp oPos.x, r0.x
exp oPos.y, r0.y
exp oPos.z, r0.z
exp oPos.w, r0.w
```

The first thing you will notice from this shader is that the compiler used four *exp* instructions to accomplish the task. This is correct, the assembly instruction to calculate an exponential can only work on a single scalar at the time and must be executed several times.

The first lesson to learn from this code is that you need to be careful with certain instructions as the number of components passed to this function can make a significant performance difference. Another classic example of performance difference would be to use the `mul` function to apply skinning to a vertex using a 4-by-4 matrix when in reality a 4-by-3 matrix is needed, causing the compiler to generate $1/3$ more code than needed since every row of the matrix multiplication generates a new assembly instruction.

This is not all. If the above shader is being compiled on 2.0 or 3.0 hardware, you are in the clear; however, if you are trying to compile the above shader on some 1.x shader hardware, you may be in for an extra surprise. If you look at Appendix A, you will notice the `exp` assembly instruction under 1.x shaders does not take a single instruction slot but actually takes ten!

Overall, this simple shader that looks innocent enough will take 41 instruction slots on 1.x hardware. This same shader will take only five instructions on 2.0 and 3.0 shader hardware.

 *Note*

When talking about performance, I use the term instruction slots in a way similar to clock cycles. Although certain hardware implementations support a limited number of instructions in a program, each instruction can take one or many instruction slots to complete.

The lesson for you at this point is that you always should profile your shaders and refer to Appendix A and B for more detailed information on the performance consequences of each shader instruction.

The Risks of Branching

In the realm of computer programming, one thing everyone takes for granted is the ability to have support for branching and looping statements. In the realm of shaders, however, the ability to branch is limited and something developers need to take into consideration when developing shaders.

The most standard form of branching supported through shader hardware is static branching. Because it is not the most common form of branching developers are accustomed to, it is worth getting into more details. Static branching is a capability within the effect framework that allows for blocks of code to be switched on or off based on a boolean shader constant. It is a convenient method for enabling or disabling code paths based on the type of object currently being rendered. Between draw calls, you can decide which features you want to support with the current shader and then set the boolean constant.

Here is a simple example of code using static branching:

```
const bool bDoLighting;

struct VS_OUTPUT
{
    float4 Pos:        POSITION;
    float2 TexCoord:   TEXCOORD0;
    float2 Color:      COLOR0;
};

float4 Light_PointDiffuse(float3 VertPos, float3 VertNorm, float3 LightPos,
                          float4 LightColor, float4 LightAttenuation)
{
    // Determine the distance from the light to the vertex and the direction
    float3 LightDir = LightPos - VertPos;
    float  Dist = length(LightDir);
    LightDir = LightDir / Dist;

    // Compute distance based attenuation. This is defined as:
    // Attenuation = 1 / ( LA.x + LA.y*Dist + LA.z*Dist*Dist )
    float DistAttn = clamp(0,1, 1 / ( LightAttenuation.x +
                                      LightAttenuation.y * Dist +
                                      LightAttenuation.z * Dist * Dist ));

    // Compute surface/light angle based attenuation defined as dot(N,L)
    float AngleAttn = clamp(0, 1, dot(VertNorm, LightDir) );

    // Compute final lighting
    return LightColor * DistAttn * AngleAttn;
}

VS_OUTPUT vs_main(float4 inPos: POSITION, float3 inNormal: NORMAL,
                  float4 inColor: COLOR0, float2 inTxr: TEXCOORD0)
{
    VS_OUTPUT Out;
    float4 Color = inColor;

    // Compute the projected position and send out the texture coordinates
    Out.Pos = mul(view_proj_matrix, inPos);
    Out.TexCoord = inTxr;

    // Compute light contribution (if needed)
    if (bDoLighting == true)
       Color += Light_PointDiffuse(inPos, inNormal, Light1_Position,
                                   Light1_Color, Light1_Attenuation);

    // Output Final Color
    Out.Color = Color;
    return Out;
}
```

In this code, you may notice that we perform the simple task of diffuse lighting a vertex. This code is essentially taken from Chapter 4 but has a little twist. There is an additional global variable named *bDoLighting* which is a boolean constant. By using this variable as a condition to the *if* statement, the HLSL compiler and effect system can dynamically enable or disable this code before using this shader since this variable is a constant and must be set before the shader is used.

You may wonder about the uses of static branching, as in the above code, you can use it to enable and disable specific features of a shader and can be used to generalize shaders into smaller units which can be enabled on demand. In addition to being able to turn features on and off, you can use static branching for other interesting tasks. For example, what if you take the above shader and want it to support multiple lights instead of a single light? This can easily be done by using a static I statement. Here is what you would get:

```
const int iNumLighting;
VS_OUTPUT vs_main(float4 inPos: POSITION, float3 inNormal: NORMAL,
                  float4 inColor: COLOR0, float2 inTxr: TEXCOORD0)
{
   VS_OUTPUT Out;
   float4 Color = inColor;

   // Compute the projected position and send out the texture coordinates
   Out.Pos = mul(view_proj_matrix, inPos);
   Out.TexCoord = inTxr;

   // Compute light contribution (if needed)
   for (int i=0; i< iNumLighting, i++)
   {
      Color += Light_PointDiffuse(inPos, inNormal, Light_Position[i],
                                  Light_Color[i], Light_Attenuation[i]);
   }

   // Output Final Color
   Out.Color = Color;
   return Out;
}
```

What you may be more accustomed to as a software developer is dynamic branching. With dynamic branching, the comparison condition resides in a variable, which means that the comparison must be calculated for each vertex or each pixel at run time.

On hardware that supports true dynamic branching (determined through the hardware capability bits), the performance hit is the cost of the branch expression plus the cost of the instructions on the side of the branch taken. For this particular case, the task of optimizing shaders using dynamic branching is similar to optimizing code that runs on a CPU.

However, on older hardware, we cannot directly do dynamic branching, but it does not mean that it cannot be accomplished. For example, take a look at the following code:

```
float4 main(float4 inPos:POSITION,
            float3 inVector:TEXCOORD0,
            float3 inVector2:TEXCOORD1,
            float3 inVector3:TEXCOORD2,
            float3 inVector4:TEXCOORD3,
            float3 inVector5:TEXCOORD4,
            float3 inVector6:TEXCOORD5
            ) : POSITION
{
  float3x3 m1 = {inVector, inVector2, inVector3};
  float3x3 m2 = {inVector4, inVector5, inVector6};
  if (inPos.w < 0.5f)
      return mul(m1, m2)._11_12_13_21;
  else
      return mul(m2, m1)._11_12_13_21;
}
```

This code does not accomplish anything practical but serves to define a basic branching example that the HLSL compiler will not optimize. If you compile this shader on a 1.x card, the compilation will not fail even though the hardware cannot accomplish the branch dynamically.

What the compiler does is evaluate both sides of the `if` statement, evaluate the result of the branching expression then take advantage of the `slt` instruction to decide which result is to be used. Below is the resulting assembly code for the above shader:

```
def c0, 0.5, 0, 0, 0

// Execute both sides of the expression
mov r1.xyz, v1
mul r0.xyz, r1.y, v5
mad r0.xyz, r1.x, v4, r0
mov r3.xyz, v2
mul r2.xy, r3.yxzw, v5
mad r0.xyz, r1.z, v6, r0
mad r0.w, r3.x, v4.x, r2.x
mad r1.w, r1.x, v5.x, r2.y
mul r2.yzw, r3.xxyz, v4.y
mad r0.w, r3.z, v6.x, r0.w
mad r1.xyz, v4.x, r1, r2.yzww
mov r2.y, v4.z
mad r1.xyz, r2.y, v3, r1
mov r2.y, v5.z
mad r1.w, r2.y, v3.x, r1.w
add r0, r0, -r1
```

```
// Execute the branch statement
slt r2.w, v0.w, c0.x
mad oPos, r2.w, r0, r1
```

In conclusion, you can accomplish dynamic branching even on hardware which doesn't support it. You need to be aware the performance hit for such use of branching is that both sides of the branch will need to be evaluated ahead of time. Although this may be useful for small calculations or to select values, you will need to be careful when dealing with expensive branches.

Taking Advantage of Preshaders

Another advantage of using the HLSL shader language versus developing them directly in assembly language comes from the fact that the shader compiler can make global optimizations on a shader. One of them is new to the DirectX SDK and is commonly called preshaders.

The idea behind a preshader is that it can be used to increase shader efficiency by pre-calculating constant shader expressions. The effect compiler automatically pulls out shader computations from the body of a shader and executes them on the CPU prior to the shader execution. For example, the following expression is simply defined from constants and can be evaluated outside of the shader before it is executed.

```
mul(World,mul(View, Projection));
```

Any shader calculation that only depends on uniform parameters; that is, the computations do not change each vertex or pixel, can be evaluated ahead of time. If you are using effects, the effect compiler will automatically generate and run a preshader for you by default. The use of preshaders can be a significant performance enhancement since it can reduce the number of instructions per shader and constant registers a shader consumes.

Think of the effect compiler as a sort of multi-processor compiler because it compiles shader code for two types of processors: a CPU and a graphics processing unit (GPU). In addition, the effect compiler is designed to move code from the GPU to the CPU and therefore improve shader performance.

The effect compiler can take shader code and separate it into both CPU and GPU components and execute them independently. In the case of preshaders, this is equivalent to pulling a static expression out of a loop. Below is a shader that transforms position from world space to projection space and copies texture coordinates:

```
float4x4 g_mWorldViewProjection;     // World * View * Projection matrix
float4x4 g_mWorldInverse;            // Inverse World matrix
float3 g_LightDir;                   // Light direction in world space
float4 g_LightDiffuse;               // Diffuse color of the light

struct VS_OUTPUT
{
    float4 Position   : POSITION;    // vertex position
    float2 TextureUV  : TEXCOORD0;   // vertex texture coords
    float4 Diffuse    : COLOR0;      // vertex diffuse color
};

VS_OUTPUT RenderSceneVS( float4 vPos : POSITION,
                         float3 vNormal : NORMAL,
                         float2 vTexCoord0 : TEXCOORD0)
{
    VS_OUTPUT Output;

    // Transform the position from object space to projection space
    Output.Position = mul(vPos, g_mWorldViewProjection);

    // Transform the light from world space to object space
    float3 vLightObjectSpace = normalize(mul(g_LightDir,
                                 (float3x3)g_mWorldInverse));

    // N dot L lighting
    Output.Diffuse = max(0,dot(vNormal, vLightObjectSpace));

    // Copy the texture coordinate
    Output.TextureUV = vTexCoord0;

    return Output;
}

technique RenderVS
{
    pass P0
    {
        VertexShader = compile vs_1_1 RenderSceneVS();
    }
}
```

If you take the above shader and compile it without preshaders, using the command-line effect compiler to compile it under vs_1_1, you will get the following results:

```
// Parameters:
//   float3 g_LightDir;
//   float4x4 g_mWorldInverse;
//   float4x4 g_mWorldViewProjection;
//
// Registers:
```

```
//   Name                   Reg   Size
//   --------------------- ----- ----
//   g_mWorldViewProjection c0      4
//   g_mWorldInverse        c4      3
//   g_LightDir             c7      1
//

    vs_1_1
    def c8, 0, 0, 0, 0
    dcl_position v0
    dcl_normal v1
    dcl_texcoord v2
    mov r1.xyz, c7
    dp3 r0.x, r1, c4
    dp3 r0.y, r1, c5
    dp3 r0.z, r1, c6
    dp4 oPos.x, v0, c0
    dp3 r1.x, r0, r0
    dp4 oPos.y, v0, c1
    rsq r0.w, r1.x
    dp4 oPos.z, v0, c2
    mul r0.xyz, r0, r0.w
    dp4 oPos.w, v0, c3
    dp3 r0.x, v1, r0
    max oD0, r0.x, c8.x
    mov oT0.xy, v2
```

As you can see, this shader uses up approximately 14 instruction slots and consumes nine constant registers. If you turn on the use of preshaders, the compiler will move the static expressions out of the shader and pre-execute them on the CPU. Taking the same shader as above and compiling it with preshaders enabled will yield the following:

```
    // Shader Instructions
    vs_1_1
    def c8, 0, 0, 0, 0
    dcl_position v0
    dcl_normal v1
    dcl_texcoord v2
    mov r1.xyz, c7

    // Preshader instructions
    // dp3 r0.x, r1, c4
    // dp3 r0.y, r1, c5
    // dp3 r0.z, r1, c6

    dp4 oPos.x, v0, c0
    dp3 r1.x, r0, r0
    dp4 oPos.y, v0, c1
    rsq r0.w, r1.x
    dp4 oPos.z, v0, c2
```

```
mul r0.xyz, r0, r0.w
dp4 oPos.w, v0, c3
dp3 r0.x, v1, r0
max oD0, r0.x, c8.x
mov oT0.xy, v2
```

The resulting shader code above in fact uses only 11 instruction slots and gives you a saving of three constant registers. Since an effect executes a preshader just before executing shader code, the result is the same functionality with increased shader performance because the number of instructions that need to be executed has been reduced.

In many cases, it is reasonable to expect a five to twenty percent performance improvement from the use of preshaders and similar savings in constant register usage.

Summary and what's next?

Creating visually stunning shaders is an arduous yet rewarding task. As a developer you must focus on not only creating great effects but also create them so they can run effectively on your target hardware. In this chapter, I have overviewed some of the basic techniques and elements you need to know to produce efficient effects.

Although the effect compiler takes care of optimizing shaders for you, it is still important to understand the consequences of using certain instructions or the impact of certain features such as the use of dynamic branching within your code. This knowledge can empower you to create more efficient shaders and gives you the knowledge to take advantage of the effect framework to its fullest.

The second point of interest is the additional optimizing features that the effect framework gives you such as pre-shaders. By taking common constant operations out of your shader and pre-executing them on the CPU you not only gain in performance but will reduce your shader constant memory usage.

So far, I have discussed a lot about the benefits of the effect framework and how the use of standard semantics can allow applications to communicate together. In the next chapter, I will show you as a developer how you can take advantage of all the different components of the DirectX effect framework to make use of shaders within your applications.

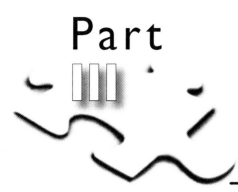

Part III

The DirectX Effect Framework

So far we have spent a great amount of time going over the HLSL language and the use of effect files. This knowledge will now come in handy as we go straight into the nuts and bolts of the how you can take advantage of the effect framework within your applications.

Over the next few chapters, we will tackle all the various components of the effect framework including the effect container, state management interfaces and even the effect compiler. Let's start with a general outline of the DirectX effect framework.

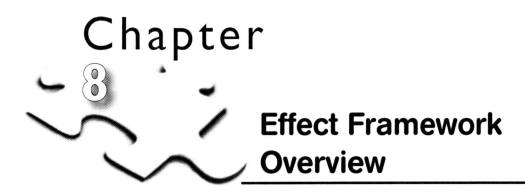

Chapter 8

Effect Framework Overview

The best way to approach any topic is to first take a global view to give you a better understanding of what is to come. The purpose of this chapter is to do a global survey of the DirectX effect framework and how you can take full advantage of it.

In the earlier days of DirectX and shaders, developers had to manage every aspect of rendering from defining and compiling the shaders to setting the appropriate textures and render states. As well as this high-level management, you had to develop your shaders in assembly language and because of this had to transfer your constants to the proper registers, making it complicated to share constants across shaders without developing your own complex shader management system.

With the arrival of DirectX 8.1, came the introduction of the effect system. The effect system didn't bloom into something truly usable until DirectX 9.0.

The effect framework introduced several important aspects to shader development such as the high-level management of shaders and render states but also the High-Level Shading Language (HLSL) allowing for development of shaders not only in a C-like language but also significantly simplifying the management of the shaders themselves and their constants.

 Note

> Microsoft has recently changed their approach towards how often they update the DirectX SDK by releasing updates a few times per year instead of every few years. The API is stable, however, and unlikely to go through any significant changes over the next few years. You can find the latest version of the DirectX SDK at http://www.msdn.com/directx.

As I have mentioned, this chapter is meant as a general overview of the effect system and some of its main functionalities. In the following chapters, I will cover more specific components and their use. So let's get going…

Why?

As a shader and graphical application developer, you have probably already realized that there is more to creating stunning visual effects than simply writing shader code. You have to set the proper render states, set up your textures and constants. In addition, with the proliferation of more performant video cards came the introduction of new shaders, which have put a new burden on developers who want to reach a broad audience. Not only do you want to have the best looking graphics, but you also need to be friendly to users who may not have the latest and greatest hardware by also developing equivalent effects to function properly on older hardware.

Your gut reaction may be to simply develop your own effect management framework, but wouldn't you rather spend your efforts on the actual effects and not their management? This is even more true today with the ever increasing graphical requirements that need more work from developers and artists.

Because of this ever increasing need, the effect framework was developed by Microsoft as part of their overall XNA initiative aimed at creating tools to help developers by giving them reusable technologies to relieve some of workload. Developers can focus on the more important task of creating their application.

The effect framework offers a wide range of features including

- Centralized management of effects which contain both shaders and their associated render states.
- Simplified shader constant management allowing efficient use of registers and sharing constants across multiple effects.
- Allows an effect to contain multiple techniques, all of which can be tested for hardware compatibility through DirectX.
- Allows for easy render state management in addition to the ability to track which states are affected by a particular effect.
- Advanced optimization techniques built-in the effect compiler, including the use of preshaders which can extract constant components of a shader and execute them ahead of time on the CPU.
- And much more…

As you can see, the effect system can do a lot in terms of facilitating your development efforts. We will explore specific components of the framework and discuss all its features in more detail.

Useful Tools

In the following sections of this chapter, I will go over all the major components of each API relevant to the effect framework and give an overview of their use and function. Let's start by talking about some important tools to use in your effect development endeavors. And believe me, they will come in handy!

Command-Line Compiler

By now, you must know something of the command-line effect compiler since it has been used in the previous chapter to illustrate how you can take advantage of shader optimizations. The command-line compiler, *fxc.exe*, can be used for several tasks, but before we look at its uses, let's go over the arguments you can use to control its behavior.

The command line format for this tool is as follows:

```
fxc.exe <options> <filename>
```

The possible options for the command-line compiler are enumerated in the Table 8-1 below.

Table 8-1 FXC.EXE Options

Option	Description
/T <profile>	Specifies the target profile, which is a single selection from the following profiles: fx_2_0 (effect profile), tx_1_0 (procedural texture profile) or any valid vertex or pixel shader profiles.
/E <name>	Defines the entrypoint function name. This parameter is used in conjunction with a vertex and pixel shader targets.
/Od	Used to disable optimizations.
/Vd	Used to disable the validation of the effect or shaders in respect to the selected target.
/Zi	Used to enable debugging information.
/Zpr	Forces the packing matrices in row-major order.
/Zpc	Forces the packing matrices in column-major order.
/Gpp	Forces the use of partial precision (16-bit floating-point).
/Fo <file>	Allows you to specify the output object file.
/Fc <file>	Allows you to specify the output assembly code listing file.
/Fx <file>	Allows you to specify the output assembly code and hex listing file.

Table 8-1 FXC.EXE Options

Option	Description
/Fh \<file\>	Allows you to specify output header containing object code.
/D \<id\> = \<text\>	Used to define a macro.
/nologo	Used to suppress the copyright message.

 Note

> You may have noticed above the inclusion of the /Gpp parameter which tells the compiler to use partial precision or 16-bits floating-point numbers. Some hardware, such as the GeForce FX series, have opted to concentrate their efforts on generating faster partial precision hardware and in some circumstances, the use of partial precision may give a significant performance boost. Also keep in mind that the functionality of the command-line compiler can be mimicked by using the DirectX SDK's effect framework functions.

As you can see, there are many options to the effect compiler. Some of the obvious features allow you to control the optimization and shader target to use for an effect, but the more useful features allow you to do a lot. Let's start with a simple effect taken from the DirectX SDK which implements a simple lighting effect and offers two techniques both for shader and fixed pipeline hardware. Below is the listing for the effect:

```
string XFile = "tiger\\tiger.x";    // model
int    BCLR = 0xff202080;           // background

// light direction (view space)
float3 lightDir <
    string UIDirectional = "Light Direction"; > = {0.577, -0.577, 0.577};

// light intensity
float4 I_a = { 0.1f, 0.1f, 0.1f, 1.0f };    // ambient
float4 I_d = { 1.0f, 1.0f, 1.0f, 1.0f };    // diffuse
float4 I_s = { 1.0f, 1.0f, 1.0f, 1.0f };    // specular

// material reflectivity
float4 k_a : MATERIALAMBIENT = { 1.0f, 1.0f, 1.0f, 1.0f };    // ambient
float4 k_d : MATERIALDIFFUSE = { 1.0f, 1.0f, 1.0f, 1.0f };    // diffuse
float4 k_s : MATERIALSPECULAR= { 1.0f, 1.0f, 1.0f, 1.0f };    // specular
float  n   : MATERIALPOWER = 32.0f;                           // power

// texture
texture Tex0 < string name = "tiger\\tiger.bmp"; >;
```

```
// transformations
float4x4 World      : WORLD;
float4x4 View       : VIEW;
float4x4 Projection : PROJECTION;

struct VS_OUTPUT
{
    float4 Pos  : POSITION;
    float4 Diff : COLOR0;
    float4 Spec : COLOR1;
    float2 Tex  : TEXCOORD0;
};

VS_OUTPUT VS(float3 Pos  : POSITION,
             float3 Norm : NORMAL,
             float2 Tex  : TEXCOORD0)
{
    VS_OUTPUT Out = (VS_OUTPUT)0;

    float3 L = -lightDir;
    float4x4 WorldView = mul(World, View);
    float3 P = mul(float4(Pos, 1), (float4x3)WorldView);
    float3 N = normalize(mul(Norm, (float3x3)WorldView));
    float3 R = normalize(2 * dot(N, L) * N - L);
    float3 V = -normalize(P);

    Out.Pos  = mul(float4(P, 1), Projection);
    Out.Diff = I_a * k_a + I_d * k_d * max(0, dot(N, L));
    Out.Spec = I_s * k_s * pow(max(0, dot(R, V)), n/4);
    Out.Tex  = Tex;
    return Out;
}

sampler Sampler = sampler_state
{
    Texture   = (Tex0);
    MipFilter = LINEAR;
    MinFilter = LINEAR;
    MagFilter = LINEAR;
};

float4 PS(float4 Diff : COLOR0,
          float4 Spec : COLOR1,
          float2 Tex  : TEXCOORD0) : COLOR
{
    return tex2D(Sampler, Tex) * Diff + Spec;
}

technique TVertexAndPixelShader
{
```

```
    pass P0
    {
        // shaders
        VertexShader = compile vs_1_1 VS();
        PixelShader  = compile ps_1_1 PS();
    }
}

technique TNoShader
{
    pass P0
    {
        // transforms
        WorldTransform[0]   = (World);
        ViewTransform       = (View);
        ProjectionTransform = (Projection);

        // material
        MaterialAmbient  = (k_a);
        MaterialDiffuse  = (k_d);
        MaterialSpecular = (k_s);
        MaterialPower    = (n);

        // lighting
        LightType[0]      = DIRECTIONAL;
        LightAmbient[0]   = (I_a);
        LightDiffuse[0]   = (I_d);
        LightSpecular[0]  = (I_s);
        LightDirection[0] = (lightDir);
        LightRange[0]     = 100000.0f;
        LightEnable[0] = TRUE;
        Lighting       = TRUE;
        SpecularEnable = TRUE;

        // samplers
        Sampler[0] = (Sampler);

        // texture stages
        ColorOp[0]   = MODULATE;
        ColorArg1[0] = TEXTURE;
        ColorArg2[0] = DIFFUSE;
        AlphaOp[0]   = MODULATE;
        AlphaArg1[0] = TEXTURE;
        AlphaArg2[0] = DIFFUSE;
        ColorOp[1]   = DISABLE;
        AlphaOp[1]   = DISABLE;

        // shaders
        VertexShader = NULL;
        PixelShader  = NULL;
    }
```

```
}
```

If you compile this effect with the */Fo* option, the command-line compiler will output an object file containing a precompiled version of the effect. This file can be used directly with the run-time effect compiler to load the effect while avoiding the compilation costs through the *D3DXCreateEffect* function.

 Note

> The command-line compiler can only compile specific shader functions for output. This implies that you will need to specify an entry point function as well as a compilation target through the */E* and the */T* parameters.

You can also compile the effect and get a text listing of the compilation result. This can be useful to determine the performance cost of a particular effect and also to see what type of manipulation the effect compiler has done to your code.

For example, compiling this effect file with the following command-line

```
fxc.exe /EVS /Tvs_1_1 /Fctest.txt simple.fx
```

tells the effect compiler to compile the VS function under *vs_1_1* and output the listing into a file, which will yield the following listing:

```
// Parameters:
//
//    float4 I_a;
//    float4 I_d;
//    float4 I_s;
//    float4x4 Projection;
//    float4x4 View;
//    float4x4 World;
//    float4 k_a;
//    float4 k_d;
//    float4 k_s;
//    float3 lightDir;
//    float n;
//
//
// Registers:
//
//    Name          Reg    Size
//    ------------  -----  ----
//    World         c0     4
//    Projection    c4     4
//    View          c8     3
```

```
//    lightDir      c11      1
//    I_a           c12      1
//    I_d           c13      1
//    I_s           c14      1
//    k_a           c15      1
//    k_d           c16      1
//    k_s           c17      1
//    n             c18      1
//
//
// Default values:
//
//    lightDir
//       c11  = { 0.577, -0.577, 0.577, 0 };
//
//    I_a
//       c12  = { 0.1, 0.1, 0.1, 1 };
//
//    I_d
//       c13  = { 1, 1, 1, 1 };
//
//    I_s
//       c14  = { 1, 1, 1, 1 };
//
//    k_a
//       c15  = { 1, 1, 1, 1 };
//
//    k_d
//       c16  = { 1, 1, 1, 1 };
//
//    k_s
//       c17  = { 1, 1, 1, 1 };
//
//    n
//       c18  = { 32, 0, 0, 0 };
//


    vs_1_1
    def c19, 1, 0, 0.25, 0
    dcl_position v0
    dcl_normal v1
    dcl_texcoord v2
    mov r0, c8
    mul r1, r0.y, c1
    mad r1, c0, r0.x, r1
    mad r1, c2, r0.z, r1
    mad r3, c3, r0.w, r1
    mad r2, v0.xyzx, c19.xxxy, c19.yyyx
    dp4 r0.x, r2, r3
    mov r4, c9
    mul r1, r4.y, c1
```

```
            dp3 r6.x, v1, r3
            mad r1, c0, r4.x, r1
            mad r5, c2, r4.z, r1
            mov r1, c10
            mul r3, r1.y, c1
            mad r4, c3, r4.w, r5
            mad r3, c0, r1.x, r3
            dp4 r0.y, r2, r4
            mad r3, c2, r1.z, r3
            dp3 r6.y, v1, r4
            mad r1, c3, r1.w, r3
            dp4 r0.z, r2, r1
            dp3 r6.z, v1, r1
            mov r0.w, c19.x
            dp3 r1.x, r6, r6
            dp4 oPos.x, r0, c4
            rsq r1.w, r1.x
            dp4 oPos.y, r0, c5
            mul r1.xyz, r6, r1.w
            dp4 oPos.z, r0, c6
            dp3 r2.x, r1, -c11
            dp4 oPos.w, r0, c7
            add r0.w, r2.x, r2.x
            max r1.w, r2.x, c19.y
            mad r1.xyz, r0.w, r1, c11
            dp3 r3.x, r0, r0
            dp3 r2.x, r1, r1
            rsq r2.w, r3.x
            rsq r0.w, r2.x
            mul r2.xyz, r0, r2.w
            mul r1.xyz, r1, r0.w
            mov r0, c13
            mul r0, r0, c16
            dp3 r2.x, r1, -r2
            mul r1, r1.w, r0
            max r0.w, r2.x, c19.y
            log r3.w, r0.w
            mov r0.w, c18.x
            mul r2.w, r0.w, c19.z
            mov r0, c12
            mad oD0, r0, c15, r1
            mul r0.w, r3.w, r2.w
            exp r1.w, r0.w
            mov r0, c14
            mul r0, r0, c17
            mul oD1, r1.w, r0
            mov oT0.xy, v2
    // approximately 74 instruction slots used
```

As you can see from the listing above, the command-line compiler can provide you with a wealth of information about a particular shader. For example, it will provide you with the complete assembly listing of the compiled shader in addition to the number of instruction slots taken by the shader and a summary of the used variables and constants from your effect file. Such a listing can come in handy when it is time to either debug or optimize a shader.

In addition to getting a complete listing of the compiled shader, you can use the */Fx* and */Fh* parameters for force the compiler to output the resulting object file in human readable format. Below is an example of the above shader compiled with the */Fx* option:

```
// 0000:  fffe0101  007cfffe  42415443  0000001c  ......|_CTAB.___
// 0010:  000001bb  fffe0101  0000000b  0000001c  .._.....___.___
// 0020:  00000100  000001b4  000000f8  000c0002  _._..__.___.._
// 0030:  00000001  000000fc  0000010c  0000011c  .___.___..__..__
// 0040:  000d0002  00000001  000000fc  00000120  ._._.___.___ ._
// ...
```

The */Fh* option performs the same task but the output will be in a form that can be used in a C/C++ program as an include file.

This little command line tool can be useful for debugging shaders or if you wish to automate the compilation or validation of shaders ahead of time.

EffectEdit

The EffectEdit tool is actually a sample that is part of the DirectX SDK but serves as a great example of how you can take advantage of the effect framework. This little application will load any effect file and give you control over which technique to display and allow you to control the variables within the effect that have the proper semantics and annotations attached to it. Figure 8.1 below illustrates EffectEdit in action.

The neat thing with EffectEdit is that it is a good example of the use of the proper annotation and semantics. For example, in

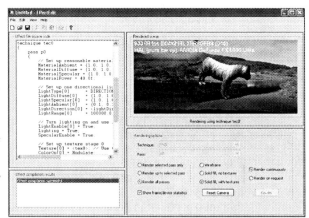

Figure 1.1: A screenshot of EffectEdit in action

the sample effect used in the previous section of this chapter, you may have noticed the use of a few annotations. For example:

```
// texture
texture Tex0 < string name = "tiger\\tiger.bmp"; >;
```

This little piece of code defines a texture, but the most interesting part is the annotation that is attached to it. The `name` annotation allows, in the case of a texture, to define which texture to use for the effect. Your application may decide itself which texture to apply as an effect may be used by multiple objects, but in this case, it allows you to define a default texture which may be used in prototyping applications such as EffectEdit so that your test objects do not show up untextured.

EffectEdit is a simple example of the use of semantics and annotations and how you can use them to make sure that multiple applications understand your shaders in the same way.

Interface Overview

Now that I have explained some of the relevant tools to the effect framework, it is time to start looking at the actual effect framework. At this point, I assume that you have a copy of the DirectX SDK and are ready to go.

In this chapter, I will go quickly over each interface in the effect framework as well as give you a simple explanation of each of the interfaces and a quick rundown of the functions within each interface. The specific details of all the interfaces will be discussed more in details in the following chapter when I start addressing the actual use of each of them.

ID3DXBaseEffect

The first interface on our agenda is the `ID3DXBaseEffect` interface. Although you will not be using this interface directly, other interfaces such as `ID3DXEffect` and `ID3DXEffectCompiler` derive from it and inherit its functionality. This interface serves as a placeholder for several functions core to the effect framework. All the members of this class, with a brief description are found in Table 8-1 below.

Table 8-1 ID3DXBaseEffect Members

Function	Description
GetAnnotation	Gets the handle of an annotation.
GetAnnotationByName	Gets the handle of an annotation by looking up its name.
GetBool	Gets a *BOOL* value.
GetBoolArray	Gets an array of *BOOL* values.
GetDesc	Gets the effect description.
GetFloat	Gets a floating-point value.
GetFloatArray	Gets an array of floating-point values.

Table 8-1 ID3DXBaseEffect Members

Function	Description
GetFunction	Gets the handle of a function.
GetFunctionByName	Gets the handle of a function by looking up its name.
GetFunctionDesc	Gets a function description.
GetInt	Gets an integer.
GetIntArray	Gets an array of integers.
GetMatrix	Gets a non-transposed matrix.
GetMatrixArray	Gets an array of non-transposed matrices.
GetMatrixPointerArray	Gets an array of pointers to non-transposed matrices.
GetMatrixTranspose	Gets a transposed matrix.
GetMatrixTransposeArray	Gets an array of transposed matrices.
GetMatrixTransposePointerArray	Sets an array of pointers to transposed matrices.
GetParameter	Gets the handle of a top-level parameter or a structure member parameter.
GetParameterByName	Gets the handle of a top-level parameter or a structure member parameter by looking up its name.
GetParameterBySemantic	Gets the handle of a top-level parameter or a structure member parameter by looking up its semantic with a case-insensitive search.
GetParameterDesc	Gets a parameter or annotation description.
GetParameterElement	Get the handle of an array element parameter.
GetPass	Gets the handle of a pass.
GetPassByName	Gets the handle of a pass by looking up its name.
GetPassDesc	Gets a pass description.
GetPixelShader	Gets a pixel shader.
GetString	Gets a string.
GetTechnique	Gets the handle of a technique.
GetTechniqueByName	Gets the handle of a technique by looking up its name.
GetTechniqueDesc	Gets a technique description.
GetTexture	Gets a texture.

Table 8-1 ID3DXBaseEffect Members

Function	Description
GetValue	Get the value of an arbitrary parameter or annotation, including simple types, structs, arrays, strings, shaders and textures. This method can be used in place of nearly all the get calls in `ID3DXBaseEffect`.
GetVector	Gets a vector.
GetVectorArray	Gets an array of vectors.
GetVertexShader	Gets a vertex shader.
SetArrayRange	Set the range of an array to pass to the device.
SetBool	Sets a `BOOL` value.
SetBoolArray	Sets an array of Boolean values.
SetFloat	Sets a floating-point value.
SetFloatArray	Sets an array of floating-point values.
SetInt	Sets an integer.
SetIntArray	Sets an array of integers.
SetMatrix	Sets a non-transposed matrix.
SetMatrixArray	Sets an array of non-transposed matrices.
SetMatrixPointerArray	Sets an array of pointers to non-transposed matrices.
SetMatrixTranspose	Sets a transposed matrix.
SetMatrixTransposeArray	Sets an array of transposed matrices.
SetMatrixTransposePointerArray	Sets an array of pointers to transposed matrices.
SetPixelShader	Sets a pixel shader.
SetString	Sets a string.
SetTexture	Sets a texture.
SetValue	Get the value of an arbitrary parameter or annotation, including simple types, structs, arrays, strings, shaders and textures. This method can be used in place of nearly all the set calls in `ID3DXBaseEffect`.
SetVector	Sets a vector.
SetVectorArray	Sets an array of vectors.
SetVertexShader	Sets a vertex shader.

Taking a look at the functions above, you can easily see that all of them serve as being get/set accessors to variables and several aspects of effects such as techniques, parameters and even annotations. Thus, the *ID3DXBaseEffect* interface serves as the foundation by which effect information will be exchanged by your applications.

I could go over every function of this interface, but in reality they all follow the same basic format. For example, the *GetBool* and *SetBool* functions follow this syntax:

```
HRESULT GetBool(
    D3DXHANDLE hParameter,
    BOOL* pb
);

HRESULT SetBool(
    D3DXHANDLE hParameter,
    BOOL b
);
```

The functions simply take a handle to a parameter and either a value, or a pointer to a value in the case of the *Get* functions. You may notice the *HRESULT* return value of all the functions. If you are familiar with DirectX, you are familiar with the use of *HRESULT* values. In the case of the accessor functions, it will return *D3D_OK* is the call succeeds and *D3DERR_INVALIDCALL* if the method fails.

This brings us to the topic of handles, effect parameters, techniques and shaders. All of them are accessed by using a handle. Handles are opaque references used to efficiently access individual components of an effect. The definition of a handle is as follows:

```
typedef LPCSTR D3DXHANDLE;
```

Handles provide an efficient means for referencing the techniques, passes, annotations, and parameters with the *ID3DXEffectCompiler* or *ID3DXEffect* interfaces. You can acquire a handle dynamically for example when you use the *GetParameterByName* function. If you look at the handle definition above, you'll notice that handles are technically string pointers. This means that in addition to dynamically generated handles, you can also use a string representing the name of the item as a handle.

This brings us to the functions used to acquire a dynamic handle to an effect component. All of theses functions simply take in a string and return a handle to the component if it exists, or *NULL* if the component cannot be found. For example, here is the definition for the *GetFunctionByName* function:

```
D3DXHANDLE GetFunctionByName(
    LPCSTR pName
);
```

Note

> Using strings as handles will allow you to easily access parameters within your shaders but are far from efficient. If you want to improve performance, especially for parameters you will often access, it is recommended that you use functions such as *GetParameterByName* to get a direct handle to the parameter when you initialize an effect.

The final category of functionality within the base interface is the parameter description functions which allow you to gather more information on individual parameter, variables and semantics. I will go over them individually over the next few sections.

ID3DXBaseEffect::GetDesc

The first function of interest,the `GetDesc` function, will return general information about the effect in general through the `D3DXEFFECT_DESC` structure. The content of the structure is defined in Table 8-2 and you can find the declaration of the `GetDesc` function below:

```
HRESULT GetDesc(
    D3DXEFFECT_DESC* pDesc
);
```

Table 8-2 D3DXEFFECT_DESC Members

Member	Type	Description
Creator	LPCSTR	String that contains the name of the effect creator.
Parameters	UINT	Number of parameters used for effect.
Techniques	UINT	Number of techniques that can render the effect.
Functions	UINT	Number of functions within the effect.

ID3DXBaseEffect::GetFunctionDesc

The second function of interest is the `GetFunctionDesc` function which will return general information about the effect in general through the `D3DXFUNCTION_DESC` structure. The content of the structure is defined in Table 8-3 and you can find the declaration of the `GetFunctionDesc` function below:

```
HRESULT GetFunctionDesc(
    D3DXHANDLE hFunction,
    D3DXFUNCTION_DESC* pDesc
);
```

Table 8-3 D3DXFUNCTION_DESC Members

Member	Type	Description
Name	LPCSTR	Function name.
Annotations	UINT	This member is currently unused and will always be zero.

ID3DXBaseEffect::GetParameterDesc

The third function of interest is the *GetParameterDesc* function which will return general information about the effect in general through the *D3DXPARAMETER_DESC* structure. The content of the structure is defined in Table 8-4 and you can find the declaration of the *GetParameterDesc* function below:

```
HRESULT GetParameterDesc(
    D3DXHANDLE hParameter,
    D3DXPARAMETER_DESC* pDesc
);
```

Table 8-4 D3DXPARAMETER_DESC Members

Member	Type	Description
Name	LPCSTR	Name of the parameter.
Semantic	LPCSTR	Semantic meaning associated with the parameter.
Class	D3DXPARAMETER_CLASS	Parameter class, as defined in *D3DX-PARAMETER_CLASS.*
Type	D3DXPARAMETER_TYPE	Parameter type, as defined in *D3DXPA-RAMETER_TYPE.*
Rows	UINT	Number of rows in the array.
Columns	UINT	Number of columns in the array.
Elements	UINT	Number of elements in the array.
Annotations	UINT	Number of annotations.
StructMembers	UINT	Number of structure members.
Flags	DWORD	Parameter attributes.
Bytes	UINT	The size of the parameter, in bytes.

From the structure definition above, you can see that a parameter can be assigned certain attributes through the *Flags* structure entry. They are defined as constants and can be one of the following:

- *D3DX_PARAMETER_ANNOTATION*: This attribute indicates that the parameter is marked as an annotation.

- *D3DX_PARAMETER_LITERAL*: This attribute indicates that the parameter is marked as a literal value. Literal parameters cannot change after compile, allowing the compiler to optimize their usage. Shared parameters cannot be marked as a literal.

- *D3DX_PARAMETER_SHARED*: This attribute indicates that the value of a parameter will be shared by all effects in the same namespace. Changing the value in one effect will change it in all shared effects. *D3DX_PARAMETER_SHARED* cannot be combined with *D3DX_PARAMETER_LITERAL* or *D3DX_PARAMETER_ANNOTATION*.

In addition to the attributes assigned to parameters, every parameter also belongs to a class and has a defined type. Theses values are defined through the *D3DXPARAMETER_CLASS* and *D3DXPARAMETER_TYPE* enumerations. The possible values for these enumerations have been enumerated below in Table 8-5 and 8-6.

Table 8-5 D3DXPARAMETER_CLASS Members

Member	Description
D3DXPC_SCALAR	Parameter is a scalar.
D3DXPC_VECTOR	Parameter is a vector.
D3DXPC_MATRIX_ROWS	Parameter is a row major matrix.
D3DXPC_MATRIX_COLUMNS	Parameter is a column major matrix.
D3DXPC_OBJECT	Parameter is an object which can be a texture, shader or a string.
D3DXPC_STRUCT	Parameter is a structure.
D3DXPC_FORCE_DWORD	Used to force enumeration to compile to 32 bits in size.

Table 8-6 D3DXPARAMETER_TYPE Members

Member	Description
D3DXPT_VOID	Parameter is a void pointer.
D3DXPT_BOOL	Parameter is a Boolean.
D3DXPT_INT	Parameter is an integer.
D3DXPT_FLOAT	Parameter is a floating-point number.
D3DXPT_STRING	Parameter is a string.
D3DXPT_TEXTURE	Parameter is a texture.
D3DXPT_TEXTURE1D	Parameter is a 1-D texture.
D3DXPT_TEXTURE2D	Parameter is a 2-D texture.
D3DXPT_TEXTURE3D	Parameter is a 3-D texture.
D3DXPT_TEXTURECUBE	Parameter is a cube texture.
D3DXPT_SAMPLER	Parameter is a sampler.
D3DXPT_SAMPLER1D	Parameter is a 1-D sampler.
D3DXPT_SAMPLER2D	Parameter is a 2-D sampler.
D3DXPT_SAMPLER3D	Parameter is a 3-D sampler.
D3DXPT_SAMPLERCUBE	Parameter is a cube sampler.
D3DXPT_PIXELSHADER	Parameter is a pixel shader.
D3DXPT_VERTEXSHADER	Parameter is a vertex shader.
D3DXPT_PIXELFRAGMENT	Parameter is a pixel shader fragment.
D3DXPT_VERTEXFRAGMENT	Parameter is a vertex shader fragment.
D3DXPT_FORCE_DWORD	Used to force this enumeration to compile to 32 bits in size.

ID3DXBaseEffect::GetPassDesc

The next informational function that is part of the *ID3DXBaseEffect* interface is the *GetPassDesc* function which will return information about the specified rendering pass. Results will be given to you through the *D3DXPASS_DESC* structure. The content of the description structure is defined in Table 8-7, and you can find the declaration of the *GetPassDesc* function below:

```
HRESULT GetPassDesc(
    D3DXHANDLE hPass,
    D3DXPASS_DESC* pDesc
);
```

Table 8-7 D3DXPASS_DESC Members

Member	Type	Description
Name	LPCSTR	String value used for the pass.
Annotations	UINT	Annotations are user-specific data that can be attached to any technique, pass, or parameter. This parameter indicates the number of annotations attached to this pass.
pVertexShaderFunction	const DWORD*	Pointer to the vertex shader function.
pPixelShaderFunction	const DWORD*	Pointer to the pixel shader function.

ID3DXBaseEffect::GetTechniqueDesc

The last of the information functions is *GetTechniqueDesc*, which will return general information about the specified technique through the *D3DXTECHNIQUE_DESC* structure. The content of the description structure is defined in Table 8-8, and you can find the declaration of the *GetTechniqueDesc* function below:

```
HRESULT GetTechniqueDesc(
    D3DXHANDLE hTechnique,
    D3DXTECHNIQUE_DESC* pDesc
);
```

Table 8-8 D3DXTECHNIQUE_DESC Members

Member	Type	Description
Name	LPCSTR	String that contains the technique name.
Passes	UINT	Number of rendering passes the technique requires.
Annotations	UINT	The number of annotations associated with this technique.

ID3DXEffect

The *ID3DXEffect* class is probably the most important class of the effect framework as it is used to contain and execute the content of an effect file. The class itself inherits from the *ID3DXBaseEffect* class but adds a few functions used to control the execution of specific effects. Although I will cover individual functions in detail later, the functions specific to this interface are enumerated in Table 8-9.

Table 8-9 ID3DXEffect Members

Function	Description
ApplyParameterBlock	Assign a state value to each effect parameter in a parameter block.
Begin	Starts an active technique.
BeginParameterBlock	Capture parameter effect state changes.
BeginPass	Begins a pass, within the active technique.
CloneEffect	Creates a clone of an effect.
CommitChanges	Propagate state changes that occur inside of an active pass to the device before rendering.
End	Ends an active technique.
EndParameterBlock	Stops capturing effect parameter state changes.
EndPass	Ends an active pass.
FindNextValidTechnique	Searches for the next valid technique, starting at the technique after the specified technique. This function will query the current device to ensure that the technique selected can be used on this device.
GetAnnotation	Gets the handle of an annotation.
GetAnnotationByName	Gets the handle of an annotation by looking up its name.
GetBool	Gets a *BOOL* value.
GetBoolArray	Gets an array of *BOOL* values.
GetCurrentTechnique	Gets the current technique.
GetDesc	Gets the effect description.
GetDevice	Retrieves the device associated with the effect.
GetFloat	Gets a floating-point value.
GetFloatArray	Gets an array of floating-point values.

Table 8-9 ID3DXEffect Members

Function	Description
GetFunction	Gets the handle of a function.
GetFunctionByName	Gets the handle of a function by looking up its name.
GetFunctionDesc	Gets a function description.
GetInt	Gets an integer.
GetIntArray	Gets an array of integers.
GetMatrix	Gets a non-transposed matrix.
GetMatrixArray	Gets an array of non-transposed matrices.
GetMatrixPointerArray	Gets an array of pointers to non-transposed matrices.
GetMatrixTranspose	Gets a transposed matrix.
GetMatrixTransposeArray	Gets an array of transposed matrices.
GetMatrixTransposePointer-Array	Sets an array of pointers to transposed matrices.
GetParameter	Gets the handle of a top-level parameter or a structure member parameter.
GetParameterByName	Gets the handle of a top-level parameter or a structure member parameter by looking up its name.
GetParameterBySemantic	Gets the handle of a top-level parameter or a structure member parameter by looking up its semantic with a case-insensitive search.
GetParameterDesc	Gets a parameter or annotation description.
GetParameterElement	Get the handle of an array element parameter.
GetPass	Gets the handle of a pass.
GetPassByName	Gets the handle of a pass by looking up its name.
GetPassDesc	Gets a pass description.
GetPixelShader	Gets a pixel shader.
GetPool	Gets a pointer to the pool of shared parameters.
GetStateManager	Gets the effect state manager.
GetString	Gets a string.
GetTechnique	Gets the handle of a technique.
GetTechniqueByName	Gets the handle of a technique by looking up its name.

Table 8-9 ID3DXEffect Members

Function	Description
GetTechniqueDesc	Gets a technique description.
GetTexture	Gets a texture.
GetValue	Gets the value of an arbitrary parameter or annotation, including simple types, structs, arrays, strings, shaders and textures. This method can be used in place of nearly all the get calls in *ID3DXBaseEffect*.
GetVector	Gets a vector.
GetVectorArray	Gets an array of vectors.
GetVertexShader	Gets a vertex shader.
IsParameterUsed	Determines if a parameter is used by the technique.
OnLostDevice	Releases all references to video memory resources and deletes all state blocks.
OnResetDevice	Should be called after the device has been reset.
SetArrayRange	Sets the range of an array to pass to the device.
SetBool	Sets a *BOOL* value.
SetBoolArray	Sets an array of *BOOL* values.
SetFloat	Sets a floating-point value.
SetFloatArray	Sets an array of floating-point values.
SetInt	Sets an integer.
SetIntArray	Sets an array of integers.
SetMatrix	Sets a non-transposed matrix.
SetMatrixArray	Sets an array of non-transposed matrices.
SetMatrixPointerArray	Sets an array of pointers to non-transposed matrices.
SetMatrixTranspose	Sets a transposed matrix.
SetMatrixTransposeArray	Sets an array of transposed matrices.
SetMatrixTransposePointer-Array	Sets an array of pointers to transposed matrices.
SetPixelShader	Sets a pixel shader.
SetStateManager	Sets the effect state manager.
SetString	Sets a string.

Table 8-9 ID3DXEffect Members

Function	Description
SetTechnique	Sets the active technique.
SetTexture	Sets a texture.
SetValue	Gets the value of an arbitrary parameter or annotation, including simple types, structs, arrays, strings, shaders and textures. This method can be used in place of nearly all the set calls in `ID3DXBaseEffect`.
SetVector	Sets a vector.
SetVectorArray	Sets an array of vectors.
SetVertexShader	Sets a vertex shader.
ValidateTechnique	Validates a technique.

Overall, this interface exposes all the functionality of the base effect interface allowing you to gather information about the effect and assign values to specific parameters. This interface also contains functionality to validate techniques such as `ValidateTechnique` and `FindNextValidTechnique`. As well, the interface exposes functionality to control the execution of effects such as `Begin/End` and `BeginPass/EndPass`.

Effects themselves are usually created based on an effect file either by using the `ID3DXEffectCompiler` interface or with one of the numerous variations of the `D3DXCreateEffect` functions.

ID3DXEffectCompiler

The `ID3DXEffectCompiler` also derives from the `ID3DXBaseEffect` interface and serves to compile individual effect. It may seem odd that such an interface exists when you can compile effects through the `D3DXCreateEffect` functions and even more bizarre that this interfaces derives from `ID3DXBaseEffect`. Although an in-depth discussion of its use is outside the scope of this chapter, you may remember a discussion earlier about static branching. The use of this interface allows the efficient compilation of variations of an effect by taking advantage of static branching. We will discuss this further in Chapter 12.

The list of functions exposed by the `ID3DXEffectCompiler` class is enumerated in Table 8-10.

Table 8-10 ID3DXEffectCompiler Members

Function	Description
CompileEffect	Compile an effect.
CompileShader	Compile a shader from an effect that contains one or more functions.
GetAnnotation	Gets the handle of an annotation.
GetAnnotationByName	Gets the handle of an annotation by looking up its name.
GetBool	Gets a BOOL value.
GetBoolArray	Gets an array of BOOL values.
GetDesc	Gets the effect description.
GetFloat	Gets a floating-point value.
GetFloatArray	Gets an array of floating-point values.
GetFunction	Gets the handle of a function.
GetFunctionByName	Gets the handle of a function by looking up its name.
GetFunctionDesc	Gets a function description.
GetInt	Gets an integer.
GetIntArray	Gets an array of integers.
GetLiteral	Gets a literal status of a parameter. A literal parameter has a value that doesn't change during the lifetime of an effect.
GetMatrix	Gets a non-transposed matrix.
GetMatrixArray	Gets an array of non-transposed matrices.
GetMatrixPointerArray	Gets an array of pointers to non-transposed matrices.
GetMatrixTranspose	Gets a transposed matrix.
GetMatrixTransposeArray	Gets an array of transposed matrices.
GetMatrixTransposePointer-Array	Sets an array of pointers to transposed matrices.
GetParameter	Gets the handle of a top-level parameter or a structure member parameter.
GetParameterByName	Gets the handle of a top-level parameter or a structure member parameter by looking up its name.

Table 8-10 ID3DXEffectCompiler Members

Function	Description
GetParameterBySemantic	Gets the handle of a top-level parameter or a structure member parameter by looking up its semantic with a case-insensitive search.
GetParameterDesc	Gets a parameter or annotation description.
GetParameterElement	Gets the handle of an array element parameter.
GetPass	Gets the handle of a pass.
GetPassByName	Gets the handle of a pass by looking up its name.
GetPassDesc	Gets a pass description.
GetPixelShader	Gets a pixel shader.
GetString	Gets a string.
GetTechnique	Gets the handle of a technique.
GetTechniqueByName	Gets the handle of a technique by looking up its name.
GetTechniqueDesc	Gets a technique description.
GetTexture	Gets a texture.
GetValue	Gets the value of an arbitrary parameter or annotation, including simple types, structs, arrays, strings, shaders and textures. This method can be used in place of nearly all the get calls in `ID3DXBaseEffect`.
GetVector	Gets a vector.
GetVectorArray	Gets an array of vectors.
GetVertexShader	Gets a vertex shader.
SetArrayRange	Sets the range of an array to pass to the device.
SetBool	Sets a `BOOL` value.
SetBoolArray	Sets an array of `BOOL` values.
SetFloat	Sets a floating-point value.
SetFloatArray	Sets an array of floating-point values.
SetInt	Sets an integer.
SetIntArray	Sets an array of integers.

Table 8-10 ID3DXEffectCompiler Members

Function	Description
SetLiteral	Toggles the literal status of a parameter. A literal parameter has a value that doesn't change during the lifetime of an effect.
SetMatrix	Sets a non-transposed matrix.
SetMatrixArray	Sets an array of non-transposed matrices.
SetMatrixPointerArray	Sets an array of pointers to non-transposed matrices.
SetMatrixTranspose	Sets a transposed matrix.
SetMatrixTransposeArray	Sets an array of transposed matrices.
SetMatrixTransposePointer-Array	Sets an array of pointers to transposed matrices.
SetPixelShader	Sets a pixel shader.
SetString	Sets a string.
SetTexture	Sets a texture.
SetValue	Gets the value of an arbitrary parameter or annotation, including simple types, structs, arrays, strings, shaders and textures. This method can be used in place of nearly all the set calls in `ID3DXBaseEffect`.
SetVector	Sets a vector.
SetVectorArray	Sets an array of vectors.
SetVertexShader	Sets a vertex shader.

ID3DXEffectPool

The `ID3DXEffectPool` interface allows effects to share parameter values. For example, all your effects will most likely have a view matrix. In the default approach, each effect would contain an instance of this variable, and you would need to ensure that each effect gets an updated version of the variable. To solve this, the `ID3DXEffect` interface allows you to specify an `ID3DXEffectPool` interface to serve as a common pool for every variable. Take note that the effect pool interface serves as a mere container and has no member functions.

ID3DXEffectStateManager

In certain architectures, you may need to keep track of what device states a particular effect will modify, if not only for debugging purposes. The *ID3DXEffectStateManager* is a user-implemented class defining a set of callbacks that you can assign to effects so you can trap all of the device state calls made to DirectX. This interface is composed only of callbacks enumerated in Table 8-11.

Table 8-11 ID3DXEffectStateManager Members

Function	Description
LightEnable	A callback function that must be implemented by a user to enable/disable a light.
SetFVF	A callback function that must be implemented by a user to set a flexible vertex format (FVF) code.
SetLight	A callback function that must be implemented by a user to set a light.
SetMaterial	A callback function that must be implemented by a user to set material state.
SetNPatchMode	A callback function that must be implemented by a user to set the number of subdivision segments for N-patches.
SetPixelShader	A callback function that must be implemented by a user to set a pixel shader.
SetPixelShaderConstantB	A callback function that must be implemented by a user to set an array of vertex shader Boolean constants.
SetPixelShaderConstantF	A callback function that must be implemented by a user to set an array of vertex shader floating-point constants.
SetPixelShaderConstantI	A callback function that must be implemented by a user to set an array of vertex shader integer constants.
SetRenderState	A callback function that must be implemented by a user to set render state.
SetSamplerState	A callback function that must be implemented by a user to set a sampler.
SetTexture	A callback function that must be implemented by a user to set a texture.
SetTextureStageState	A callback function that must be implemented by a user to set the texture stage state.

Table 8-11 ID3DXEffectStateManager Members

Function	Description
SetTransform	A callback function that must be implemented by a user to set a transform.
SetVertexShader	A callback function that must be implemented by a user to set a vertex shader.
SetVertexShaderConstantB	A callback function that must be implemented by a user to set an array of vertex shader Boolean constants.
SetVertexShaderConstantF	A callback function that must be implemented by a user to set an array of vertex shader floating-point constants.
SetVertexShaderConstantI	A callback function that must be implemented by a user to set an array of vertex shader integer constants.

ID3DXInclude

If you take a look at the variety of `D3DXCreateEffect` functions, you notice that they take your effect source code from various sources. What happens if your shader tries to use an `#include` statement when it is loaded from a memory buffer? Depending on your effect management strategy, you may want to have control over where shaders come from. The `ID3DXInclude` interface allows you to control the compiler's behavior when it encounters `#include` statement. The interface is user-implemented and only contains the two members listed below:

- **Close**: A user-implemented method for closing an effect `#include` file.
- **Open**: A user-implemented method for opening and reading the contents of an effect `#include` file.

Summary and what's next?

At first glance, you see that the effect framework has a lot to offer in terms of helping you manage your shaders and effects, but there is more than meet the eye! Over the next few chapters, I will go over the specific functionality attached with different components of the framework.

In the next chapter, I will explain the core interface of the framework, `ID3DXEffect`. This is the centerpiece of the framework as it is the container that controls and executes individual effects. You will not only learn how to use effects but how to manipulate their parameters, compile them and debug effects efficiently.

Chapter 9

The Effect

Whether you have simple or complex shading needs, the effect framework can go a long way to make your life easier and facilitate the task of developing shaders. The most important component of the whole effect framework is the `ID3DXEffect` interface which is meant to enclose shaders and their related functionality. In addition to taking the general management of shaders in hand, this interface also handles several other management aspects of rendering effects such as handling render states and shader variables.

In this chapter, I will discuss in-depth the `ID3DXEffect` interface along with its functions, but most importantly its use and how you can take advantage of it. In addition, I will briefly overview how effects can be compiled and how you can use the effect framework to debug shaders efficiently.

Compiling Effects

Although this topic will be discussed in-depth in Chapter 12, it makes sense to at least have a quick discussion of how you will create an `ID3DXEffect` interface before you learn how to use it.

Of course the first step to creating an effect is to write various shaders, techniques and passes within an .FX file. Such a file actually needs to be compiled into a usable form by the effect framework. The run-time component to the effect framework can create effects in two distinct ways.

The most obvious and convenient way to create an effect interface is to take advantage of the various `D3DXEffecrCreate` functions. Although there are many variations of this function, they all serve the same purpose. Each of them will take a raw effect in some form and generate a matching `ID3DXEffectInterface`. For example, take a look at the interface for the `D3DXCreateEffectFromFile` function:

```
HRESULT WINAPI D3DXCreateEffectFromFile(
    LPDIRECT3DDEVICE9 pDevice,
    LPCTSTR pSrcFile,
    const D3DXMACRO *pDefines,
    LPD3DXINCLUDE pInclude,
    DWORD Flags,
```

```
            LPD3DXEFFECTPOOL pPool,
            LPD3DXEFFECT *ppEffect,
            LPD3DXBUFFER *ppCompilationErrors
    );
```

This function will take an effect defined within the supplied text file supplied by the *pSrcFile* parameter. The function also takes many accessory parameters, which will be discussed more in details in Chapter 12.

The second, less obvious, approach to compiling effects is to create an instance of the *ID3DXEffectCompiler* interface. If you take a look at the interface itself, there does not seem to be much of interest as it supports all the functionality of the *ID3DXBaseEffect* class and adds a *CompileEffect* function to its repertoire.

The main advantage of using this interface is that it can be used to optimize the compilation of the same effect with a multiple varieties due to static branching as the compiler can precompile all the necessary components and assemble the final effect based on your choice of variables.

Effect Validation

Although compiling effects is the first step to using them, another reality is that not all video hardware supports every shader model or feature supported by DirectX. You may have an effect composed of multiple techniques. For example, take a look at the following effect:

```
string XFile = "tiger\\tiger.x";   // model
int    BCLR = 0xff202080;          // background

// … More variables removed for simplicity…

VS_OUTPUT VS(
     float3 Pos  : POSITION,
     float3 Norm : NORMAL,
     float2 Tex  : TEXCOORD0)
{
     VS_OUTPUT Out = (VS_OUTPUT)0;

     float3 L = -lightDir;
     float4x4 WorldView = mul(World, View);
     float3 P = mul(float4(Pos, 1), (float4x3)WorldView);
     float3 N = normalize(mul(Norm, (float3x3)WorldView));
     float3 R = normalize(2 * dot(N, L) * N - L);
     float3 V = -normalize(P);

     Out.Pos  = mul(float4(P, 1), Projection);
     Out.Diff = I_a * k_a + I_d * k_d * max(0, dot(N, L));
     Out.Spec = I_s * k_s * pow(max(0, dot(R, V)), n/4);
     Out.Tex  = Tex;
```

```
            return Out;
    }

    float4 PS(
        float4 Diff : COLOR0,
        float4 Spec : COLOR1,
        float2 Tex  : TEXCOORD0) : COLOR
    {
        return tex2D(Sampler, Tex) * Diff + Spec;
    }

    technique TVertexAndPixelShader
    {
        pass P0
        {
            // shaders
            VertexShader = compile vs_1_1 VS();
            PixelShader  = compile ps_1_1 PS();
        }
    }

    technique TNoShader
    {
        pass P0

        {
            // transforms
            WorldTransform[0]   = (World);
            ViewTransform       = (View);
            ProjectionTransform = (Projection);

            // material
            MaterialAmbient  = (k_a);
            MaterialDiffuse  = (k_d);
            MaterialSpecular = (k_s);
            MaterialPower    = (n);

            // lighting
            LightType[0]      = DIRECTIONAL;
            LightAmbient[0]   = (I_a);
            LightDiffuse[0]   = (I_d);
            LightSpecular[0]  = (I_s);
            LightDirection[0] = (lightDir);
            LightRange[0]     = 100000.0f;

            LightEnable[0] = TRUE;
            Lighting       = TRUE;
            SpecularEnable = TRUE;

            // samplers
```

```
        Sampler[0] = (Sampler);

        // texture stages
        ColorOp[0]    = MODULATE;
        ColorArg1[0]  = TEXTURE;
        ColorArg2[0]  = DIFFUSE;
        AlphaOp[0]    = MODULATE;
        AlphaArg1[0]  = TEXTURE;
        AlphaArg2[0]  = DIFFUSE;

        ColorOp[1]    = DISABLE;
        AlphaOp[1]    = DISABLE;

        // shaders
        VertexShader = NULL;
        PixelShader  = NULL;
    }
}
```

This effect makes use of two techniques. The first one is implemented using the 1.x shader model. The second technique in this effect makes use of the fixed pipeline. Although most new video cards will support both techniques, older cards do not have hardware accelerated shader support.

To render geometry using an effect, you will need to pick a particular technique to use, but how can you know which ones are supported by your current hardware? You are in luck as Direct3D asks the video device for you.

The first and most convenient approach to validating effects is to simply ask which of the techniques within the effect are considered valid. This can easily be done by using the *FindNextValidTechnique* function part of the *ID3DXEffect* interface which is defined below:

```
HRESULT FindNextValidTechnique(
    D3DXHANDLE hTechnique,
    D3DXHANDLE* pTechnique
);
```

The first parameter to this function is a pointer of the current technique for which you need to find the next valid technique. If this parameter is set to *NULL*, the function starts looking at the first technique in the effect. The second parameter, *pTechnique*, is a pointer to a handle used to contain the pointer to the next valid effect. This value is returned as *NULL* if there is no next valid technique.

Using this function, you can easily go through all the techniques within an effect and list only the ones which will work on the current hardware. A second approach to determine if an effect is valid on a particular piece of hardware is to simply get the handle to a specific technique and call the *ValidateTechnique* method of the *ID3DXEffect* interface. Below is the declaration of the *ValidateTechnique* function:

```
HRESULT ValidateTechnique(
    D3DXHANDLE hTechnique
);
```

This function simply takes in the handle to a technique within the effect and will return *D3D_OK* if the effect is supported by the current hardware device.

API Overview

You know how to create an effect and make sure which of its techniques will work on the current hardware, you need to learn how to take advantage of the effect framework and the *ID3DXEffect* interface to render effects. Although I have quickly covered the list of functions which are part of this interface in the previous chapter; this time, I will go into more details as to what each of the functions can accomplish for you.

As you know, the *ID3DXEffect* interface is based on the *ID3DXBaseEffect* interface and thus inherits its functionality consisting mostly of functions used to set and get effect parameters. If we take a look at the functionality added by the *ID3DXEffect* interface, we can condense it to the list of function in the Table 9-1 below.

Table 9-1 Simplified ID3DXEffect Member List

Function	Description
ApplyParameterBlock	Assigns a state value to each effect parameter defined within a parameter block.
Begin	Starts the current active technique.
BeginParameterBlock	Used to capture parameter effect state changes.
BeginPass	Begins a pass, within the active technique.
CloneEffect	Creates a clone of the current effect.
CommitChanges	Used to propagate state changes that occur inside of an active pass to the device before rendering new geometry.
End	Ends the currently active technique.
EndParameterBlock	Stops capturing effect parameter state changes and generates a corresponding parameter block.

Table 9-1 Simplified ID3DXEffect Member List

Function	Description
EndPass	Used to end the active pass of the current active technique.
FindNextValidTechnique	Searches for the next valid technique, starting at the technique after the specified technique. It will query the current device to ensure that the technique selected can be used on this device.
IsParameterUsed	Used to determine if the specified parameter is used by the technique.
OnLostDevice	This function is to be called when the video device is lost and will release all references to video memory resources and deletes all state blocks.
OnResetDevice	This function is to be called after the device has been reset after if has been lost.
ValidateTechnique	Used to validate a technique.

Although the above table can be handy, it makes sense to look at each of the function's usage before we can use them in a real-world use context.

IID3DXEffect::ApplyParameterBlock

This function is meant to assign a state value to each effect parameters contained within a parameter block. Parameter blocks in general are discussed later in this chapter. The declaration for this function uses the following syntax:

```
HRESULT ApplyParameterBlock(
    D3DXHANDLE hParameterBlock
);
```

The *hParameterBlock* parameter is a handle to the parameter block to be applied. This is the handle returned by the *ID3DXEffect::EndParameterBlock* function. This function returns a standard *HRESULT* value and the possible return values for this function are as follows:

- *D3D_OK*: The function succeeded.
- *D3DERR_INVALIDCALL*: The method call is invalid. For example, a method's parameter may have an invalid value.
- *D3DXERR_INVALIDDATA*: The data is invalid.

IID3DXEffect::Begin

This function is used to start rendering using the currently active technique within the effect. Note that this function prepares for the render but must always be completed with an *ID3DXEffect::End* call. Also note that you must always call *ID3DXEffect::Begin* before you call *ID3DXEffect::BeginPass*. The declaration for this function uses the following syntax:

```
HRESULT Begin(
    UINT* pPasses,
    DWORD Flags
);
```

The *pPasses* parameter is a pointer to a *UINT* type variable filled by the function to indicate the number of passes associated to the current technique. The *Flags* parameter determines if state modified by an effect is saved and restored. The default value of zero specifies that *ID3DXEffect::Begin* and *ID3DXEffect::End* will save and restore all state modified by the effect. Valid flags for this parameter are listed below:

- *D3DXFX_DONOTSAVESTATE*: No render states are saved when calling *ID3DXEffect::Begin* or restored when calling *ID3DXEffect::End*.
- *D3DXFX_DONOTSAVESAMPLERSTATE*: A stateblock saves all states with the exception of texture sampler states when calling *ID3DXEffect::Begin*. The saved stated will be restored when calling *ID3DXEffect::End*.
- *D3DXFX_DONOTSAVESHADERSTATE*: A stateblock saves all state states with the exception of shaders and shader constants when calling *ID3DXEffect::Begin*. The saved states will be restored when calling *ID3DXEffect::End*.

This function returns a standard *HRESULT* value and the possible return values for this function are as follows:

- *D3D_OK*: The function succeeded.
- *D3DERR_INVALIDCALL*: The method call is invalid. For example, a method's parameter may have an invalid value.
- *D3DXERR_INVALIDDATA*: The data is invalid.

IID3DXEffect::BeginParameterBlock

This function is meant to begin the capture of effect state changes into a parameter block. The use of parameter blocks is discussed later in this chapter. The declaration for this function uses the following syntax:

```
HRESULT BeginParameterBlock(VOID);
```

This function returns a standard *HRESULT* value and the possible return values for this function are as follows:

- *D3D_OK*: The function succeeded.
- *D3DERR_INVALIDCALL*: The method call is invalid. For example, a method's parameter may have an invalid value.
- *D3DXERR_INVALIDDATA*: The data is invalid.

IID3DXEffect::BeginPass

This function is meant to begin a specific render pass using the currently active technique. The declaration for this function uses the following syntax:

```
HRESULT BeginPass(
    UINT Pass
);
```

The *Pass* parameter is the pass of the current technique to be used. This function returns a standard *HRESULT* value and the possible return values for this function are as follows:

- *D3D_OK*: The function succeeded.
- *D3DERR_INVALIDCALL*: The method call is invalid. For example, a method's parameter may have an invalid value.
- *D3DXERR_INVALIDDATA*: The data is invalid.

IID3DXEffect::CloneEffect

This function is used to create a clone of the effect. The declaration for this function uses the following syntax:

```
HRESULT CloneEffect(
    LPDIRECT3DDEVICE9 pDevice,
    LPD3DXEFFECT* ppEffect
);
```

The *pDevice* parameter is a pointer to a Direct3D device handle. This device will become associated to the specified device. The second parameter, *ppEffect* is a pointer to an *ID3DXEffect* interface containing the cloned interface. This function returns a standard *HRESULT* value, and the possible return values for this function are as follows:

- *D3D_OK*: The function succeeded.
- *D3DERR_INVALIDCALL*: The method call is invalid. For example, a method's parameter may have an invalid value.
- *D3DXERR_INVALIDDATA*: The data is invalid.

IID3DXEffect::CommitChanges

This function is used to propagate state changes that occur within an active pass to the device before rendering. The declaration for this function uses the following syntax:

```
HRESULT CommitChanges(VOID);
```

When an application changes any effect state using any of the *ID3DXEffect::SetXXX* methods inside of an *ID3DXEffect::BeginPass/ID3DXEffect::EndPass* pair, the corresponding states are not automatically sent to the hardware for efficiency reasons. The application must call *ID3DXEffect::CommitChanges* before any *DrawXXXPrimitive* call to propagate state changes to the device before rendering. This function returns a standard *HRESULT* value, and the possible return values for this function are as follows:

- *D3D_OK*: The function succeeded.
- *D3DERR_INVALIDCALL*: The method call is invalid. For example, a method's parameter may have an invalid value.
- *D3DXERR_INVALIDDATA*: The data is invalid.

IID3DXEffect::End

This function is used to end the current active technique. The declaration for this function uses the following syntax:

```
HRESULT End(VOID);
```

When all the rendering using an effect is done within a matching pair of *ID3DXEffect::Begin* and *ID3DXEffect::End* calls. The effect system uses the state block created when *ID3DXEffect::Begin* was called to automatically restore the pipeline's state to what it was called before *ID3DXEffect::Begin* was called. This function returns a standard *HRESULT* value however will always return *D3D_OK*.

IID3DXEffect::EndParameterBlock

This function is used to stop capturing effect parameter state changes which was initiated by calling *ID3DXEffect::BeginParameterBlock*. All effect parameters that changed state will be saved in an effect parameter state block which can later be reapplied through the `ID3DXEffect::ApplyParameterBlock` function. The declaration for this function uses the following syntax:

```
D3DXHANDLE EndParameterBlock(VOID);
```

This function returns a simple `D3DXHANDLE` to a state block resource to be reused later on. Take note that this function is assumed to never fail.

IID3DXEffect::EndPass

This function is used to end rendering of the active pass from the currently active technique. This function works in tandem and must always be used in conjunction to the `ID3DXEffect::BeginPass` function. The declaration for this function uses the following syntax:

```
HRESULT EndPass(VOID);
```

This function returns a standard `HRESULT` value but will currently always succeed and return `D3D_OK`.

IID3DXEffect::FindNextValidTechnique

This function searches for the next valid technique, starting from the specified technique. This function will query the current device to ensure that the technique selected can be used on this device. The declaration for this function uses the following syntax:

```
HRESULT FindNextValidTechnique(
    D3DXHANDLE hTechnique,
    D3DXHANDLE* pTechnique
);
```

The first parameter to this function, `hTechnique`, is a pointer of the current technique for where the function will start looking for the next valid one. If this parameter is set to `NULL`, the function will start looking at the first technique in the effect. The second parameter, `pTechnique`, is a pointer to a handle used to contain the pointer to the next valid effect. If this value is `NULL` then the function could not find another valid technique. This function also returns a standard `HRESULT` value and the possible return values for this function are as follows:

- `D3D_OK`: The function succeeded.
- `D3DERR_INVALIDCALL`: The method call has failed.

IID3DXEffect::IsParameterUsed

This function call can be used to determine if a parameter within an effect is used by the specified technique. The declaration for this function uses the following syntax:

```
BOOL IsParameterUsed(
    D3DXHANDLE hParameter,
    D3DXHANDLE hTechnique
);
```

The *hParameter* parameter is a handle to the parameter for which you wish to check the usage. The second parameter, hTechnique, is also a simple handle pointing to the technique at which you wish to look for parameter usage. This function returns a boolean value indicating if the specified parameter is used within the supplied technique.

IID3DXEffect::OnLostDevice

This function is used to release all references to video memory resources and deletes all state blocks. The need to call this function occurs when a Direct3D device is lost and releases all unused resources before calling the *ID3DXEffect::OnResetDevice* function. A more in-depth discussion of device losses is included later in this chapter. The declaration for this function uses the following syntax:

```
HRESULT OnLostDevice(VOID);
```

This function returns a standard *HRESULT* value. The possible return values for this function are as follows:

- *D3D_OK*: The function succeeded.
- *D3DERR_INVALIDCALL*: The method call has failed.

IID3DXEffect::OnResetDevice

This function should be called every time that a device has been reset with the *ID3DDevice9::Reset* function. Doing so will allow the effect to recreate the proper resources which were associated to the device before it was reset. A more in-depth discussion of device losses is included later in this chapter. The declaration for this function uses the following syntax:

```
HRESULT OnResetDevice(VOID);
```

This function returns a standard *HRESULT* value. The possible return values for this function are as follows:

- *D3D_OK*: The function succeeded.
- *D3DERR_INVALIDCALL*: The method call has failed.

IID3DXEffect::ValidateTechnique

This function is used to validate a technique to ensure that it can currently be executed on the rendering device. The declaration for this function uses the following syntax:

```
HRESULT ValidateTechnique(
    D3DXHANDLE hTechnique
);
```

The *hTechnique* parameter is a handle to the technique needing to be validated. This function returns a standard *HRESULT* value. The possible return values for this function are as follows:

- *D3D_OK*: The function succeeded.
- *D3DERR_INVALIDCALL*: The method call failed, which generally means that the specified technique did not pass the validation by the rendering device.

Using effects

From the previous section, you can see that the *ID3DXEffect* API is fairly hefty, but it is in fact easy to use. In this section, I will go over how the effect system can be used with more details. We have already covered the topics of effect creation and validation earlier in this chapter, but there is still more to do.

You will need to learn how to use the *ID3DXEffect* to render geometry with the effect of your choice. You will also need to be able to work with parameters, either by setting them manually or by taking advantage of effect parameter blocks. To make your application interoperate with other applications, you will not only need to set parameters but also determine their meaning by using semantics and annotations.

Rendering With Effects

Probably the most important part of the effect framework is the ability to render geometry using your effects. Fortunately, this process is easy and will seem intuitive. The first step, covered earlier, is to create an effect and to pick an appropriate rendering technique. Although this was covered earlier, the following sample code illustrates how you can easily load up and create an *ID3DXEffect* interface from an effect file.

```
HRESULT hr = S_OK;
hr = CreateEffectFromFile( pd3dDevice, str, NULL, NULL,
```

```
        g_dwShaderFlags, g_pEffectPool, pEffect, NULL );

    // If the loading of the effect succeeded, find the first valid
    // technique and apply it to the effect.
    if( !pEffect )
    {
        D3DXHANDLE hTech;
        pEffect->FindNextValidTechnique( NULL, &hTech );
        pEffect->SetTechnique( hTech );
    }
```

Simply create an effect then find which technique works for you and assign it as the currently active technique. Within a more complete application, you will always want to validate your results to make sure that your effect actually compiled and that more importantly, the current rendering device can support at least one of the techniques within your effect file.

As you remember, an effect is composed of techniques, which in turn are constructed with one or multiple rendering passes. When rendering using an effect, you will need to take in consideration that a technique may have multiple passes. This is easily determined when calling the *ID3DXEffect::Begin* function. The code below illustrates how you can take an effect and render some geometry using the currently active technique.

```
    UINT cPasses;
    HRESULT hr;

    // Begin using the effect, the number of render passes
    // within the technique is returned in cPasses
    hr = pEffect->Begin( &cPasses, 0 );

    // If this succeeded, go off and render all the
    // passes given by the Begin function.
    If ( hr == D3D_OK )
    {
        // Iterate through all passes
        for( UINT p = 0; p < cPasses; ++p )
        {
            // Begin the rendering pass
            pEffect->BeginPass( p );

            // Render your geometry here…

            // End the rendering pass
            pEffect->EndPass();
        }

        // Finish off rendering and restore the effect
        // states captured on the Begin call.
        pEffect->End();
    }
```

Pretty easy, huh? Rendering using effects is simple and can be quickly integrated into any applications. At this point, you may be wondering about effect parameters. In fact, right now, we've blindly rendered some geometry using an effect without considering its parameters. No need to worry, this is the topic I will be covering in the next section.

Dealing with Parameters

In the previous section, we have rendered geometry through an effect but have omitted an important part. In this section, I will discuss the topic of parameters and how they can be accessed easily and efficiently.

Each effect will have a rich set of parameters to control the behavior of the rendering. Some are obvious and necessary such as your geometry's transformation matrix and the texture samplers used within your pixel shader. Some parameters will also control other behaviors such as lighting and animation and will need to be setup before you use your effects.

Setting parameters within an effect is simple task which involves calling the appropriate *ID3DXEffect::SetXXX* function and passing it to the necessary data. For example, if you have a variable named *WorldMatrix* within your effect which is a 4-by-4 matrix, you can easily set its value using the following code:

```
D3DXMATRIXA16 mWorldMatrix;

// Set your matrix to a valid value and pass it to the effect
pEffect->SetMatrix( "WorldMatrix", &mWorldMatrix );
```

You can use the name of a variable directly as a handle to the parameter within an effect, however, this implies that the effect system will need to go through all the parameters of your effect and determine the appropriate one based on its name. This can work fine for some one-time parameter but can be inefficient if you are setting multiple parameters for each effect. One alternative is to retrieve a real handle to the parameter through the *ID3DXEffect::GetParameterByName* function call. Below is the same example code as above, converted to make use of effect parameter handles:

```
D3DXMATRIXA16 mWorldMatrix;
D3DXHANDLE hWorldMatrix;

// Get the handle to our parameter
hWorldMatrix = pEffect->GetParameterByName( NULL, "WorldMatrix");

// Set your matrix to a valid value and pass it to the effect
pEffect->SetMatrix( hWorldMatrix, &mWorldMatrix );
```

Parameters can also be defined as structures within your effect files. In such case, you can also set individual elements of the structure but will need to take a few extra steps. For example, if you have the following structure and variable within your effect file,

```
struct LightStruct
{
    float4 Pos;
    float4 Color;
};
LightStruct Light;
```

you can set a particular element of the structured variable by first fetching the variable and then fetching the element structure as illustrated below:

```
D3DXVECTOR4 vLightColor( 1.0f, 1.0f, 1.0f, 0.0f );
D3DXHANDLE hLight, hLightColor;

// Get the handle to our structure parameter
hLight = pEffect->GetParameterByName( NULL, "Light");
hLightColor = pEffect->GetParameterByName( hLight, "Color");

// Set the value of the effect parameter
pEffect->SetVector( hLightColor, &vLightColor );
```

Another situation that may arise when your effect has multiple lights and that the light structure variable is an array as in the following:

```
LightStruct Light[4];
```

In this particular case, you will not only need to access the structure element but get to the appropriate array element. This can easily done with the `ID3DXEffect::GetParameterElement` function call. Below is the same example code which sets the color of the first light element within the array:

```
D3DXVECTOR4 vLightColor( 1.0f, 1.0f, 1.0f, 0.0f );
D3DXHANDLE hLight, hLightElement, hLightColor;

// Get the handle to our structure parameter
hLight = pEffect->GetParameterByName( NULL, "Light");
hLightElement = pEffect->GetParameterElement( hLight, 0);
hLightColor = pEffect->GetParameterByName( hLightElement, "Color");

// Set the value of the effect parameter
pEffect->SetVector( hLightColor, &vLightColor );
```

There we go! Using parameters is an easy task. I will address the issue of semantics in the next section. I have addressed the issue of efficiency using parameter handles, however, what if your effect contains many of the same parameters for a particular geometry that are constant or at least change infrequently? Doing all of those `ID3DXEffect::SetXXX` calls can become expensive and the effect framework allows you to group such parameter values together into what is called a parameter block.

Creating parameter blocks is simply a matter of wrapping your standard parameter settings within a set of `ID3DXEffect::BeginParameterBlock` and `ID3DXEffect::EndParameterBlock` function calls. This will give you back a handle to the parameter block which can be applied to the current effect at any time using the `ID3DXEffect::ApplyParameterBlock` function call. Below is a simple example of the construction of a parameter block for our above lighting example:

```
D3DXVECTOR4 vLightColor( 1.0f, 1.0f, 1.0f, 0.0f );
D3DXVECTOR4 vLightPostion( 0.0f, 0.0f, 0.0f, 0.0f );
D3DXHANDLE hLight, hLightColor, hLightPosition;
D3DXHANDLE hLightParamBlock;

// Get the handle to our structure parameter
hLight = pEffect->GetParameterByName( NULL, "Light");
hLightColor = pEffect->GetParameterByName( hLight, "Color");
hLightPosition = pEffect->GetParameterByName( hLight, "Position");

// Build a parameter block
pEffect->BeginParameterBlock();
pEffect->SetVector( hLightColor, &vLightColor );
pEffect->SetVector( hLightPosition, &vLightPosition );
hLightParamBlock = pEffect->EndParameterBlock();

// Apply the parameter block to the effect
pEffect->ApplyParameterBlock();
```

One last thing I would like to mention about parameters is what happens to the parameter values when you set them. When you set a variable, the effect framework keeps track of the value and the fact that it has been changed. Next time you start the effect by using the `ID3DXEffect::Begin` call, all the relevant parameters to the current techniques will be passed down to the hardware and used as needed.

If your render loop begins an effect and renders multiple pieces of geometry using the same effect, you may need to change some parameters (such as a transform matrix) as you render. The problem is that you are already within a `ID3DXEffect::Begin` call and your parameter changes will not get propagated to the hardware until you call `ID3DXEffect::Begin` again. The alternative to this particular situation is to call the `ID3DXEffect::CommitChanges` function. This function will cause any changed parameters to be forcefully propagated to the hardware.

The whole process of setting effect parameters is easy and straightforward. However, unless you use a consistent naming convention within your effects, your application will need a way to know the meaning of all the parameters within an effect so it can set them to the proper value. This is the purpose of semantics and annotations.

Using Semantics and Annotations

Preparing your effects for render involves going through all the parameters associated with your effect and assigning the proper values. Unless you wish to stick with predefined names, it can be difficult to determine the meaning of a parameter, especially if some of your effects can be defined by third parties outside your application and thus outside of your control.

As discussed in Chapter 6, this is exactly why semantics and annotations were created. They allow for developers to separate the name of a parameter from its actual meaning or function. Although there is a set of predefined semantics intended to cover most standard rendering needs (See Appendix C), you can easily define your own semantics to address the specific needs of your application.

If we take the examples used in the previous section, our transformation matrix was named *WorldMatrix*, which implied in itself that the parameter was the world transform matrix. This also implied that you would have to stick to this precise name for each of your effects if you wanted your application to work properly. If you were to change the definition of the parameter to the following:

```
float4x4 WorldMatrix        : WORLD;
```

you can see that we now have tacked a standard *WORLD* semantic to our variable, meaning that the name of the variable is now irrelevant to your application. Of course, this implies that your application sets its parameters based on the semantic of a variable instead of its name. This can easily be accomplished with the *ID3DXEffect::GetParameterBySemantic* function call. Below is the one of our previous samples which has been converted to take advantage of semantics:

```
D3DXMATRIXA16 mWorldMatrix;
D3DXHANDLE hWorldMatrix;

// Get the handle to our parameter by its semantic
hWorldMatrix = pEffect->GetParameterBySemantic( NULL, "WORLD");

// Set your matrix to a valid value and pass it to the effect
pEffect->SetMatrix( hWorldMatrix, &mWorldMatrix );
```

Another approach to the same problem, depending on how you wish to structure your application is to gather all the parameters within an effect and get their semantics through the *ID3DXEffect::GetParameterDesc* function. The structure returned by this function contains the semantic associated with each parameter and allows you build a cache of all relevant parameters to an effect and associate them with their meaning within your application. The sample code below will go through all the parameters of an effect and find the parameter to match the *WORLD* semantic.

```
D3DXMATRIXA16 mWorldMatrix;

// Determine the number of parameters and iterate through
// all of them
D3DXEFFECT_DESC EffectDesc;
pEffect->GetDesc(&EffectDesc);
for (int i=0; i<EffectDesc.Parameters; i++)
{
    D3DXHANDLE hParameter;
    D3DXPARAMETER_DESC ParameterDesc;

    // Get the handle to our parameter by its semantic
    hParameter = pEffect->GetParameter ( NULL, i );

    // Get the description of the parameter
    pEffect->GetParameterDesc( hParameter, &ParameterDesc );

    // Check if the parameter semantics matches our semantics
    if (strcmp( ParameterDesc.Semantic, "WORLD" ) == 0 )
    {
        pEffect->SetMatrix( hParameter, &mWorldMatrix );
    }
}
```

Annotations are used to give additional information about the use of a particular parameter. For example, it can be used to define the user interface associated with a parameter to allow an application to enable its user to dynamically change the value of an effect. Since a parameter can have multiple annotations associated with it, you will need to determine the number of annotations associated to a parameter through the *ID3DXEffect::GetParameterDesc* function and then calling *ID3DXEffect::GetAnnotation* to retrieve each of the annotations. For example, for the following effect parameter:

```
texture Tex0 < string name = "tiger.bmp"; >;
```

We define a texture for which we assign an annotation of *name*. In this context, the annotation indicates the default texture file to use for this effect. The below example shows how you can look for this particular annotation to load up a texture:

```
// Determine the number of parameters and iterate through
// all of them
D3DXEFFECT_DESC EffectDesc;
pEffect->GetDesc(&EffectDesc);
for (int i=0; i<EffectDesc.Parameters; i++)
{
    D3DXHANDLE hParameter;
```

```
D3DXPARAMETER_DESC ParameterDesc;

// Get the handle to our parameter by its semantic
hParameter = pEffect->GetParameter ( NULL, i );

// Get the description of the parameter
pEffect->GetParameterDesc( hParameter, &ParameterDesc );

// Check all annotations for something we understand
D3DXHANDLE hAnnot;
for( UINT iAnnot = 0; iAnnot < ParamDesc.Annotations; iAnnot++ )
{
    hAnnot = m_pEffect->GetAnnotation ( hParam, iAnnot );
    m_pEffect->GetParameterDesc( hAnnot, &AnnotDesc );
    if( _strcmpi( AnnotDesc.Name, "name" ) == 0 )
    {
        pEffect->GetString( hAnnot, &pstrName );
        // Load the texture…
    }
}
}
```

Defining the use of semantics and annotations is very application centric, but with what I have covered above, adding support for annotation and semantics to your application should be a straightforward matter.

Debugging Techniques

Possibly one of the most tedious aspects of shader and effect development is figuring out what is wrong when your effect is not functioning as expected. When dealing with regular code, you can take advantage of debugging features offered by your compiler environment, such as Visual Studio to debug and troubleshoot your code.

The first approach to deducing problems with your effects is to have the effect framework give you a listing of the compiled effect and shaders. As you know, this can be done with the command-line compiler but also performed with the various *D3DXCreateEffect* functions covered in more detail in Chapter 12.

Of course, this approach has no guaranties and will require you to have an understanding of the appropriate vertex and pixel shader assembly languages. A complete reference of the vertex and pixel shader instructions, as well as their performance implications, has been included in Appendix A.

Another approach to debugging effects is to use it by hand and take advantage of the rendering output to see intermediate results. By taking portions of your shader code and isolating them, you can output various intermediate results of your shader operation to your display. For example, you can output the surface normals of an object as color to see visually that the results correspond to what you are expecting.

Of course, all these approaches can be tedious and time consuming. If you use Visual Studio .NET as your development environment, you may be able to take advantage of the DirectX extensions to efficiently debug your shaders.

DirectX VS.NET Extensions

The DirextX extensions for Visual Studio .NET are a set of tools that integrate into the IDE to facilitate the development and debugging of graphical applications. The extensions are part of the DirectX SDK and will install automatically if you install the SDK and have Visual Studio present. The extensions give you a lot of functionality including

- Debug vertex and pixel shaders both in assembly and in HLSL form.
- Look at the contents of variables, registers, and device state.
- Use the IDE to run the code, single step through code, or break where necessary. Breakpoints can be set both on line or specific on-screen pixel areas.
- View the assembly code generated by the HLSL compiler.
- View loaded texture(s) on the Microsoft Direct3D device.
- View render target(s) as pixel shaders write to them.
- See syntax coloring for recognized file types, including: .FX (effects files), .VSH (assembly vertex shader files), and .PSH (assembly pixel shader files).

To take advantage of the extension your application must be running in software mode. You will not be able to take advantage of hardware acceleration when debugging shaders and effects.

The first step to using the DirectX extensions is enabling them within DirectX itself. To do so, you will need to fire up the DirectX Control Panel applet and enable both the *Debug Version of Direct3D* and the *Enable Shader Debugging* options. Next, create your Direct3D device so that the vertex and pixel processing is done on the CPU. This will generally imply creating your device using the reference rasterizer with software vertex processing. Take a look at the documentation on *IDirect3D9::CreateDevice* for more information.

At this point, you are set to debug your application. To run the DirectX debugger within Visual Studio, go to the *Debug->Direct3D* menu and pick the *Start with Direct3D Debugging* option.

Now, you can easily add breakpoints to your effects by opening the .FX files and placing the breakpoints. In fact, the process is the same as it would be if you were to debug a regular application. In addition, you can manually place a function breakpoint for both `IDirect3D9::BeginScene` and `IDirect3D9::EndScene` so you can trap the beginning and end of a scene render.

You can also add breakpoints to be triggered when certain areas of the screen are updated. This can be done simply by going to the breakpoint menu and adding a variable breakpoint and specifying *(x, y)* for a specific pixel or *(left, top)-(right, bottom)* for a region of the screen.

In addition, you can see specific registers and even the device state within the watch window of the debugger. To see shader registers or variables, you can simply type in the name of the variable. To see the current rendering device state, you can add the `$DeviceState` variable to your watch window.

As you can see, debugging shaders is easy with the DirectX extensions; however, keep in mind that because you must run in software emulation, rendering of your application can be significantly slower.

Summary and what's next?

Using the effect framework can dramatically simplify the process of managing shaders and effects. When dealing with applications needing to support a wide range of hardware, the concept of technique is critical. The `ID3DXEffect` interface is at the center stage of the effect framework and allows you not only to render using effects but also to manage all the parameters associated with your effects.

In the next chapter, I will discuss the topic of parameter sharing. The reality is that many shaders will share parameters in common such as transformation matrices or textures. Under normal circumstances, however, each effect will have an instance of all its variables. The effect framework allows sharing parameters for more efficient processing of multiple effects by using the proper effect framework interfaces.

Chapter 10

Sharing Parameters

When developing graphical applications, you will likely use more than a single effect. Each of your objects may use various shaders to represent different types of materials, thus requiring several different effects to accomplish the task. As you may have noticed from the standard semantics and annotations, many basic types of parameters can be used in effects.

The reality is that many of your effects will use some of the same parameter. For example, most of your effects will use a transformation matrix. Many of your effects may share the same lighting parameters; however, since each instance of an *ID3DXEffect* is created independently, each of these common parameters will have a separate instance within each of your effects.

This has a few consequences for you as a developer. First of all, this is inefficient memory-wise as the effect framework has to keep track of all those redundant variables. More importantly, since each of these variables are independent from effect to effect, you will need to update each of them for every effect even if their values have not changed from one render to another.

To solve this issue, the DirectX team has created a new interface *ID3DXEffectPool* to allow selective sharing of common parameters between effects.

ID3DXEffectPool

To facilitate the sharing of parameters among effects, the DirectX team has created the *ID3DXEffectPool* interface. This interface has no members but is used as a container in which shared parameters will remain. In essence, you will need to create a single instance of this interface for each pool of parameters you wish to create. You can create a new effect parameter pool simply by calling the *D3DXCreateEffectPool* function with the the following declaration:

```
HRESULT WINAPI D3DXCreateEffectPool(
    LPD3DXEFFECTPOOL* ppPool
);
```

This function creates and returns a new effect pool instance through the *ppPool* parameter. Assigning an effect to a particular pool is straightforward but must be done on creation of the effect using one of the *D3DXCreateEffect* functions.

```
HRESULT WINAPI D3DXCreateEffect(
    LPDIRECT3DDEVICE9 pDevice,
    LPCVOID pSrcData,
    UINT SrcDataLen,
    const D3DXMACRO *pDefines,
    LPD3DXINCLUDE pInclude,
    DWORD Flags,
    LPD3DXEFFECTPOOL pPool,
    LPD3DXEFFECT *ppEffect,
    LPD3DXBUFFER *ppCompilationErrors
);
```

Notice that the seventh parameter to the function is a pointer to an effect pool. If you do not wish to have your effect share parameters, you can easily pass *NULL* to this parameter. This is equivalent to having the effect framework create a new *ID3DXEffectPool* for each new effect.

The basic task of sharing parameters amongst your effects is straightforward,but before you make full use of this feature, there are a few restrictions you need to be aware of:

- A parameter is added to the pool the first time an effect containing that parameter is added to the pool.
- A pool gets initial values from the first instance of a shared parameter. Any parameters shared subsequently get their initial values from the pool.
- A parameter is deleted from the pool only when all effect references to the shared parameter are released.
- All effects in the pool that contain the same (shared) device-dependent parameter must use the same device.

Another restriction that you must be aware of is that effects sharing parameters must use the same device. This is enforced to prevent the sharing of device-dependent parameters (such as shaders or textures) across different rendering devices. This means that cross device sharing of parameters is disallowed.

Controlling Shared Parameters

Although effect parameter sharing is a nifty feature, you may not want all the parameters of your effect to be shared across all instances. For example, there may be specific textures for use in one effect that does not apply to all your other effects. This implies that you need some form of control on the sharing of parameters, so you may decide which ones deserve sharing.

The effect parameters which can be shared are all the non-static variables declared within an effect. This includes both global variables and annotations. By default, all non-static effect parameters are not shared even if the effect is created with an *ID3DXEffectPool* interface instance. You can enable the sharing of parameters between different effects by declaring them with the *shared* keyword and then associating the effect to an effect pool when creating it.

Below is a portion of an effect file specifying some shared parameters:

```
// light intensity
shared float4 LightAmbientIntensity    = { 0.8f, 0.8f, 0.8f, 1.0f };
shared float4 LightDiffuseColor        = { 1.0f, 0.9f, 0.8f, 1.0f };
shared float4 LightSpecularColor       = { 1.0f, 1.0f, 1.0f, 1.0f };

// material reflectivity
float4 MaterialAmbientIntensity = { 0.5f, 0.5f, 0.5f, 1.0f };   // ambient
float4 MaterialDiffuseColor     = { 0.4f, 0.4f, 0.4f, 1.0f };   // diffuse
float4 MaterialSpecularColor    = { 0.2f, 0.2f, 0.2f, 1.0f };   // specular
int    MaterialSpecularPower    = 32;                           // power

// transformations
float4x3 World  : WORLD;
shared float4x3 View    : VIEW;
shared float4x4 ViewProjection : VIEWPROJECTION;
shared float3 CameraPos : CAMERAPOSITION;
```

From the example above, you can see some of the circumstances in which it makes sense to share parameters. For example, it makes sense to share basic lighting parameters as they will likely be the same for objects in the same vicinity. For transformation matrices, it makes sense to share the camera and view related matrices since they do not change over a scene. It may make sense to keep the world matrix separate as it will likely be different for every object in your scene.

Using the shared parameters in this context is now straightforward. You can create all your effects using the same *ID3DXEffectPool* interface and then only setup the parameters once. Below is a practical example of what this may look like within your application:

```
HRESULT hr = S_OK;
ID3DXEffectPool *pEffectPool;

// Create the common effect pool
hr = CreateEffectPool( &pEffectPool );

// Create two effects sharing common parameters
hr = CreateEffectFromFile( pd3dDevice, str1, NULL, NULL,
    g_dwShaderFlags, pEffectPool, pEffect1, NULL );
hr = CreateEffectFromFile( pd3dDevice, str2, NULL, NULL,
    g_dwShaderFlags, pEffectPool, pEffect2, NULL );

// Find the best techniques for both effects
```

```
D3DXHANDLE hTech;
if( !pEffect1 )
{
    pEffect1->FindNextValidTechnique( NULL, &hTech );
    pEffect1->SetTechnique( hTech );
}
if( !pEffect2 )
{
    pEffect2->FindNextValidTechnique( NULL, &hTech );
    pEffect2->SetTechnique( hTech );
}

// Set the common parameters to the effect
D3DXMATRIXA16 mViewMatrix;
D3DXHANDLE hViewMatrix;

// Get the handle to our parameter by its semantic
hViewMatrix = pEffect1->GetParameterBySemantic( NULL, "VIEW");
pEffect1->SetMatrix( hWorldMatrix, &mWorldMatrix );

// Render using an effect
UINT cPasses;
hr = pEffect2->Begin( &cPasses, 0 ) );

// If this succeded, go off and render all the
// passes given by the Begin function.
If ( hr == D3D_OK )
{
    // Iterate through all passes
    for( UINT p = 0; p < cPasses; ++p )
    {
        // Begin the rendering pass
        pEffect2->BeginPass( p );

        // Render your geometry here...

        // End the rendering pass
        pEffect2->EndPass();
    }

    // Finish off rendering and restore the effect
    // states captured on the Begin call.
    pEffect2->End();
}
```

Effect Cloning

Although the topic of effect cloning might have been more relevant to the previous chapter, some restrictions and details portray to the sharing of parameters. First, any effect can easily be cloned with the `ID3DXEffect::CloneEffect`. The definition of the function is given below:

```
HRESULT CloneEffect(
    LPDIRECT3DDEVICE9 pDevice,
    LPD3DXEFFECT* ppEffect
);
```

The `CloneEffect` function takes in a Direct3D device and will return a pointer to a new instance of the effect. Cloned effects are identical to the original effect and all parameters; even dynamically added annotations will be cloned. One interesting point to note is the clone function allows the specification of a Direct3D device, thus allowing cloning effects across devices. With effect cloning and parameter sharing, however, there are a few restrictions.

- Clones inherit the original effect's pool.
- Clones inherit the original effect's techniques, passes, parameters, and annotations; including all annotations dynamically added through the `ID3DXEffect` interface.
- Cloning onto a new device will fail if the original effect's pool was not `NULL` and the original effect contained a shared device-dependent parameter.

Summary and what's next?

Sharing parameters among effects is more a matter of performance and efficiency. It allows developers to chain effects together in a more natural way. All of this can easily be accomplished through the proper use of the `ID3DXEffectPool` interface and the use of the `shared` keyword within your effect files.

In the next chapter, I will discuss the topic render state management. Effect files can define a set of render states to be modified and updated; however, the application has little to no knowledge of what is going on. The render state management system allows the application to place itself between the effect framework and Direct3D, thus allowing the application to keep track of the current rendering device state.

Chapter

11

Effect State Manager

When developing graphical applications using the effect framework, various device states will be setup by your effects, but unless you look at the source effect files, you have no clue about what individual device states will be set by a particular effect. If your application uses effects exclusively, this may not pose any problems. There are cases, however, where either for debugging or for the purpose of your engine, you may need to know the current state of the hardware.

One solution would be to simply query the Direct3D device as needed using one of the *GetXXX* functions. Most of theses functions will only work when your Direct3D device is not created as a *PURE* device and may have some performance implications to your application. In addition, you may need in special cases to trap certain states and modify them as needed by your application.

Because of this, the effect framework defines an interface called *ID3DXEffectStateManager* used to keep track of device state changes as they happen. In the next sections, I'll go over the interface and describe all of its functions.

ID3DXEffectStateManager

The *ID3DXEffectStateManager* interface is user implemented and provides an intermediate between the effect framework and the Direct3D device. This allows you not only to keep track of state changes but alter them as they transit from your effect to the Direct3D device. Table 11-1 below is the list of all the members part of the *ID3DXEffectStateManager*:

Table 11-1 ID3DXEffectStateManager Members

Function	Description
LightEnable	A callback function that must be implemented by a user to enable/disable a light.
SetFVF	A callback function that must be implemented by a user to set a flexible vertex format (FVF) code.
SetLight	A callback function that must be implemented by a user to set a light.
SetMaterial	A callback function that must be implemented by a user to set material state.
SetNPatchMode	A callback function that must be implemented by a user to set the number of subdivision segments for N-patches.
SetPixelShader	A callback function that must be implemented by a user to set a pixel shader.
SetPixelShaderConstantB	A callback function that must be implemented by a user to set an array of vertex shader Boolean constants.
SetPixelShaderConstantF	A callback function that must be implemented by a user to set an array of vertex shader floating-point constants.
SetPixelShaderConstantI	A callback function that must be implemented by a user to set an array of vertex shader integer constants.
SetRenderState	A callback function that must be implemented by a user to set render state.
SetSamplerState	A callback function that must be implemented by a user to set a sampler.
SetTexture	A callback function that must be implemented by a user to set a texture.
SetTextureStageState	A callback function that must be implemented by a user to set the texture stage state.
SetTransform	A callback function that must be implemented by a user to set a transform.
SetVertexShader	A callback function that must be implemented by a user to set a vertex shader.
SetVertexShaderConstantB	A callback function that must be implemented by a user to set an array of vertex shader Boolean constants.

Table 11-1 ID3DXEffectStateManager Members

Function	Description
SetVertexShaderConstantF	A callback function that must be implemented by a user to set an array of vertex shader floating-point constants.
SetVertexShaderConstantI	A callback function that must be implemented by a user to set an array of vertex shader integer constants.

All of the functions listed above are callbacks that will be called by an effect to setup the appropriate states. For an effect to take advantage of a state manager, you simply need to call the *ID3DXEffect::SetStateManager* which has the following definition:

```
HRESULT SetStateManager(
    LPD3DXEFFECTSTATEMANAGER pManager
);
```

The function takes a pointer to an instance of your custom state manager. From this point on, all state related calls from an effect will go through your manager. To go back to the default behavior for an effect, simply set the manager to *NULL*.

Over the next few sections, I will go more in-depth with each of the members of the *ID3DXEffectStateManager* and explain which states they manage. Before I kick it off, a quick note, each of these callback functions return a *HRESULT* value which must be *D3D_OK* or the effect itself will fail.

IID3DXEffectStateManager::LightEnable

This callback function is called by the effect framework when enabling fixed pipeline lights. This function is the Direct3D equivalent to *IDirect3D9::LightEnable*. The declaration for this function uses the following syntax:

```
HRESULT LightEnable(
    DWORD Index,
    BOOL Enable
);
```

The first parameter is the index of the light, *Index*, is the index to the light that will be enabled by the second parameter, *Enable*. The value of the index is the same index as used by the *IDirect3D9::SetLight* function.

A sample implementation of the function which simply relays the states to Direct3D is as follows:

```
STDMETHOD(LightEnable)(THIS_ DWORD Index, BOOL Enable )
{
    return m_pDevice->LightEnable( Index, Enable );
}
```

IID3DXEffectStateManager::SetFVF

This callback function is called by the effect framework when setting the flexible vertex format, or FVF. This function is the Direct3D equivalent to *IDirect3D9::SetFVF*. The declaration for this function uses the following syntax:

```
HRESULT SetFVF(
    DWORD FVF,
);
```

The only parameter to this function is the new FVF telling Direct3D how to interpret vertex data. A sample implementation of the function relaying the states to Direct3D is as follows:

```
STDMETHOD(SetFVF)(THIS_ DWORD dwFVF )
{
    return m_pDevice->SetFVF( dwFVF );
}
```

IID3DXEffectStateManager::SetLight

This callback function is called by the effect framework when setting the fixed pipeline lighting parameters. This function is the Direct3D equivalent to *IDirect3D9::SetLight*. The declaration for this function uses the following syntax:

```
HRESULT SetLight(
    DWORD Index,
    CONST D3DLIGHT9* pLight
);
```

The first parameter is the index of the light, *Index*, is the index to the light that will be enabled by the second parameter, *pLight*, an instance of the *D3DLIGHT9* structure.

A sample implementation of the function relaying the states to Direct3D is as follows:

```
STDMETHOD(SetLight)(THIS_ DWORD Index, CONST D3DLIGHT9 *pLight )
{
    return m_pDevice->SetLight( Index, pLight );
}
```

IID3DXEffectStateManager::SetMaterial

This callback function is called by the effect framework when setting material states. This function is the Direct3D equivalent to *IDirect3D9::SetMaterial*. The declaration for this function uses the following syntax:

```
HRESULT SetMaterial(
    CONST D3DMATERIAL9* pMaterial
);
```

The only parameter to this function, pMaterial, is an instance of the *D3DMATERIAL9*. A sample implementation of the function relaying the states to Direct3D is as follows:

```
STDMETHOD(SetMaterial)(THIS_ CONST D3DMATERIAL9 *pMaterial )
{
    return m_pDevice->SetMaterial( pMaterial );
}
```

IID3DXEffectStateManager::SetNPatchMode

This callback function is called by the effect framework when setting the number of subdivision segments and rendering N-patches. This function is the Direct3D equivalent to *IDirect3D9::SttNPatchMode*. The declaration for this function uses the following syntax:

```
HRESULT SetNPatchMode(
    FLOAT nSegments
);
```

The only parameter to this function, *nSegments*, indicates the number of segments in which the patch must be divided on render. A sample implementation of the function relaying the states to Direct3D is as follows:

```
STDMETHOD(SetNPatchMode)(THIS_ FLOAT NumSegments )
{
    m_nTotalStateChanges++;
    return m_pDevice->SetNPatchMode( NumSegments );
}
```

IID3DXEffectStateManager::SetPixelShader

This callback function is called by the effect framework when setting the current pixel shader. This function is the Direct3D equivalent to *IDirect3D9::SetPixelShader*. The declaration for this function uses the following syntax:

```
HRESULT SetPixelShader(
    LPDIRECT3DPIXELSHADER9 pShader
);
```

The only parameter to this function, *pShader*, is an instance of the pixel shader that will be used by the effect. A sample implementation of the function relaying the states to Direct3D is as follows:

```
STDMETHOD(SetPixelShader)(THIS_ LPDIRECT3DPIXELSHADER9 pShader )
{
    return m_pDevice->SetPixelShader( pShader );
}
```

IID3DXEffectStateManager:: SetPixelShaderConstantB

This callback function is called by the effect framework to set an array of pixel shader boolean constants. This function is the Direct3D equivalent to *IDirect3D9::SetPixelShaderConstantB*. The declaration for this function uses the following syntax:

```
HRESULT SetPixelShaderConstantB(
    UINT StartRegister,
    CONST BOOL* pConstantData,
    UINT RegisterCount
);
```

The first parameter, *StartRegister*, indicates the memory location where the constant array should be applied. The second parameter, *pConstantData* is a pointer to the shader constant data. The last parameter, *RegisterCount*, indicates the number of registers to be filled.

A sample implementation of the function relaying the states to Direct3D is as follows:

```
STDMETHOD(SetPixelShaderConstantB)(THIS_ UINT RegisterIndex,
                                   CONST BOOL *pConstantData,
                                   UINT RegisterCount )
{
    return m_pDevice->SetPixelShaderConstantB( RegisterIndex,
                                               pConstantData,
                                               RegisterCount );
}
```

IID3DXEffectStateManager:: SetPixelShaderConstantF

This callback function is called by the effect framework to set an array of pixel shader float constants. This function is the Direct3D equivalent to *IDirect3D9::SetPixelShaderConstantF*. The declaration for this function uses the following syntax:

```
HRESULT SetPixelShaderConstantF(
    UINT StartRegister,
    CONST FLOAT* pConstantData,
    UINT RegisterCount
);
```

The first parameter, *StartRegister*, indicates the memory location where the constant array should be applied. The second parameter, *pConstantData* is a pointer to the actual shader constant data. The last parameter, *RegisterCount*, indicates the number of registers to be filled.

A sample implementation of the function relaying the states to Direct3D is as follows:

```
STDMETHOD(SetPixelShaderConstantF)(THIS_ UINT RegisterIndex,
                                   CONST FLOAT *pConstantData,
                                   UINT RegisterCount )
{
    return m_pDevice->SetPixelShaderConstantF( RegisterIndex,
                                               pConstantData,
                                               RegisterCount );
}
```

IID3DXEffectStateManager:: SetPixelShaderConstantI

This callback function is called by the effect framework to set an array of pixel shader integer constants. This function is the Direct3D equivalent to *IDirect3D9::SetPixelShaderConstantI*. The declaration for this function uses the following syntax:

```
HRESULT SetPixelShaderConstantI(
    UINT StartRegister,
    CONST INT* pConstantData,
    UINT RegisterCount
);
```

The first parameter, *StartRegister*, indicates the memory location where the constant array should be applied. The second parameter, *pConstantData* is a pointer to the shader constant data. The last parameter, *RegisterCount*, indicates the number of registers to be filled.

A sample implementation of the function relaying the states to Direct3D is as follows:

```
STDMETHOD(SetPixelShaderConstantI)(THIS_ UINT RegisterIndex,
                                   CONST INT *pConstantData,
                                   UINT RegisterCount )
{
    return m_pDevice->SetPixelShaderConstantI( RegisterIndex,
                                               pConstantData,
                                               RegisterCount );
}
```

IID3DXEffectStateManager::SetRenderState

This callback function is called by the effect framework when a render state needs to be set. This function is the Direct3D equivalent to *IDirect3D9::SetRenderState*. The declaration for this function uses the following syntax:

```
HRESULT SetRenderState(
    D3DRENDERSTATETYPE State,
    DWORD Value
);
```

The first parameter, *State*, is the *D3DRENDERSTATETYPE* needing to be set and the second parameter, *Value*, indicated the value the render state needs to be set. The value of the index is the same index as used by the *IDirect3D9::SetRenderState* function.

A sample implementation of the function relaying the states to Direct3D is as follows:

```
STDMETHOD(SetRenderState)(THIS_ D3DRENDERSTATETYPE d3dRenderState,
                          DWORD dwValue )
{
    return m_pDevice->SetRenderState( d3dRenderState, dwValue );
}
```

IID3DXEffectStateManager::SetSamplerState

This callback function is called by the effect framework when setting a sampler. This function is the Direct3D equivalent to *IDirect3D9::SetSamplerState*. The declaration for this function uses the following syntax:

```
HRESULT SetSamplerState(
    DWORD Sampler,
```

```
        D3DSAMPLERSTATETYPE Type,
        DWORD Value
);
```

The first parameter, *Sampler*, is the zero-based index to the sampler. The remaining parameters, *Type* and *Value*, define the sampler state and its value.

A sample implementation of the function relaying the states to Direct3D is as follows:

```
STDMETHOD(SetSamplerState)(THIS_ DWORD dwStage,
                           D3DSAMPLERSTATETYPE d3dSamplerState,
                           DWORD dwValue )
{
    return m_pDevice->SetSamplerState( dwStage, d3dSamplerState, dwValue );
}
```

IID3DXEffectStateManager::SetTexture

This callback function is called by the effect framework when the effect selects a texture. This function is the Direct3D equivalent to *IDirect3D9::SetTexture*. The declaration for this function uses the following syntax:

```
HRESULT SetTexture(
    DWORD Stage,
    LPDIRECT3DBASETEXTURE9 pTexture
);
```

The first parameter, *Stage*, is the index to the texture state to be set. The value of the texture state is the same index as used by the *IDirect3D9::SetTexture* and *IDirect3D9::SetTexture StageState* function.

A sample implementation of the function relaying the states to Direct3D is as follows:

```
STDMETHOD(SetTexture)(THIS_ DWORD dwStage, LPDIRECT3DBASETEXTURE9 pTexture )
{
    m_nTotalStateChanges++;
    return m_pDevice->SetTexture( dwStage, pTexture );
}
```

IID3DXEffectStateManager:: SetTextureStageState

This callback function is called by the effect framework when setting a texture stage state. This function is the Direct3D equivalent to *IDirect3D9::SetTextureStageState*. The declaration for this function uses the following syntax:

```
HRESULT SetTextureStageState(
    DWORD Stage,
    D3DTEXTURESTAGESTATETYPE Type,
    DWORD Value
);
```

The first parameter, *Stage*, is the index to the texture state to be set. The value of the texture state is the same index as used by the *IDirect3D9::SetTexture* and *IDirect3D9::SetTexture StageState* function. The remaining parameters, *Type* and *Value*, define the texture stage state and its value.

A sample implementation of the function relaying the states to Direct3D is as follows:

```
STDMETHOD(SetTextureStageState)(THIS_ DWORD dwStage,
                                D3DTEXTURESTAGESTATETYPE State,
                                DWORD dwValue )
{
    return m_pDevice->SetTextureStageState( dwStage,
                                            State,
                                            dwValue );
}
```

IID3DXEffectStateManager::SetTransform

This callback function is called by the effect framework when a transform matrix is set. This function is the Direct3D equivalent to *IDirect3D9::SetTransform*. The declaration for this function uses the following syntax:

```
HRESULT SetTransform(
    D3DTRANSFORMSTATETYPE State,
    CONST D3DMATRIX* pMatrix
);
```

The first parameter, *State*, is the type of transform matrix to be set and the second parameter, *pMatrix*, is the matrix to which the transform state will be set.

A sample implementation of the function relaying the states to Direct3D is as follows:

```
STDMETHOD(SetTransform)(THIS_ D3DTRANSFORMSTATETYPE State,
                        CONST D3DMATRIX *pMatrix )
{
    return m_pDevice->SetTransform( State, pMatrix );
}
```

IID3DXEffectStateManager::SetVertexShader

This callback function is called by the effect framework when setting the current vertex shader. This function is the Direct3D equivalent to *IDirect3D9::SetVertexShader*. The declaration for this function uses the following syntax:

```
HRESULT SetVertexShader(

    LPDIRECT3DVERTEXSHADER9 pShader

);
```

The only parameter to this function, *pShader*, is an instance of the vertex shader that will be used by the effect.

A sample implementation of the function relaying the states to Direct3D is as follows:

```
STDMETHOD(SetVertexShader)(THIS_ LPDIRECT3DVERTEXSHADER9 pShader )

{

    return m_pDevice->SetVertexShader( pShader );

}
```

IID3DXEffectStateManager:: SetVertexShaderConstantB

This callback function is called by the effect framework to set an array of vertex shader boolean constants. This function is the Direct3D equivalent to *IDirect3D9::SetVertexShaderConstantB*. The declaration for this function uses the following syntax:

```
HRESULT SetVertexShaderConstantB(
    UINT StartRegister,
    CONST BOOL* pConstantData,
    UINT RegisterCount
);
```

The first parameter, *StartRegister*, indicates the memory location where the constant array should be applied. The second parameter, *pConstantData* is a pointer to the shader constant data. The last parameter, *RegisterCount*, indicates the number of registers to be filled.

A sample implementation of the function relaying the states to Direct3D is as follows:

```
STDMETHOD(SetVertexShaderConstantB)(THIS_ UINT RegisterIndex,
```

```
                              CONST BOOL *pConstantData,
                              UINT RegisterCount )
    {
        return m_pDevice->SetVertexShaderConstantB( RegisterIndex,
                                                    pConstantData,
                                                    RegisterCount );
    }
```

IID3DXEffectStateManager:: SetVertexShaderConstantF

This callback function is called by the effect framework to set an array of vertex shader float constants. This function is the Direct3D equivalent to *IDirect3D9::SetVertexShaderConstant F*. The declaration for this function uses the following syntax:

```
HRESULT SetVertexShaderConstantF(
    UINT StartRegister,
    CONST FLOAT* pConstantData,
    UINT RegisterCount
);
```

The first parameter, *StartRegister*, indicates the memory location where the constant array should be applied. The second parameter, *pConstantData* is a pointer to the shader constant data. The last parameter, *RegisterCount*, indicates the number of registers to be filled.

A sample implementation of the function relaying the states to Direct3D is as follows:

```
STDMETHOD(SetVertexShaderConstantF)(THIS_ UINT RegisterIndex,
                                    CONST FLOAT *pConstantData,
                                    UINT RegisterCount )
    {
        return m_pDevice->SetVertexShaderConstantF( RegisterIndex,
                                                    pConstantData,
                                                    RegisterCount );
    }
```

IID3DXEffectStateManager:: SetVertexShaderConstantI

This callback function is called by the effect framework to set an array of pixel shader integer constants. This function is the Direct3D equivalent to *IDirect3D9::SetVertexShaderConstant I*. The declaration for this function uses the following syntax:

```
HRESULT SetVertexShaderConstantI(
    UINT StartRegister,
    CONST INT* pConstantData,
    UINT RegisterCount
);
```

The first parameter, *StartRegister*, indicates the memory location where the constant array should be applied. The second parameter, `pConstantData` is a pointer to the shader constant data. The last parameter, `RegisterCount`, indicates the number of registers to be filled.

A sample implementation of the function relaying the states to Direct3D is as follows:

```
STDMETHOD(SetVertexShaderConstantI)(THIS_ UINT RegisterIndex,
                                    CONST INT *pConstantData,
                                    UINT RegisterCount )
{
    return m_pDevice->SetVertexShaderConstantI( RegisterIndex,
                                                pConstantData,
                                                RegisterCount );
}
```

Why Manage States?

You may wonder why there is a need to manage states in the first place and why the `ID3DXEffectStateManager` interface exists. In fact, there are a few scenarios in which the use of such an interface makes sense. Before I move any farther, I have to remind you that the state management functions only apply to states set through an effect file.

When compiling your rendering in your application in retail mode, you may wish to create your Direct3D device as *PURE*. In such mode, Direct3D reduces its work and attempts to talk directly to the device driver. One consequence of a *PURE* device is that the content of many of the device states aren't cached and passed directly to the hardware. Although it may make sense from a performance point of view in some cases, it may still be more performant to manually cache the render state changes from the effect system. For example, the following code sample illustrates how parameter caching can be accomplished for the *ID3DXEffectStateManager::SetRenderState* function:

```
STDMETHOD(SetRenderState)(THIS_ D3DRENDERSTATETYPE d3dRenderState,
                          DWORD dwValue )
{
    // Update the render state cache
    if( cacheRenderStates.set_val( d3dRenderState, dwValue ) )
        return m_pDevice->SetRenderState( d3dRenderState, dwValue );

    return S_OK;
}
```

Another scenario where state management would make sense is where you might need to override a specific state. For example, your effects might define a value for the fill mode. Although you want your fill mode to be solid, you may want to override the mode to wireframe for debugging purposes. The following code illustrates how you can accomplish this:

```
STDMETHOD(SetRenderState)(THIS_ D3DRENDERSTATETYPE d3dRenderState,
                          DWORD dwValue )
{
    // Update render state except for the wireframe mode which
    // always come from a global variable
    if( d3dRenderState == D3DRS_FILLMODE )
        return m_pDevice->SetRenderState( d3dRenderState,
                                          g_WireFrame ? D3DFILL_WIREFRAME
                                                      : D3DFILL_SOLID );
    else
        return m_pDevice->SetRenderState( d3dRenderState, dwValue );
}
```

Summary and what's next?

The concept of managing all device states coming through the effect system is a powerful tool. Through the *ID3DXEffectStateManager* interface, you not only capture every state change triggered by an effect, but you can also relay the information to Direct3D and even manipulate it. Whether you use it only for debugging purposes or to improve performance by caching render states to avoid duplicate calls, the *ID3DXEffectStateManager* interface is a great tool allowing your application to place itself between the effect framework and Direct3D.

In the next chapter, I will discuss more advanced topics relating to the compilation of effects and how you can manage including files within your effects. By using the effect compiler interface, you not only fine-tune the compilation process but also optimize the processing of all your effect files by avoiding redundant recompilations.

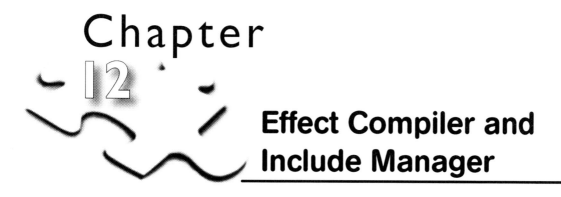

Chapter 12

Effect Compiler and Include Manager

Y ou may wonder why there is a dedicated chapter on the effect compiler since the topic of effect compilation has already been covered several in this book. Up until now, we have only focused on the compilation of effects through the various *D3DXEffectCreate* functions. The effect framework also offers an interface, *ID3DXEffectCompiler*, which can also be used to compile effects, and it has additional advantages overusing the function-based compiler.

In addition, effect file can include other files by using *#include* directives. Because of the various *D3DXEffectCreate* functions, the source of the original effect file may not be an actual physical file. How is the effect system supposed to know where to find the proper include files? The effect framework allows you to control include behavior with the *ID3DXInclude* interface, which we will cover later in this chapter.

But for now, let's start by taking a look at the effect compiler interface and see how you can take advantage of it within your applications.

ID3DXEffectCompiler

The *ID3DXEffectCompiler* interface is based upon the *ID3DXBaseEffect* interface, which may seem like an odd choice as the base interface of an effect compiler. When you consider the reasons behind wanting to use this compiler interface, however, it does make good sense.

The big advantage of wanting to use the *ID3DXEffectCompiler* interface is that the compiler can be used to compile several variations of the same effect file by taking advantage of static branching. The effect compiler will pre-compile several components of the shader and then put all of them together as needed based on the current parameters of the effect. I will explain this in more detail a little later.

To start, you will need to create an instance of the *ID3DXEffectCompiler* interface. This can be accomplished by using one of the various *D3DXCreateEffectCompiler* functions. The function is similar to the regular effect compiling functions and has the following declaration:

```
HRESULT WINAPI D3DXCreateEffectCompiler(
    LPCSTR pSrcData,
    UINT SrcDataLen,
    const D3DXMACRO *pDefines,
    LPD3DXINCLUDE pInclude,
    DWORD Flags,
    LPD3DXEFFECTCOMPILER *ppEffectCompiler,
    LPD3DXBUFFER *ppParseErrors
);
```

As you can see, the declaration to this function is almost the same to the declaration of *D3DXCreateEffect*. The only major difference being that the function returns an instance to an effect compiler instead of an effect. This effect compiler can then be used to compile several effects stemming from the same effect file.

For now, let me go over the functions which are specific to the *ID3DXEffectCompiler* interface: *CompileEffect*, *CompileShader*, *SetLiteral* and *GetLiteral*...

ID3DXEffectCompiler::CompileEffect

This function is used to compile an effect based on the current parameters and has the following syntax:

```
HRESULT CompileEffect(
    DWORD Flags,
    LPD3DXBUFFER *ppEffect,
    LPD3DXBUFFER *ppErrorMsgs
);
```

The first parameter to the function, *Flags*, is the same set of flags used with the various *D3DXCreateEffect* and controls aspects of the compilation process such as the use of preshaders and optimizations. The second parameter, *ppEffect*, is a pointer to the resulting effect. Finally, *ppErrorMsgs* is a buffer filled with at least the first compilation error, if any.

ID3DXEffectCompiler::CompileShader

This function is used to compile any shader function within an effect as a standalone shader. The declaration to this function uses the following syntax:

```
HRESULT CompileShader(
    D3DXHANDLE hFunction,
    LPCSTR pTarget,
    DWORD Flags,
    LPD3DXBUFFER* ppShader,
    LPD3DXBUFFER* ppErrorMsgs,
```

```
        LPD3DXCONSTANTTABLE* ppConstantTable
    );
```

The first parameter to the function, *hFunction*, is a handle to the effect function that you wish to compile as a standalone shader. The second parameter, *pTarget*, is a string indicating the target platform for the shader. The *Flags* parameter is any of the standard effect compilation flags which may also apply to the compilation of this shader. The *ppShader* parameter is simply a buffer meant to contain the *DWORD* stream resulting from the shader compilation. The *ppErrorMsgs* parameter is a buffer, which will be filled with at least the first compilation error, if any. And finally, the *ppConstantTable* parameter is an instance of the *ID3DXConstantTable* interface and is used to provide information about all the constants used by the shader resulting from the compilation. Below is a list of the possible targets for use with the *ID3DXEffectCompiler::CompileShader* function:

- **Vertex shader targets**: vs_1_1, vs_2_0, vs_2_sw, vs_3_0.
- **Pixel shader targets**: ps_1_1, ps_1_2, ps_1_3, ps_1_4, ps_2_0, ps_2_sw, ps_3_0.
- **Texture fill targets**: tx_0, tx_1.

ID3DXEffectCompiler::GetLiteral

This function is used to determine whether the parameter is a literal. Literals are parameters that do not change during the lifetime of an effect, such as constants. The function can be used in combination with *SetLiteral* to change the value of constants in your effects with the goal of controlling static branching when compiling your effects. This function has the following syntax:

```
HRESULT GetLiteral(
    D3DXHANDLE hParameter,
    BOOL* pLiteral
);
```

The first parameter to the function, *hParameter*, is the handle to the parameter for which you wish to verify the literal status. The literal status of the parameter will be put in the second parameter, *pLiteral*. Take note that this function only allows you to check if a parameter is a literal. To set the parameter's value you will need to use one of the various *SetXXX* functions part of the *ID3DXBaseEffect* interface.

ID3DXEffectCompiler::SetLiteral

This function is used to specify if a parameter will be considered as a literal. Literals are parameters that do not change during the lifetime of an effect, such as a constant. This function has the following syntax:

```
HRESULT SetLiteral(
    D3DXHANDLE hParameter,
    BOOL* Literal
);
```

The first parameter to the function, *hParameter*, is the handle to the parameter for which you wish to change the literal status. The literal status of the parameter will be defined by the second parameter, *Literal*. Take note that this function only allows you to check if a parameter is a literal/ To set the parameter you will need to use one of the various *SetXXX* functions.

Taking Advantage of the Compiler Interface

As mentioned early on in this chapter, the initial purpose behind the *ID3DXEffectCompiler* interface may seem obscure as you can easily call one of the various framework functions to compile your effects. The use of the effect compiler starts making more sense when you deal with specific situations such as when you wish to take advantage of static branching to create generic multipurpose effects.

The main advantage of using the effect compiler in such cases is that the compiler will preprocess your effect file once upon creation of the *ID3DXEffectCompiler* interface but allow you to create multiple effect variations from the same file with the *ID3DXEffectCompiler::CompileEffect* function. Let me show you how this works with a practical example. Take a look at the following effect:

```
// Constant used to affect the use of bumpmapping within
// the effect
const bool bDoBumpmap = true;

// Note: All other effect variables omitted for
// reader simplicity.

// Vertex output structure
struct VS_OUTPUT
{
    float4 Pos:        POSITION;
    float2 TexCoord:   TEXCOORD0;
    float4 LightDir:   TEXCOORD1;
    float3 HalfVect:   TEXCOORD2;
};

VS_OUTPUT vs_main(float4 inPos: POSITION, float3 inNormal: NORMAL,
                  float3 inTangent:TANGENT, float3 inBinormal:BINORMAL,
                  float2 inTxr: TEXCOORD0)
{
```

```
    VS_OUTPUT Out;

    // Compute the projected position and send out the texture coordinates
    Out.Pos = mul(view_proj_matrix, inPos);
    Out.TexCoord = inTxr;

    // Determine the distance from the light to the vertex and the direction
    float4 LightDir;
    LightDir.xyz = mul(inv_view_matrix,float3(80,00,-80)) - inPos;
    float  Dist = length(LightDir.xyz);
    LightDir.xyz = LightDir.xyz / Dist;

    // Compute the per-vertex distance based attenuation
    LightDir.w = clamp(0,1, 1 / ( Light1_Attenuation.x +
                                  Light1_Attenuation.y * Dist +
                                  Light1_Attenuation.z * Dist * Dist ));


    // Determine the eye vector
    float3 EyeVector = normalize(view_position-inPos);

    // Transform to tangent space and output
    // half vector and light direction
    float3x3 TangentSpace;
    TangentSpace[0] = inTangent;
    TangentSpace[1] = inBinormal;
    TangentSpace[2] = inNormal;
    Out.HalfVect = mul(TangentSpace,normalize(LightDir.xyz+EyeVector));
    Out.LightDir = float4(mul(TangentSpace,LightDir.xyz),LightDir.w);

    return Out;
}

float4 Light_Point(float3 Normal, float3 HalfVect, float4 LightDir,
                   float4 LightColor)
{
    // Compute both specular and diffuse factors
    float SpecularAttn =  pow( clamp(0, 1,dot(Normal, HalfVect)),16);
    float DiffuseAttn =  clamp(0, 1,dot(Normal, LightDir));

    // Compute final lighting
    return LightColor * LightDir.w * (SpecularAttn+DiffuseAttn);
}

float4 ps_main(float2 inTxr:TEXCOORD0,float4 LightDir:TEXCOORD1,
               float3 HalfVect:TEXCOORD2) : COLOR
{
    // Read bump and influence the normal (if we need to)
    float3 normal(0,1,0);
    If (bDoBumpmap == true)
        float3 normal = tex2D(Bump,inTxr) * 2 - 1;
```

```
        // Simply route the vertex color to the output
        return tex2D(Texture0,inTxr)*
               (0.15+Light_Point(normal,HalfVect,LightDir,Light1_Color));
    }

    technique TBaseMaterial
    {
        pass P0
        {
            // shaders
            VertexShader = compile vs_2_0 vs_main();
            PixelShader  = compile ps_2_0 ps_main();
        }
    }
```

This effect is fairly simple. It takes the bumpmapping shader developed in Chapter 4 and exposes it through a simple one-pass technique. Although most of the effect parameters have been omitted for simplicity, you may have noticed the following parameter.

```
const bool bDoBumpmap = true;
```

This parameter is a constant, or literal, which is set to a value of *true*. The intent is to take advantage of this parameter to determine whether our effect should apply bumpmapping when rendering. To accomplish this, the pixel shader has been modified to accomplish a static branch on this parameter, simply omitting the bumpmapping if the parameter is set to *false*. Here is the segment of code executing the static branch:

```
float3 normal(0,1,0);
If (bDoBumpmap == true)
    float3 normal = tex2D(Bump,inTxr) * 2 - 1;
```

Although the situation in this effect is simple and could be easily implemented using two separate effects, things do get complicated as you add more features to the effect. If you were to add support for two lights, you would then need to support four effects and so on. Since each of the effects would share most of the same code, the maintenance requirements would be bothersome. This can lead to quite complicated effects but also increases code reuse and reduces the number of various effects needed. The compromise is a choice that you as a developer will have to make.

By developing your effects with static branching, you can take advantage of the effect compiler to create all variations to your effect on the fly by creating an instance of the *ID3DXEffectCompiler* for your effect file and then changing the value of the constant parameter for each of the effect variations.

The sample code below illustrates how this can be accomplished:

```
// Create the effect compiler
ID3DXEffectCompiler* pEffectCompiler;
D3DXCreateEffectCompilerFromFile( "MyEffect.FX",
    NULL, NULL, 0, &pEffectCompiler, NULL);

// Create the non-bumped effect
ID3DXEffect* pEffect;
pEffectCompiler->SetBool("bDoBumpmap", FALSE);
pEffectCompiler->CompileEffect( 0, &pEffect, NULL);

// Create the bumped effect
ID3DXEffect* pEffectBump;
pEffectCompiler->SetBool("bDoBumpmap", TRUE);
pEffectCompiler->CompileEffect( 0, &pEffectBump, NULL);
```

As you see, the `ID3DXEffectCompiler` approach is straightforward. The biggest advantage of using this technique is that the effect compiler will precompile the components of the effect file and assemble them together on-the-fly when you call `ID3DXEffectCompiler::CompileEffect`. The overall performance of compiling both effects would be significantly better than compiling separate effect files.

Effect Includes

As you know by now, when compiling effects or shaders, there is a variety of functions that will compile your data from one of many sources such as a file, resource or a location in memory. One problem you may encounter is that your shaders or effects may include other files with `#include` directives.

This may seem straightforward when dealing with effects located within files, but what is the effect system supposed to do if the effect data is located in memory? Where is the effect system supposed to fetch your includes from?

To work around this problem, the effect framework exposes an interface named `ID3DXInclude`, which you can implement and pass as a parameter to one of the several effect and shader compilation functions such as `D3DXCompileShader`, `D3DXAssembleShader`, `D3DXCreateEffect` or `D3DXCreateEffectCompiler`.

The `ID3DXEffect` interface is a user-implemented interface in which you will control the include process through its member functions. The `ID3DXEffect` interface is composed of two members:

- **Close**: This method is called for closing an `#include` file.
- **Open**: This method is called for opening and reading the contents of an `#include` file.

Implementing the interface is simple. Take a look at next few sections as I go over the use of each of the member functions.

ID3DXInclude::Close

This is called when the effect framework whishes to close an include file. The purpose of the function is to destroy the resources allocated when opening the include file and has the following syntax:

```
HRESULT Close(
    LPCVOID pData
);
```

The first parameter to the function, *pData*, is a pointer to the block of data allocated during the *#include* open process. This data must be freed appropriately to avoid memory leaks.

The sample implementation below simply needs to take care of deleting the data buffer allocated during the call to *ID3DXEffect::Open* call:

```
HRESULT CInclude::Close(LPCVOID pData)
{
    BYTE* pData2 = (BYTE*)pData;
    If ( pData2 )
        delete [] pData2;
    return S_OK;
}
```

ID3DXInclude::Open

This is called when the effect framework wishes to close an include file. The purpose of the function is to destroy the resources allocated when opening the include file and has the following syntax:

```
HRESULT Open(
    D3DXINCLUDE_TYPE IncludeType,
    LPCSTR pFileName,
    LPCVOID pParentData,
    LPCVOID *ppData,
    UINT *pBytes
);
```

The first parameter to the function, *IncludeType*, comes from the effect file to indicate how the include file name should be treated. This value must be one of the following:

- *D3DXINC_LOCAL*: Look in the local project for the include file.

- *D3DXINC_SYSTEM*: Look in the system path for the include file.

The second parameter, *pFileName*, is a pointer to the name of the include file to be opened. The third parameter, *pParentData*, is a pointer to the container that is including this new *#include* file.

The last two parameters, *ppData* and *pBytes*, are meant to contain the data from the include file. The first parameter will contain the data buffer you create and fill with the data from your include file. The second parameter is to tell the effect framework the size of the data contained in *ppData*.

The sample implementation below will open the specified file name, create and fill a buffer with the data from the include file:

```
HRESULT CIncludeManager::Open(D3DXINCLUDE_TYPE IncludeType,
                              LPCSTR pName,
                              LPCVOID pParentData,
                              LPCVOID *ppData,
                              UINT *pBytes)
{
    CFile f;
    WCHAR strFile[MAX_PATH];

    MultiByteToWideChar( CP_ACP, 0, pName, -1, strFile, MAX_PATH );

    if( !f.Open( strFileFull, CFile::modeRead ) )
        return E_FAIL;

    UINT size = (UINT)f.GetLength();

    BYTE* pData = new BYTE[size];
    if( pData == NULL )
        return E_OUTOFMEMORY;

    f.Read( pData, size );

    *ppData = pData;
    *pBytes = size;

    return S_OK;
}
```

Summary and what's next?

By taking advantage of the features of the *ID3DXEffectCompiler* interface, you not only optimize your effect compilation process but also reduce the total number of effect files needed by your application. Using this approach, you can put your general effects together using effect parameters and static branching to select which code path to use when generating an effect.

In addition, since the effect compiler can process data coming from various sources such as files or system resources, the effect compiler might need to get data from various *#include* files. How can the effect framework know where to get the included data? By using the *ID3DXInclude* interface, you can control the behavior of the effect framework when dealing with *#include* statements.

Moving forward, it is now time for the all-famous appendixes. In the following chapters, you will find various references for different components of the effect framework such as the HLSL instructions and a complete reference to the standard semantics and annotations.

Part IV

Appendices

This section is filled with extra information and reference materials that will be useful as you take advantage of the effect framework. The appendices include references to the shader assembly instructions, the built-in HLSL functions and the standard semantics.

It has been a fun and thrilling journey writing this book. I hope the knowledge I have conveyed to you will be helpful and allow you to create the most stunning graphics applications!

Appendix A

Shader Assembly Instruction Reference

This chapter serves as a reference manual for the shader assembly instructions for both vertex and pixel shaders. Although this book focuses mostly on the High-Level Shading Language (HLSL), having a basic understanding of the basic instruction set which can be very useful when debugging or optimizing shaders.

You are bound to encounter shaders that do not work the way you expected, or you may wish to squeeze out every little drop of performance out of your shaders. By using either the command line shader compiler *fxc.exe* or requesting a listing from DirectX, you will need to have a basic understanding of the instructions, their meaning and their performance implications.

Throughout this appendix, I will introduce the instruction set of every version of the vertex and pixel shaders supported through the HLSL compiler and give you a simple description of their functionality and a description of their performance costs. The data will mostly be arranged in the form of a table to make it easier for you to reference it when you need it most.

This reference manual is loosely inspired by the DirectX 9.0 documentation. For a more complete reference, we suggest reading the full reference included as part of the DirectX 9.0 SDK's documentation.

Vertex Shader Version 1.1

The first thing you may notice is that the only vertex shader in the 1.x range mentioned here is the 1.1 version. This is because all subsequent versions do have the same instruction set, the only improvement being the number of instructions which can be used as well as the number of registers available.

Setup instructions do not actually do anything beyond preparing the shader, for example defining some constants to be set into the constant registers. Below is the list of setup instructions supported in the 1.1 vertex shader instruction set.

- *dcl_usage*: Used to declare input vertex registers.
- *def*: Used to define constants.
- *vs*: Used to retrieve the shader version.

The vertex shader 1.x model offers a wide range of instructions. Below, in Table A-1, you will find a complete listing of shader instructions along with a quick description of their functionality and the number of instruction slots taken by the instruction.

Table A-1 Vertex Shader 1.1 Assembly Instructions

Name	Description	Slots
add	Add two vectors together	1
dp3	Three-component dot product	1
dp4	Four-component dot product	1
dst	Calculate the distance vector used for lighting. The first source operand is assumed to be the vector *(ignored, d*d, d*d, ignored)* and the second source operand is assumed to be the vector *(ignored, $1/_d$, ignored, $1/_d$)*. The destination will contain *(1, d, d*d, $1/_d$)*	1
exp	Full precision 2^x	10
expp	Partial precision 2^x. Partial precision is done at 16-bits instead of 32-bits	1
frc	Returns the fractional component of the input. For *vs_1_1*, the instruction can only write to *.y* and *.xy*	3
lit	Returns the partial lighting calculation by calculating lighting coefficients from two dot products and an exponent.	1
log	Full precision log2(x)	10
logp	Partial precision log2(x). Partial precision operates at 16-bits instead of 32-bits.	1
m3x2	Computes the product of a 3-component vector and a 2×3 matrix.	2
m3x3	Computes the product of a 3-component vector and a 3×3 matrix.	3
m3x4	Computes the product of a 3-component vector and a 4×3 matrix.	4
m4x3	Computes the product of a 4-component vector and a 3×4 matrix.	3
m4x4	Computes the product of a 4-component vector and a 4×4 matrix.	4
mad	Multiplies two inputs together and add the result to the third input.	1
max	Returns the maximum between two inputs.	1

Table A-1 Vertex Shader 1.1 Assembly Instructions

Name	Description	Slots
min	Returns the minimum between two inputs.	1
mov	Moves data from one register to another.	1
mul	Multiplies two inputs together.	1
nop	No operation. This is sometimes needed to avoid stalls.	1
rcp	Returns the reciprocal of the input, or if you prefer $1/_{input}$.	1
rsq	Reciprocal square root, or $1/_{sqrt(input)}$.	1
sge	Greater than or equal compare. The output for this instruction will be either 0 or 1.	1
slt	Less than compare. The output of this instruction will be either 0 or 1.	1
sub	Subtracts two inputs from each other.	1

Vertex Shader Version 2.0

Vertex shader 2.0 is the first version allowing for a limited set of flow control instructions, thus putting this shader model closer to the capabilities of a general purpose processor. In addition to the flow control instructions, this new model also allows for the definition of integer and boolean variable types.

As with the 1.0 vertex shader model, the 2.0 model also contains setup instructions. Below is the list of setup instructions supported in the 2.0 vertex shader instruction set.

- `dcl_usage`: Used to declare input vertex registers.
- `def`: Used to define constants.
- `defb`: Used to define boolean constants.
- `deif`: Used to define integer constants.
- `label`: Used to define label within the shader code which can be used for flow conrol.
- `vs`: Used to retrieve the shader version.

The vertex shader 2.0 model offers a wide range of instructions. Below, in Table A-2, you will find a complete listing of all shader instructions along with a quick description of their functionality, the number of instruction slots taken by the instruction and whether the instruction is arithmetic in nature or used for flow control.

Table A-2 Vertex Shader 2.0 Assembly Instructions

Name	Description	Slots	Type
abs	Returns the per-component absolute value of the input.	1	Arithmetic
add	Adds two vectors together.	1	Arithmetic
call	Calls a subroutine. This function will push the current onto the return address stack and continue execution at the specified label.	2	Flow Control
callnz_bool	Calls a subroutine if a boolean register is not zero.	3	Flow Control
crs	Cross product of two vectors.	2	Arithmetic
dp3	Three-component vector dot product.	1	Arithmetic
dp4	Four-component vector dot product.	1	Arithmetic
dst	Calculates the distance vector used for lighting. The first source operand is assumed to be the vector *(ignored, d*d, d*d, ignored)* and the second source operand is assumed to be the vector *(ignored, $1/_d$, ignored, $1/_d$)*. The destination will contain *(1, d, d*d, $1/_d$)*.	1	Arithmetic
else	Begins an `else` block.	1	Flow Control
endif	Ends an `if`/`else` block.	1	Flow Control
endloop	End of a `loop`/`endloop` block.	2	Flow Control
endrep	End of a `repeat` block.	2	Flow Control
exp	Full precision 2^x.	1	Arithmetic
expp	Partial precision 2^x, meaning it will operate at 16-bits instead of 32-bits.	1	Arithmetic
frc	Returns the fractional component of the input.	1	Arithmetic
if_bool	Begins an `if`/`else`/`endif` block (using a boolean condition).	3	Flow Control
lit	Returns the partial lighting calculation by calculating lighting coefficients from two dot products and an exponent.	3	Arithmetic
log	Full precision log2(x).	1	Arithmetic
logp	Partial precision log2(x), meaning it will operate at 16-bits instead of 32-bits	1	Arithmetic
loop	Start a `loop`/`endloop` block.	3	Flow Control
lrp	Linearly interpolates between two input vectors.	2	Arithmetic

Table A-2 Vertex Shader 2.0 Assembly Instructions

Name	Description	Slots	Type
m3x2	Product of a 3-component vector and a 2×3 matrix.	2	Arithmetic
m3x3	Product of a 3-component vector and a 3×3 matrix.	3	Arithmetic
m3x4	Product of a 3-component vector and a 4×3 matrix.	4	Arithmetic
m4x3	Product of a 4-component vector and a 3×4 matrix.	3	Arithmetic
m4x4	Product of a 4-component vector and a 4×4 matrix.	4	Arithmetic
mad	Multiplies two inputs together and add the result to the third input.	1	Arithmetic
max	Returns the maximum between two inputs.	1	Arithmetic
min	Returns the minimum between two inputs.	1	Arithmetic
mov	Moves data from one register to another.	1	Arithmetic
mova	Moves data from a floating-point register to the address register	1	Arithmetic
mul	Multiplies two inputs together.	1	Arithmetic
nop	No operation. This is sometimes needed to avoid stalls.	1	
nrm	Normalizes a four-component vector. Equivalent to $input/_{length(input)}$.	3	Arithmetic
pow	Returns the first input to the power of the second, or x^y.	3	Arithmetic
rcp	Returns the reciprocal of the input, or $1/_{input}$.	1	Arithmetic
rep	Starts a `rep` / `endrep` block.	3	Flow Control
ret	End of either a subroutine or main.	1	Flow Control
rsq	Reciprocal square root, or $1/_{sqrt(input)}$.	1	Arithmetic
sge	Greater than or equal compare. The output for this instruction will be either 0 or 1.	1	Arithmetic
sgn	This function returns the sign of the input. It will return -1 for a negative input and 1 for a positive input.	3	Arithmetic
sincos	This function computes both the sine and cosine.	8	Arithmetic
slt	Less than compare.	1	Arithmetic
sub	Subtracts two inputs from each other.	1	Arithmetic

Vertex Shader Version 2.x

Vertex shader 2.x is a simple extension to the 2.0 vertex shader model. It adds a few flow control instructions such as *if_comp*, *break* and *break_comp* in addition to adding the concept of predication.

As with the 2.0 vertex shader model, the 2.x model also contains setup instructions. Below is the list of setup instructions supported in the 2.x vertex shader instruction set.

- *dcl_usage*: Used to declare input vertex registers.
- *def*: Used to define constants.
- *defb*: Used to define Boolean constants.
- *deif*: Used to define integer constants.
- *label*: Used to define label within the shader code which can be used for flow conrol.
- *vs*: Used to retrieve the shader version.

The vertex shader 2.x model offers a wide range of instructions. Below, in Table A-3, you will find a complete listing of shader instructions along with a quick description of their functionality, the number of instruction slots taken by the instruction and whether the instruction is arithmetic in nature or used for flow control.

Table A-3 Vertex Shader 2.x Assembly Instructions

Name	Description	Slots	Type
abs	Returns the per-component absolute value of the input.	1	Arithmetic
add	Adds two vectors together.	1	Arithmetic
break	Breaks out of a *loop* / *endloop* or *rep* / *endrep* block.	1	Flow Control
break_comp	Conditionally break out of a *loop*/*endloop* or *rep*/*endrep* block, with a comparison.	3	Flow Control
breakp	Break out of a *loop*/*endloop* or *rep*/*endrep* block, based on a predicate.	3	Flow Control
call	Calls a subroutine. This function will push the current onto the return address stack and continue execution at the specified label.	2	Flow Control
callnz_bool	Calls a subroutine if a boolean register is not zero.	3	Flow Control

Table A-3 Vertex Shader 2.x Assembly Instructions

Name	Description	Slots	Type
crs	Cross product of two vectors.	2	Arithmetic
dp3	Three-component vector dot product.	1	Arithmetic
dp4	Four-component vector dot product.	1	Arithmetic
dst	Calculates the distance vector used for lighting. The first source operand is assumed to be the vector *(ignored, d*d, d*d, ignored)* and the second source operand is assumed to be the vector *(ignored, $1/_d$, ignored, $1/_d$)*. The destination will contain *(1, d, d*d, $1/_d$)*.	1	Arithmetic
else	Begins an `else` block.	1	Flow Control
endif	Ends an `if`/`else` block.	1	Flow Control
endloop	End of a `loop`/`endloop` block.	2	Flow Control
endrep	End of a `repeat` block.	2	Flow Control
exp	Full precision 2^x.	1	Arithmetic
expp	Partial precision 2^x, meaning it will operate at 16-bits instead of 32-bits.	1	Arithmetic
frc	Returns the fractional component of the input.	1	Arithmetic
if_bool	Begins an `if`/`else`/`endif` block (using a boolean condition).	3	Flow Control
if_comp	Begins an `if` block, with a comparison.	3	Flow Control
if_pred	Begins an `if` block with a predicate condition.	3	Flow Control
lit	Returns the partial lighting calculation by calculating lighting coefficients from two dot products and an exponent.	3	Arithmetic
log	Full precision log2(x).	1	Arithmetic
logp	Partial precision log2(x), meaning it will operate at 16-bits instead of 32-bits	1	Arithmetic
loop	Starts a `loop`/`endloop` block.	3	Flow Control
lrp	Linearly interpolates between two input vectors.	2	Arithmetic
m3x2	Product of a 3-component vector and a 2×3 matrix.	2	Arithmetic
m3x3	Product of a 3-component vector and a 3×3 matrix.	3	Arithmetic
m3x4	Product of a 3-component vector and a 4×3 matrix.	4	Arithmetic

Table A-3 Vertex Shader 2.x Assembly Instructions

Name	Description	Slots	Type
m4x3	Product of a 4-component vector and a 3×4 matrix.	3	Arithmetic
m4x4	Product of a 4-component vector and a 4×4 matrix.	4	Arithmetic
mad	Multiplies two inputs together and add the result to the third input.	1	
max	Returns the maximum between two inputs.	1	Arithmetic
min	Returns the minimum between two inputs.	1	Arithmetic
mov	Moves data from one register to another.	1	Arithmetic
mova	Moves data from a floating-point register to the address register	1	Arithmetic
mul	Multiplies two inputs together.	1	Arithmetic
nop	No operation. This is sometimes needed to avoid stalls.	1	Arithmetic
nrm	Normalizes a four component vector. This instruction is equivalent to $input/_{length(input)}$.	3	Arithmetic
pow	Returns the first input to the power of the second, or x^y.	3	Arithmetic
rcp	Returns the reciprocal of the input, or $1/_{input}$.	1	Arithmetic
rep	Starts a `rep` / `endrep` block.	3	Flow Control
ret	End of either a subroutine or main.	1	Flow Control
rsq	Reciprocal square root, or $1/_{sqrt(input)}$.	1	Arithmetic
setp_comp	Sets the predicate register.	1	Flow Control
sge	Greater than or equal compare. The output for this instruction will be either 0 or 1.	1	Arithmetic
sgn	This instruction returns the sign of the input. It will return -1 for a negative input and 1 for a positive input.	3	Arithmetic
sincos	This function computes both the sine and cosine.	8	Arithmetic
slt	Less than compare. The output of this instruction will be either 0 or 1.	1	Arithmetic
sub	Subtracts two inputs from each other.	1	Arithmetic

Vertex Shader Version 3.0

Vertex shader 3.0 is an extension to the 2.x vertex shader model adding support for new indexing registers but more importantly support for reading textures within a vertex shader though the use of the *texldl* instruction.

As with the 2.x vertex shader model, the 3.0 model also contains setup instructions. Below is the list of setup instructions supported in the 3.0 vertex shader instruction set.

- *dcl_usage*: Used to declare input vertex registers and texture samplers.
- *def*: Used to define constants.
- *defb*: Used to define boolean constants.
- *deif*: Used to define integer constants.
- *label*: Used to define label within the shader code which can be used for flow conrol.
- *vs*: Used to retrieve the shader version.

The vertex shader 3.0 model offers a wide range of instructions. Below, in Table A-4, you will find a complete listing of all shader instructions along with a quick description of their functionality, the number of instruction slots taken by the instruction and whether the instruction is arithmetic, for flow control or a texture access instruction.

Table A-4 Vertex Shader 3.0 Assembly Instructions

Name	Description	Slots	Type
abs	Returns the per-component absolute value of the input.	1	Arithmetic
add	Adds two vectors together.	1	Arithmetic
break	Breaks out of a *loop* / *endloop* or *rep* / *endrep* block.	1	Flow Control
break_comp	Conditionally breaks out of a *loop* / *endloop* or *rep* / *endrep* block, with a comparison.	3	Flow Control
breakp	Breaks out of a *loop* / *endloop* or *rep* / *endrep* block, based on a predicate.	3	Flow Control
call	Calls a subroutine. This function will push the current onto the return address stack and continue execution at the specified label.	2	Flow Control
callnz_bool	Calls a subroutine if a boolean register is not zero.	3	Flow Control
crs	Cross product of two vectors.	2	Arithmetic

Table A-4 Vertex Shader 3.0 Assembly Instructions

Name	Description	Slots	Type
dp3	Three-component vector dot product.	1	Arithmetic
dp4	Four-component vector dot product.	1	Arithmetic
dst	Calculates the distance vector used for lighting. The first source operand is assumed to be the vector *(ignored, d*d, d*d, ignored)* and the second source operand is assumed to be the vector *(ignored, $1/_d$, ignored, $1/_d$)*. The destination will contain *(1, d, d*d, $1/_d$)*.	1	Arithmetic
else	Begins an `else` block.	1	Flow Control
endif	Ends an `if`/`else` block.	1	Flow Control
endloop	End of a `loop`/`endloop` block.	2	Flow Control
endrep	End of a `repeat` block.	2	Flow Control
exp	Full precision 2^x.	1	Arithmetic
expp	Partial precision 2^x, meaning it will operate at 16-bits instead of 32-bits.	1	Arithmetic
frc	Returns the fractional component of the input.	1	Arithmetic
if_bool	Begins an `if`/`else`/`endif` block (using a boolean condition).	3	Flow Control
if_comp	Begins an `if` block, with a comparison.	3	Flow Control
if_pred	Begins an `if` block with a predicate condition.	3	Flow Control
lit	Returns the partial lighting calculation by calculating lighting coefficients from two dot products and an exponent.	3	Arithmetic
log	Full precision log2(x).	1	Arithmetic
logp	Partial precision log2(x), meaning it will operate at 16-bits instead of 32-bits	1	Arithmetic
loop	Starts a `loop`/`endloop` block.	3	Flow Control
lrp	Linearly interpolates between two input vectors.	2	Arithmetic
m3x2	Product of a 3-component vector and a 2×3 matrix.	2	Arithmetic
m3x3	Product of a 3-component vector and a 3x3 matrix.	3	Arithmetic
m3x4	Product of a 3-component vector and a 4×3 matrix.	4	Arithmetic
m4x3	Product of a 4-component vector and a 3×4 matrix.	3	Arithmetic

Table A-4 Vertex Shader 3.0 Assembly Instructions

Name	Description	Slots	Type
m4x4	Product of a 4-component vector and a 4×4 matrix.	4	Arithmetic
mad	Multiplies two inputs together and add the result to the third input.	1	
max	Returns the maximum between two inputs.	1	Arithmetic
min	Returns the minimum between two inputs.	1	Arithmetic
mov	Moves data from one register to another.	1	Arithmetic
mova	Moves data from a floating-point register to the address register	1	Arithmetic
mul	Multiplies two inputs together.	1	Arithmetic
nop	No operation. This is sometimes needed to avoid stalls.	1	Arithmetic
nrm	Normalizes a four-component vector. Equivalent to $input/_{length(input)}$.	3	Arithmetic
pow	Returns the first input to the power of the second, or x^y.	3	Arithmetic
rcp	Returns the reciprocal of the input, or $1/_{input}$.	1	Arithmetic
rep	Starts a `rep` / `endrep` block.	3	Flow Control
ret	End of either a subroutine or main.	1	Flow Control
rsq	Reciprocal square root, or $1/_{sqrt(input)}$.	1	Arithmetic
setp_comp	Sets the predicate register.	1	Flow Control
sge	Greater than or equal compare. The output for this instruction will be either 0 or 1.	1	Arithmetic
sgn	Returns the sign of the input. The function will return -1 for a negative input and 1 for a positive input.	3	Arithmetic
sincos	This function computes both the sine and cosine.	8	Arithmetic
slt	Less than compare. The output of this instruction will be either 0 or 1.	1	Arithmetic
sub	Subtracts two inputs from each other.	1	Arithmetic
texldl	Loads a texture with user-adjustable mipmap.	*	Texture

* 2 slots for regular textures, 5 slots for cubemaps.

Pixel Shaders Version 1.1 Thru 1.4

In this section I will overview the instruction sets defined for the pixel shader 1.x model. Since most of the 1.x pixel shader versions (1.1, 1.2, 1.3 and 1.4) are similar in functionality, their instructions have been grouped.

Setup instructions do not actually do anything beyond preparing the shader, for example defining some constants to be set into the constant registers. Below is the list of setup instructions supported in the 1.x pixel shader instruction set.

- *phase*: Transition between phase 1 and phase 2 shader code.
- *def*: Used to define constants.
- *ps*: Used to retrieve the shader version.

The pixel shader 1.x model offers a wide range of instructions. Below, in Table A-5, you will find a complete listing of all arithmetic shader instructions along with a quick description of their functionality, the number of instruction slots taken by the instruction and shader version for which these instructions are available.

Table A-5 Pixel Shader 1.1-1.4 Arithmetic Assembly Instructions

Name	Description	Slots	1.1	1.2	1.3	1.4
add	Adds two vectors together.	1	■	■	■	■
bem	Apply a fake bump environment-map transform	2				■
cmp	Compares source vector to 0.	2(f1.2 and 1.3) 1(for 1.4)		■	■	■
cnd	Compares source vector to 0.5.	1	■	■	■	
dp3	Three-component vector dot product.	1	■	■	■	
dp4	Four-component dot product	2(for 1.2 and 1.3) 1(for 1.4)		■	■	■
lrp	Linear interpolate of two input vectors.	1	■	■	■	■
mad	Multiplies two inputs together and add the result to the third input.	1	■	■	■	■
mov	Moves data from one register to another.	1	■	■	■	■
mul	Multiplies two inputs together.	1	■	■	■	■
nop	No operation.	0	■	■	■	■
sub	Subtracts a vector from another.	1	■	■	■	■

In addition to arithmetic instructions, the pixel shader 1.x model offers a wide range of texture accessing instructions. Below, in Table A-6, you will find a complete listing of texture access instructions along with a quick description of their functionality, the number of instruction slots taken and for which version of the pixel shader model 1.x the instruction is available.

Table A-6 Pixel Shader 1.1-1.4 Texture Assembly Instructions

Name	Description	Slots	1.1	1.2	1.3	1.4
tex	Sample a texture.	1	■	■	■	
texbem	Apply a fake bump environment-map.	1	■	■	■	
texbeml	Apply a fake bump environment-map transform with luminance correction.	2	■	■	■	
texcoord	Interpret texture coordinate data as color data.	1	■	■	■	
texcrd	Copy texture coordinate data as color data.	1		■		■
texdepth	Calculates depth values.	1		■		■
texdp3	Three-component dot product between texture data and the texture coordinates.	1		■	■	
texdp3tex	Three-component dot product and 1-D texture lookup.	1		■	■	
texkill	Cancels rendering of pixels based on a comparison.	1	■	■	■	■
texld	Sample a texture.	1				■
texm3x2depth	Calculates per-pixel depth values.	1			■	
texm3x2pad	First row matrix multiply of a two-row matrix multiply.	1	■	■	■	
texm3x2tex	Final row matrix multiply of a two-row matrix multiply.	1	■	■	■	
texm3x3	3×3 matrix multiply.	1		■	■	
texm3x3pad	First or second row multiply of a three-row matrix multiply.	1	■	■	■	
texm3x3spec	Final row multiply of a three-row matrix multiply.	1	■	■	■	
texm3x3tex	Texture look up using a 3×3 matrix.	1	■	■	■	

Table A-6 Pixel Shader 1.1-1.4 Texture Assembly Instructions

Name	Description	Slots	1.1	1.2	1.3	1.4
texm3x3vspec	Texture look up using a 3×3 matrix multiply, with non-constant eye-ray vector.	1				
texreg2ar	Sample a texture using the alpha and red components.	1				
texreg2gb	Sample a texture using the gb components.	1				
texreg2rgb	Sample a texture using the rgb components.	1				

Pixel Shader Version 2.0

In this section I will outline the instruction sets defined for the pixel shader 2.0 model. In this model, the choice of instruction set is more closely related to the instruction set in the 2.0 vertex shader model. The only exception is that the 2.0 pixel shader instruction set does not allow for any flow control instructions.

Setup instructions do not actually do anything beyond preparing the shader, for example defining some constants to be set into the constant registers. Below is the list of setup instructions supported in the 2.0 pixel shader instruction set.

- `dcl`: Declares the association between vertex shader output registers and pixel shader input registers.
- `dc_samplerTyp1`: Declares the texture dimension for a sampler.
- `def`: Used to define constants.
- `ps`: Used to retrieve the shader version.

The pixel shader 2.0 model offers a wide range of instructions. Below, in Table A-7, you will find a complete listing of all the arithmetic shader instructions along with a quick description of their functionality, the number of instruction slots taken by the instruction.

Table A-7 Pixel Shader 2.0 Assembly Instructions

Name	Description	Slots	Type
abs	Returns the per-component absolute value of the input.	1	Arithmetic
add	Adds two vectors together.	1	Arithmetic
cmp	Compares source to 0.	1	Arithmetic
crs	Cross product of two vectors.	2	Arithmetic
dp2add	2-D dot product and add.	2	Arithmetic
dp3	Three-component vector dot product.	1	Arithmetic
dp4	Four-component vector dot product.	1	Arithmetic
exp	Full precision 2^x.	1	Arithmetic
frc	Returns the fractional component of the input.	1	Arithmetic
log	Full precision log2(x).	1	Arithmetic
lrp	Linearly interpolates between two input vectors.	2	Arithmetic
m3x2	Computes the product of a 3-component vector and a 2×3 matrix.	2	Arithmetic
m3x3	Computes the product of a 3-component vector and a 3×3 matrix.	3	Arithmetic
m3x4	Computes the product of a 3-component vector and a 4×3 matrix.	4	Arithmetic
m4x3	Computes the product of a 4-component vector and a 3×4 matrix.	3	Arithmetic
m4x4	Computes the product of a 4-component vector and a 4×4 matrix.	4	Arithmetic
mad	Multiplies two inputs together and add the result to the third input.	1	Arithmeic
max	Returns the maximum between two inputs.	1	Arithmetic
min	Returns the minimum between two inputs.	1	Arithmetic
mov	Moves data from one register to another.	1	Arithmetic
mul	Multiplies two inputs together.	1	Arithmetic
nop	No operation. This is sometimes needed to avoid stalls.	1	Arithmetic

Table A-7 Pixel Shader 2.0 Assembly Instructions

Name	Description	Slots	Type
nrm	Normalizes a four-component vector. Equivalent to $input/_{length(input)}$.	3	Arithmetic
pow	Returns the first input to the power of the second, or x^y.	3	Arithmetic
rcp	Returns the reciprocal of the input, or $1/_{input}$.	1	Arithmetic
rsq	Reciprocal square root, or $1/_{sqrt(input)}$.	1	Arithmetic
sincos	This function computes both the sine and cosine.	8	Arithmetic
sub	Subtracts two inputs from each other.	1	Arithmetic
texkill	Cancels rendering of the current pixel if any of components of the texture coordinates is less than zero.	1	Texture
texld	Sample a texture.	1	Texture
texldb	Texture sampling with level of detail bias from w-component of the texture coordinates.	1	Texture
texldp	Texture sampling with projective divide by w-component.	1	Texture

Pixel Shader Version 2.x

Pixel shader version 2.x is a simple extension to the 2.0 shader model. Extensions to the language mostly come in the form of support for flow control instructions and predication.

Setup instructions do not actually do anything beyond preparing the shader, for example defining some constants to be set into the constant registers. Below is the list of setup instructions supported in the 2.x pixel shader instruction set.

- `dcl`: Declares the association between vertex shader output registers and pixel shader input registers.
- `dc_samplerTypl`: Declares the texture dimension for a sampler.
- `def`: Used to define constants.
- `defb`: Used to define boolean constants.
- `defi`: Used to define integer constants.
- `label`: Used to define label within the shader code which can be used for flow conrol.
- `ps`: Used to retrieve the shader version.

The pixel shader 2.x model offers a wide range of instructions. Below, in Table A-8, you will find a complete listing of arithmetic shader instructions along with a quick description of their functionality and the number of instruction slots taken by the instruction.

Table A-8 Pixel Shader 2.x Assembly Instructions

Name	Description	Slots	Type
abs	Returns the per-component absolute value of the input.	1	Arithmetic
add	Adds two vectors together.	1	Arithmetic
break	Breaks out of a *loop*/*endloop* or *rep*/*endrep* block.	1	Flow Control
break_comp	Conditionally breaks out of a *loop* / *endloop* or *rep*/*endrep* block, with a comparison.	3	Flow Control
breakp	Breaks out of a *loop* / *endloop* or *rep* / *endrep* block, based on a predicate.	3	Flow Control
call	Calls a subroutine. This function will push the current onto the return address stack and continue execution at the specified label.	2	Flow Control
callnz_bool	Calls a subroutine if a boolean register is not zero.	3	Flow Control
callnz_pred	Calls a subroutine if a predicate register is not zero.	3	Flow Control
cmp	Compares source to 0.	1	Arithmetic
crs	Cross product of two vectors.	2	Arithmetic
dp2add	2-D dot product and add.	2	Arithmetic
dp3	Three-component vector dot product.	1	Arithmetic
dp4	Four-component vector dot product.	1	Arithmetic
dsx	Rate of change in the x direction.	1	Arithmetic
dsy	Rate of change in the y direction.	1	Arithmetic
else	Begins an *else* block.	1	Flow Control
endif	Ends an *if* / *else* block.	1	Flow Control
endloop	End of a *loop*/*endloop* block.	2	Flow Control
endrep	End of a *repeat* block.	2	Flow Control
exp	Full precision 2^x.	1	Arithmetic
frc	Returns the fractional component of the input.	1	Arithmetic

Table A-8 Pixel Shader 2.x Assembly Instructions

Name	Description	Slots	Type
if_bool	Begins an *if* / *else* / *endif* block (using a boolean condition).	3	Flow Control
if_comp	Begins an *if* block, with a comparison.	3	Flow Control
if_pred	Begins an *if* block with a predicate condition.	3	Flow Control
log	Full precision log2(x).	1	Arithmetic
lrp	Linearly interpolates between two input vectors.	2	Arithmetic
m3x2	Computes the product of a 3-component vector and a 2×3 matrix.	2	Arithmetic
m3x3	Computes the product of a 3-component vector and a 3×3 matrix.	3	Arithmetic
m3x4	Computes the product of a 3-component vector and a 4×3 matrix.	4	Arithmetic
m4x3	Computes the product of a 4-component vector and a 3×4 matrix.	3	Arithmetic
m4x4	Computes the product of a 4-component vector and a 4×4 matrix.	4	Arithmetic
mad	Multiplies two inputs together and add the result to the third input.	1	Arithmetic
max	Returns the maximum between two inputs.	1	Arithmetic
min	Returns the minimum between two inputs.	1	Arithmetic
mov	Moves data from one register to another.	1	Arithmetic
mul	Multiplies two inputs together.	1	Arithmetic
nop	No operation. This is sometimes needed to avoid stalls.	1	Arithmetic
nrm	Normalizes a four-component vector. Equivalent to $input/_{length(input)}$.	3	Arithmetic
pow	Returns the first input to the power of the second, or x^y.	3	Arithmetic
rcp	Returns the reciprocal of the input, or $1/_{input}$.	1	Arithmetic
rep	Starts a *rep* / *endrep* block.	3	Flow Control
ret	End of either a subroutine or main.	1	Flow Control

Table A-8 Pixel Shader 2.x Assembly Instructions

Name	Description	Slots	Type
rsq	Reciprocal square root, or $1/_{sqrt(input)}$.	1	Arithmetic
setp_comp	Sets the predicate register.	1	Flow Control
sincos	This function computes both the sine and cosine.	8	Arithmetic
sub	Subtracts two inputs from each other.	1	Arithmetic
texkill	Cancels rendering of the current pixel if any of the first three components of the texture coordinates is less than zero.	Note 1	Texture
texld	Sample a texture.	Note 2	Texture
texldb	Texture sampling with level of detail bias from w-component of the texture coordinates.	Note 3	Texture
texldd	Texture sampling with user-provided gradients.	3	Texture
texldp	Texture sampling with projective divide by w-component.	Note 4	Texture

Note 1: If *D3DPS20CAPS_NOTEXINSTRUCTIONLIMIT* is set, slots = 2; otherwise slots = 1.

Note 2: If *D3DPS20CAPS_NOTEXINSTRUCTIONLIMIT* is set and the texture is a cube map, slots = 4; otherwise slot = 1.

Note 3: If *D3DPS20CAPS_NOTEXINSTRUCTIONLIMIT* is set, slots = 6; otherwise slots = 1.

Note 4: If *D3DPS20CAPS_NOTEXINSTRUCTIONLIMIT* is not set, slots = 1; otherwise: if the texture is a cube map, slots = 4; if the texture is *not* a cube map, slots = 3.

Pixel Shader Version 3.0

In this section I will overview the instruction sets defined for the pixel shader 3.0 model which is an extension to the 2.0 model. Setup instructions do not actually do anything beyond preparing the shader, for example defining some constants to be set into the constant registers. Below is the list of setup instructions supported in the 3.0 pixel shader instruction set.

- *dcl_usage*: Declares the association between vertex shader output registers and pixel shader input registers.
- *dc_samplerTyp1*: Declares the texture dimension for a sampler.
- *def*: Used to define constants.
- *defb*: Used to define Boolean constants.
- *defi*: Used to define integer constants.

- *label*: Used to define label within the shader code which can be used for flow conrol.
- *ps*: Used to retrieve the shader version.

The pixel shader 3.0 model offers a wide range of instructions. Below, in Table A-9, you will find a complete listing of all arithmetic shader instructions along with a quick description of their functionality and the number of instruction slots taken by the instruction.

Table A-9 Pixel Shader 3.0 Assembly Instructions

Name	Description	Slots	Type
abs	Returns the per-component absolute value of the input.	1	Arithmetic
add	Adds two vectors together.	1	Arithmetic
break	Breaks out of a *loop* / *endloop* or *rep* / *endrep* block.	1	Flow Control
break_comp	Conditionally breaks out of a *loop* / *endloop* or *rep* / *endrep* block with a comparison.	3	Flow Control
breakp	Breaks out of a *loop/endloop* or *rep/endrep* block, based on a predicate.	3	Flow Control
call	Calls a subroutine. This function will push the current onto the return address stack and continue execution at the specified label.	2	Flow Control
callnz_bool	Calls a subroutine if a boolean register is not zero.	3	Flow Control
callnz_pred	Call a subroutine if a predicate register is not zero.	3	Flow Control
cmp	Compares source to 0.	1	Arithmetic
crs	Cross product of two vectors.	2	Arithmetic
dp2add	2-D dot product and add.	2	Arithmetic
dp3	Three-component vector dot product.	1	Arithmetic
dp4	Four-component vector dot product.	1	Arithmetic
dsx	Rate of change in the x direction.	1	Arithmetic
dsy	Rate of change in the y direction.	1	Arithmetic
else	Begins an *else* block.	1	Flow Control
endif	Ends an *if* / *else* block.	1	Flow Control
endloop	End of a *loop* / *endloop* block.	2	Flow Control
endrep	End of a *repeat* block.	2	Flow Control

Table A-9 Pixel Shader 3.0 Assembly Instructions

Name	Description	Slots	Type
exp	Full precision 2^x.	1	Arithmetic
frc	Returns the fractional component of the input.	1	Arithmetic
if_bool	Begins an `if` / `else` / `endif` block (using a boolean condition).	3	Flow Control
if_comp	Begins an `if` block, with a comparison.	3	Flow Control
if_pred	Begins an `if` block with a predicate condition.	3	Flow Control
log	Full precision log2(x).	1	Arithmetic
loop	Starts a `loop` / `endloop` block.	3	Flow Control
lrp	Linearly interpolates between two input vectors.	2	Arithmetic
m3x2	Product of a 3-component vector and a 2×3 matrix.	2	Arithmetic
m3x3	Product of a 3-component vector and a 3×3 matrix.	3	Arithmetic
m3x4	Product of a 3-component vector and a 4×3 matrix.	4	Arithmetic
m4x3	Product of a 4-component vector and a 3×4 matrix.	3	Arithmetic
m4x4	Product of a 4-component vector and a 4×4 matrix.	4	Arithmetic
mad	Multiplies two inputs together and add the result to the third input.	1	Arithmetic
max	Returns the maximum between two inputs.	1	Arithmetic
min	Returns the minimum between two inputs.	1	Arithmetic
mov	Moves data from one register to another.	1	Arithmetic
mul	Multiplies two inputs together.	1	Arithmetic
nop	No operation. This is sometimes needed to avoid stalls.	1	Arithmetic
nrm	Normalizes a four-component vector. Equivalent to $input/_{length(input)}$.	3	Arithmetic
pow	Returns the first input to the power of the second, or x^y.	3	Arithmetic
rcp	Returns the reciprocal of the input, or $^1/_{input}$.	1	Arithmetic
rep	Starts a `rep` / `endrep` block.	3	Flow Control
ret	End of either a subroutine or main.	1	Flow Control

Table A-9 Pixel Shader 3.0 Assembly Instructions

Name	Description	Slots	Type
rsq	Reciprocal square root, or $1/_{sqrt(input)}$.	1	Arithmetic
setp_comp	Sets the predicate register.	1	Flow Control
sincos	This function computes both the sine and cosine.	8	Arithmetic
sub	Subtracts two inputs from each other.	1	Arithmetic
texkill	Cancels rendering of the current pixel if any of the first three components of the texture coordinates is less than zero.	2	Texture
texld	Sample a texture.	Note 1	Texture
texldb	Texture sampling with level of detail bias from w-component of the texture coordinates.	6	Texture
texldl	Texture sampling with LOD from w-component.	Note 2	Texture
texldd	Texture sampling with user-provided gradients.	3	Texture
texldp	Texture sampling with projective divide by w-component.	Note 3	Texture

Note 1: If the texture is a cube map, slots = 4; otherwise slots = 1.

Note 2: If the texture is a cube map, slots = 5; otherwise slots = 2.

Note 3: If the texture is a cube map, slots = 4; otherwise slots = 3.

Appendix B

HLSL Intrinsic Function Reference

This chapter serves as a reference manual for the High-Level Shader Language from Microsoft. Although HLSL was introduced as part of the DirectX 9.0 SDK, I chose this language because of its simplicity and versatility compared to writing shaders in pure assembly. Also, with the introduction of the Cg shading language, which is compatible with HLSL, the knowledge you will gain with this book is portable to other rendering APIs and platforms without any major modifications.

The big advantage of HLSL over its assembly counterpart is that it brings shaders to you in a more accessible way. It allows you to separate yourself from specific shader version support, register allocation and turning over optimization decisions to the compiler.

The high-level shader language brings you the development of shaders in a language similar to C. It offers a rich set of features including functions, statements, user defined data types and a wide collection of built-in functions for you to use. All this making shader development more oriented towards algorithm design and less with figuring out how to code your algorithm.

Keep in mind that this reference manual is loosely inspired by the HLSL reference in DirectX9's documentation. For a more complete reference, we suggest reading the full reference included as part of the DirectX 9.0 SDK's documentation.

ret abs(x)

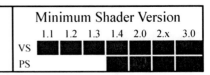

Parameters

Name	In/Out	Template Type	Component Type	Size
x	in	scalar, vector or matrix	float, int	any
ret	out	same as input *x*	same as input *x*	same as input *x*

Description

This function returns the absolute value of its inputs. This function will operate per-component for vectors or matrices.

For example, the code below

```
float2 res = abs(1.1, -2.5);
```

yields the following result: 1.1, 2.5

Special Considerations

The absolute value instruction does not exist natively on shader profiles below vs_2_0 and ps_2_0. To achieve a similar result on hardware not supporting natively the computation of an absolute value, the processor will take advantage of the max instruction.

For example, the following code:

```
float4 main(float4 inPos:POSITION) : POSITION
{
   return abs(inPos);
}
```

generates the following under vs_2_0

```
abs oPos, v0
```

but will generate the following under vs_1_1:

```
max oPos, -v0, v0
```

ret acos(x)

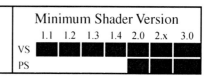

Parameters

Name	In/Out	Template Type	Component Type	Size
x	in	scalar, vector or matrix	float, int	any
ret	out	same as input *x*	same as input *x*	same as input *x*

Description

This function returns the arccosine value of its inputs. The arccosine is defined as the reverse operation of a cosine. This function will operate per-component on vector or matrix inputs. The results for this function are only defined for inputs in the range [-1, 1]. For example, the following code:

```
float4 main(float4 inPos: POSITION) : POSITION
{
   return acos(float4(-1.0, -0.5, 0.25, 0.75));
}
```

Will yield the following result: 3.14159274, 2.09439516, 1.31811607, 0.722734272

Special Considerations

The arccosine function is not supported natively on any hardware. This has significant performance considerations as the compiler will take the instruction and evaluate it using an estimation (usually a Taylor series). For example, on *vs_1_1*, the following code:

```
float4 main(float4 inPos:POSITION) : POSITION
{
   return acos(inPos);
}
```

will generate shader assembly taking 17 instructions as follows:

```
def c0, 1, -0.0187292993, 0.0742610022, -0.212114394
def c1, 1.57072878, -2, 3.14159274, 0
abs r2, v0
mad r0, r2, c0.y, c0.z
add r1, -r2, c0.x
mad r0, r0, r2, c0.w
rsq r1.x, r1.x
rsq r1.y, r1.y
rsq r1.z, r1.z
rsq r1.w, r1.w
mad r0, r0, r2, c1.x
```

```
rcp r1.x, r1.x
rcp r1.y, r1.y
rcp r1.z, r1.z
rcp r1.w, r1.w
mul r2, r0, r1
mad r0, r2, c1.y, c1.z
slt r1, v0, -v0
mad oPos, r0, r1, r2
```

ret all(x)

Minimum Shader Version

	1.1	1.2	1.3	1.4	2.0	2.x	3.0
VS	■	■	■	■	■	■	■
PS					■	■	■

Parameters

Name	In/Out	Template Type	Component Type	Size
x	in	scalar, vector or matrix	float, int, bool	any
ret	out	scalar	bool	1

Description

This function tests if all the components of the input x are nonzero. For example, the following code

```
float4 main(float4 inPos:POSITION) : POSITION
{
   bool R1 = all( float4(1,2,3,4) );
   bool R2 = all( float4(0,1,2,3) );
   return float4(R1, R1, R1, R2);
}
```

the value of R1 will be true and the value of R2 will be false.

Special Considerations

The all function does not have any native hardware support. This function is generally evaluated by taking the value, squaring it, using the sge instruction with the value and its negative. This will give us a nonzero result for any nonzero input value. Taking this result and doing a dot product with itself, we can determine that all the components are nonzero. For example, the following code

```
float4 main(float4 inPos:POSITION) : POSITION
{
   return float4(0,0,0,all(inPos));
}
```

will generate the following shader assembly under vs_1_1:

```
mul r0, v0, v0
sge r0, -r0, r0
dp4 r0.w, r0, r0
sge oPos.w, -r0.w, r0.w
mov oPos.xyz, c0.x
```

ret any(x)

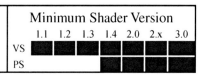

Parameters

Name	In/Out	Template Type	Component Type	Size
x	in	scalar, vector or matrix	float, int, bool	any
ret	out	scalar	bool	1

Description

This function tests if any of the components of the input *x* are nonzero. For example, the following code

```
float4 main(float4 inPos:POSITION) : POSITION
{
  bool R1 = any( float4(1,2,3,0) );
  bool R2 = any( float4(0,0,0,0) );
  return float4(R1, R1, R1, R2);
}
```

the value of *R1* will be *true* and the value of *R2* will be *false*.

Special Considerations

The *any* function is generally evaluated by using a combination of the *slt* and *dp4* instructions. For example, the following code:

```
float4 main(float4 inPos:POSITION) : POSITION
{
  return float4(0,0,0,any(inPos));
}
```

will generate the following shader assembly under *vs_1_1*:

```
dp4 r0.w, v0, v0
slt oPos.w, -r0.w, r0.w
mov oPos.xyz, c0.x
```

ret asin(x)

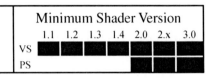

	Minimum Shader Version
	1.1 1.2 1.3 1.4 2.0 2.x 3.0
VS	███████
PS	███

Parameters

Name	In/Out	Template Type	Component Type	Size
x	in	scalar, vector or matrix	float	any
ret	out	same as input x	float	same as input x

Description

This function returns the arcsine value of its inputs. The arcsine is defined as the reverse operation of a sine. This function will operate per-component on vector or matrix inputs. The result for this function is only defined for inputs in the range $[-\pi/2, \pi/2]$. For example, the following code

```
float4 main(float4 inPos:POSITION) : POSITION
{
   return asin(float4(-1.0,- 0.25, 0.5, 0.75));
}
```

will yield the following result: -1.57079637, -0.252680242, 0.52359879, 0.848062098

Special Considerations

The `asin` function is not supported natively on any hardware. This has significant performance considerations as the compiler will take the instruction and evaluate it using an approximation (usually a Taylor series). For example, on `vs_1_1`, the following code

```
float4 main(float4 inPos:POSITION) : POSITION
{
   return asin(inPos);
}
```

will generate shader assembly taking 18 instructions as follows:

```
def c0, 1, -0.0187292993, 0.0742610022, -0.212114394
def c1, 1.57072878, -2, 3.14159274, 1.57079637
max r2, -v0, v0
mad r0, r2, c0.y, c0.z
add r1, -r2, c0.x
mad r0, r0, r2, c0.w
rsq r1.x, r1.x
rsq r1.y, r1.y
rsq r1.z, r1.z
rsq r1.w, r1.w
mad r0, r0, r2, c1.x
```

```
rcp r1.x, r1.x
rcp r1.y, r1.y
rcp r1.z, r1.z
rcp r1.w, r1.w
mul r2, r0, r1
mad r0, r2, c1.y, c1.z
slt r1, v0, -v0
mad r0, r0, r1, r2
add oPos, -r0, c1.w
```

ret atan(x)

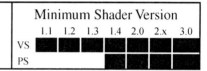

Minimum Shader Version							
	1.1	1.2	1.3	1.4	2.0	2.x	3.0
VS	■	■	■	■	■	■	■
PS				■	■	■	■

Parameters

Name	In/Out	Template Type	Component Type	Size
x	in	scalar, vector or matrix	float	any
ret	out	same as input x	float	same as input x

Description

This function returns the arctangent value of its inputs. The arctangent is defined as the reverse operation of a tangent. This function will operate per-component on vector or matrix inputs. The result for this function will be in the range $[-\pi/2, \pi/2]$. For example, the following code

```
float4 main(float4 inPos:POSITION) : POSITION
{
    return atan(float4(-10.0,-2.25, 0.5, 75));
}
```

will yield the following result: -1.47112763, -1.15257204, 0.463647604, 1.55746377

Special Considerations

The `atan` function is not supported natively on any hardware. This has significant performance considerations as the compiler will take the instruction and evaluate it using an approximation (usually a Taylor series). For example, on `vs_1_1`, the following code

```
float4 main(float4 inPos:POSITION) : POSITION
{
    return atan(inPos);
}
```

will generate shader assembly taking 21 instructions as follows:

```
def c0, 1, 0.0208350997, -0.0851330012, 0.180141002
def c1, -0.330299497, 0.999866009, -2, 1.57079637
max r0, -v0, v0
max r1, r0, c0.x
rcp r2.x, r1.x
rcp r2.y, r1.y
rcp r2.z, r1.z
rcp r2.w, r1.w
min r1, r0, c0.x
mul r1, r2, r1
mul r2, r1, r1
mad r3, r2, c0.y, c0.z
mad r3, r2, r3, c0.w
mad r3, r2, r3, c1.x
mad r2, r2, r3, c1.y
mul r2, r1, r2
slt r1, c0.x, r0
mad r0, r2, c1.z, c1.w
mad r2, r0, r1, r2
min r0, v0, c0.x
add r1, r2, r2
slt r0, r0, -r0
mad oPos, r0, -r1, r2
```

ret atan2(x,y)

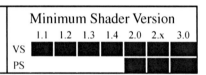

Parameters

Name	In/Out	Template Type	Component Type	Size
x	in	scalar, vector or matrix	float	any
y	in	same as input x	float	same as input x
ret	out	same as input x	float	same as input x

Description

This function returns the arctangent value of x/y. The signs of the inputs x and y will be used to determine in which quadrant the arctan will occur, giving results in the range $[-\pi/2, \pi/2]$. This function will operate per-component on vector or matrix inputs. For example, the following code

```
float4 main(float4 inPos:POSITION) : POSITION
{
    return atan2(float4(-10.0,-2.25, 0.5, 75), float4(-2.0, 0.25, 5.0, -1.0));
}
```

will yield the following result: -1.76819193, -1.46013916, 0.0996686518, 1.58412886

Special Considerations

The *atan2* function is not supported natively on any hardware and has significant performance considerations as the compiler evaluate it using an approximation. For example, on *vs_1_1*, the following code

```
float4 main(float4 inPos:POSITION) : POSITION
{
   return atan2(inPos, float4(0.2, -10.0, 1.0, 0.1));
}
```

will generate shader assembly taking 25 instructions as follows:

```
max r0, -v0, v0
max r1, r0, c3
rcp r2.x, r1.x
rcp r2.y, r1.y
rcp r2.z, r1.z
rcp r2.w, r1.w
min r1, r0, c3
mul r1, r2, r1
mul r2, r1, r1
mad r3, r2, c1.x, c1.y
mad r3, r2, r3, c1.z
mad r3, r2, r3, c1.w
mad r2, r2, r3, c2.x
mul r2, r1, r2
slt r1, c3, r0
mad r0, r2, c2.y, c2.z
mad r0, r0, r1, r2
add r2, r0, c4.xyxx
min r0, v0, c0
max r1, v0, c0
slt r0, r0, -r0
sge r3, r1, -r1
add r1, r2, r2
mul r0, r0, r3
mad oPos, r0, -r1, r2
```

ret ceil(x)

Parameters

Name	In/Out	Template Type	Component Type	Size
x	in	scalar, vector or matrix	float	any
ret	out	same as input *x*	float	same as input *x*

Description

This function returns the integer greater or equal to the input. This function will operate per-component for vector and matrix inputs. For example, the following code

```
float4 main(float4 inPos:POSITION) : POSITION
{
    return ceil(float4(1.0, -1.1, 2.2, 10.001));
}
```

will return the following: 1, -1, 3, 11

Special Considerations

The `ceil` function does not have direct native hardware support;however the task can easily be accomplished by taking the fractional part of the input using the `frc` instruction and subtracting it from the initial input. For example, the following code

```
float4 main(float4 inPos:POSITION) : POSITION
{
    return ceil(inPos);
}
```

will generate the following shader assembly under `vs_2_0`:

```
frc r0, -v0
add oPos, r0, v0
```

Note that under `vs_1_1`, the compiler will generate the following:

```
frc r1.xy, -v0.zwzw
mov r0.zw, r1.xyxy
frc r0.xy, -v0
add oPos, r0, v0
```

ret clamp(ret, min, max)

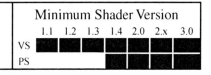

	Minimum Shader Version						
	1.1	1.2	1.3	1.4	2.0	2.x	3.0
VS	■	■	■	■	■	■	■
PS					■	■	■

Parameters

Name	In/Out	Template Type	Component Type	Size
x	in	scalar, vector or matrix	float, int	any
min	in	same as input x	same as input x	same as input x
max	in	same as input x	same as input x	same as input x
ret	out	same as input x	same as input x	same as input x

Description

This function returns the input x clamped to the range [min, max]. This function is useful to constrain a value to a certain range and will operate per-component on inputs of vector or matrix types. For example, the following code

```
float4 main(float4 inPos:POSITION) : POSITION
{
  return clamp(float4(0.2, -0.1, 2.2, 0.75), 0, 1);
}
```

will return the following: 0.200000003, 0, 1, 0.75

Special Considerations

The clamp function does not have a direct hardware equivalent. The task can easily accomplished in two instructions with the min and max instructions. For example, the following code

```
float4 main(float4 inPos:POSITION) : POSITION
{
  return clamp(inPos, -2, 2);
}
```

will generate the following under vs_1_1:

```
def c0, -2, 2, 0, 0
max r0, v0, c0.x
min oPos, r0, c0.y
```

clip(x)

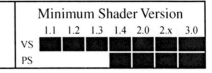

Parameters

Name	In/Out	Template Type	Component Type	Size
x	in	scalar, vector or matrix	float	any

Description

This function is only applicable to pixel shaders and will discard the current pixel if any of components of the input x is less than zero. This function is generally used to simulate clip planes by putting the distances of a pixel from the plane inside the input values.

Special Considerations

This function is supported natively in hardware; however you will need to consider that discarded pixels are still rasterized and tested against the z-buffer since there is no guarantee the pixel will be discarded. For hardware supporting user clip planes, it will generally be efficient to take advantage of theses instead of using the *clip* function.

ret cos(x)

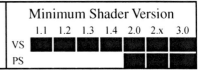

Parameters

Name	In/Out	Template Type	Component Type	Size
x	in	scalar, vector or matrix	float	any
ret	out	same as input x	float	same as input x

Description

This function returns the cosine of x. It will operate per-component for vector and matrix inputs. For example, the following code

```
float4 main(float4 inPos:POSITION) : POSITION
{
    return cos(float4(-1.0,- 0.25, 0.5, 0.75));
}
```

will return the following: 0.540302277, 0.968912423, 0.87758255, 0.731688857

Special Considerations

As with the sine and other trigonometric functions, there is no native support for the *cos* function, and it will be emulated using a Taylor series. For example, the following code

```
float4 main(float4 inPos:POSITION) : POSITION
{
    return cos(inPos);
}
```

will compile to the following 15 instructions under *vs_1_1*:

```
mad r1, v0, c1.x, c1.y
frc r2.xy, r1.zwzw
mov r0.zw, r2.xyxy
frc r0.xy, r1
mad r0, r0, c1.z, c1.w
mul r0, r0, r0
mad r1, r0, c2.x, c2.y
mad r1, r0, r1, c2.z
mad r1, r0, r1, c2.w
mad r1, r0, r1, c0.x
mad oPos, r0, r1, c0.y
```

ret cosh(x)

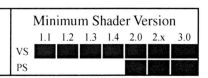

Parameters

Name	In/Out	Template Type	Component Type	Size
x	in	scalar, vector or matrix	float	any
ret	out	same as input x	float	same as input x

Description

This function returns the hyperbolic cosine of x. It will operate per-component for vector and matrix inputs. For example, the following code

```
float4 main(float4 inPos:POSITION) : POSITION
{
    return cosh(float4(-1.0,- 0.25, 0.5, 0.75));
}
```

will return the following: 1.54308069, 1.03141308, 1.12762594, 1.29468334

Special Considerations

The `cosh` function does not have native support on current shader hardware. The compiler will emulate the functionality by using a numerical approximation. For example, the following code

```
float4 main(float4 inPos:POSITION) : POSITION
{
    return cosh(inPos);
}
```

will compile to the following under `vs_1_1`:

```
def c0, 1.44269502, 0.5, 0, 0
mul r1, v0, c0.x
exp r0.x, r1.x
exp r0.y, r1.y
exp r0.z, r1.z
exp r0.w, r1.w
exp r1.x, -r1.x
exp r1.y, -r1.y
exp r1.z, -r1.z
exp r1.w, -r1.w
add r0, r0, r1
mul oPos, r0, c0.y
```

Take note that the `exp` instruction is more expensive on `vs_1_x` and will cause stalls, generally leading to an execution of about 83 instruction slots versus 11 instruction slots on `vs_2_x` and `vs_3_x`.

ret cross(x,y)

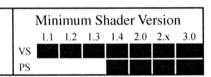

	Minimum Shader Version						
	1.1	1.2	1.3	1.4	2.0	2.x	3.0
VS	■	■	■	■	■	■	■
PS					■	■	■

Parameters

Name	In/Out	Template Type	Component Type	Size
x	in	vector	float	3
y	in	vector	float	3
ret	out	vector	float	3

Description

This function will execute the cross product between two 3-D vectors. The cross product of two vectors will yield a vector perpendicular to the two source vector. The cross product is executed using the right hand rule equivalent to

```
dest.x = src0.y * src1.z - src0.z * src1.y;
dest.y = src0.z * src1.x - src0.x * src1.z;
dest.z = src0.x * src1.y - src0.y * src1.x;
```

Special Considerations

The cross product does have native hardware support starting with *vs_2_0* and *ps_2_0* using the *crs* instruction. For lesser hardware, however, the compiler will evaluate the cross product using the above equations. For example, the following code

```
float4 main(float4 inPos:POSITION,
            float3 inVector:TEXCOORD0,
            float3 inVector2:TEXCOORD1) : POSITION
{
   return float4(cross(inVector2, inVector),1);
}
```

will yield the following under *vs_1_1*:

```
def c0, 1, 0, 0, 0
mov r0.xyz, v1
mul r1.xyz, r0.zxyw, v0.yzxw
mad oPos.xyz, r0.yzxw, v0.zxyw, -r1
mov oPos.w, c0.x
```

ret D3DCOLORtoUBYTE(x)

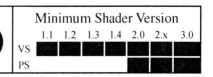

Parameters

Name	In/Out	Template Type	Component Type	Size
x	in	vector	float	4
ret	out	vector	float	4

Description

This function will swizzle and scale a *D3DCOLOR* 4D vector correctly to compensate for the lack of *UBYTE* vertex format on some hardware. This function will in essence bring the input from the [0, 1] range to the [0, 255] range and rearrange the components so that *ret = x.zyxw*. For example

```
float4 main(float4 inPos:POSITION) : POSITION
{
   return D3DCOLORtoUBYTE4(float4(0.0,0.25, 0.5, 0.75));
}
```

will yield 127, 63, 0, 191

Special Considerations

This function is not natively supported on the hardware, but it can easily be computed with the `mul` instruction and some swizzle operations. The following code

```
float4 main(float4 inPos:POSITION) : POSITION
{
   return D3DCOLORtoUBYTE4(inPos);
}
```

will generate the following under `vs_1_1`:

```
def c0, 255.001953, 0, 0, 0
mul oPos, v0.zyxw, c0.x
```

	Minimum Shader Version
ret ddx(x)	1.1 1.2 1.3 1.4 2.0 2.x 3.0

	1.1	1.2	1.3	1.4	2.0	2.x	3.0
VS							
PS						■	■

Parameters

Name	In/Out	Template Type	Component Type	Size
x	in	scalar, vector or matrix	float	any
ret	out	same as input x	float	same as input x

Description

This function will return the partial derivate of the input x with respect to the screen space x coordinate. This functionality is only applicable to pixel shaders, and the result will be estimated based on the interpolation results from neighboring pixels.

Special Considerations

This functionality is an optional feature of the pixel shader 2.0 model. You will need to verify the device capabilities to see if you can use `ddx`. In addition, since the derivate is determined from neighboring pixel input interpolation, you may only use this function on pixel shader inputs.

ret ddy(x)

	Minimum Shader Version
	1.1 1.2 1.3 1.4 2.0 2.x 3.0
VS	
PS	▮▮

Parameters

Name	In/Out	Template Type	Component Type	Size
x	in	scalar, vector or matrix	float	any
ret	out	same as input *x*	float	same as input *x*

Description

This function will return the partial derivate of the input *x* with respect to the screen space y coordinate. This functionality is only applicable to pixel shaders, and the result will be estimated based on the interpolation results from neighboring pixels.

Special Considerations

This functionality is an optional feature of the pixel shader 2.0 model. You will need to verify the device capabilities to see if you can use *ddy*. In addition, since the derivate is determined from neighboring pixel input interpolation, you may only use this function on pixel shader inputs.

---

ret degrees(x)

	Minimum Shader Version
	1.1 1.2 1.3 1.4 2.0 2.x 3.0
VS	▮▮▮▮▮▮
PS	▮▮▮

Parameters

Name	In/Out	Template Type	Component Type	Size
x	in	scalar, vector or matrix	float	any
ret	out	same as input *x*	float	same as input *x*

Description

This function will convert the input x from radians to degrees. This is done by taking the input and multiplying it by a constant of $180/_\pi$. For example, the following code

```
float4 main(float4 inPos:POSITION) : POSITION
{
  return degrees(float4(0.0, 1.0, 2.0, 3.14));
}
```

will yield the following result: 0, 57.2957764, 114.591553, 179.908737

Special Considerations

There is no native support for this function on the shader hardware. However, it can easily be computed in a single instruction with the *mul* instruction.

	Minimum Shader Version
# ret determinant(x)	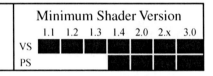

Parameters

Name	In/Out	Template Type	Component Type	Size
x	in	matrix	float	any (rows == columns)
ret	out	scalar	float	1

Description

This function returns the determinant of the input matrix *x*. Because of the nature of determinants, the input value must be a square matrix. Determinants are used to determine if a matrix defined from a set of linear equations has a single solution. For example, the determinant of a 3-by-3 matrix *x* is defined below:

```
x[0][0] * x[1][1] * x[2][2] - x[0][0] * x[1][2] * x[2][1] +
x[0][1] * x[1][0] * x[2][2] - x[0][1] * x[1][2] * x[2][0] +
x[0][2] * x[1][0] * x[2][1] - x[0][2] * x[1][1] * x[2][0]
```

Special Considerations

The determinant function is not natively supported on any shader hardware; it is evaluated by taking the input data and applying the above equation. For example, the following vertex shader code computing the determinant on a 3-by-3 matrix:

```
float4 main(float4 inPos:POSITION,
            float3 inT1:TEXCOORD0,
            float3 inT2:TEXCOORD1,
            float3 inT3:TEXCOORD2) : POSITION
{
   float3x3 mat = {inT1, inT2, inT3};
   return determinant(mat);
}
```

will generate the following 12 instructions under *vs_1_1*:

```
mov r0.z, v1.y
mov r0.x, v2.y
mov r0.y, v0.y
mov r1.y, v2.z
mov r1.z, v0.z
mov r1.x, v1.z
mul r2.xyz, r0, r1
mad r0.xyz, r0.zxyw, r1.yzxw, -r2
mov r1.x, v0.x
mov r1.y, v1.x
mov r1.z, v2.x
dp3 oPos, r0, r1
```

ret distance(x,y)

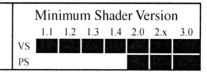

Minimum Shader Version

	1.1	1.2	1.3	1.4	2.0	2.x	3.0
VS	■	■	■	■	■	■	■
PS					■	■	■

Parameters

Name	In/Out	Template Type	Component Type	Size
x	in	vector	float	any
y	in	vector	float	same as input x
ret	out	scalar	float	1

Description

This function will compute the distance between the two input points x and y. The distance between two points is defined as the square root of the product of the corresponding components of both inputs.

```
Dist = sqrt( x.x*y.x + x.y*y.y + …)
```

Special Considerations

There is no direct hardware support for this instruction; however, the square distance of two points can easily be computed with the dot-product instruction $dp4$. Also note that the hardware does not have support for a direct square root but can accomplish the same result by combining a reciprocal square root (rsq) along with a reciprocal (rcp). For example, the following code

```
float4 main(float4 inPos:POSITION,
            float3 inVector:TEXCOORD0,
            float3 inVector2:TEXCOORD1) : POSITION
{
    return distance(inVector2, inVector);
}
```

will generate the following five instructions under vs_1_1:

```
mov r0.xyz, v1
add r0.xyz, r0, -v0
dp3 r0.x, r0, r0
rsq r0.w, r0.x
rcp oPos, r0.w
```

ret dot(x,y)

	Minimum Shader Version
	1.1 1.2 1.3 1.4 2.0 2.x 3.0
VS	■ ■ ■ ■ ■ ■ ■
PS	■ ■ ■

Parameters

Name	In/Out	Template Type	Component Type	Size
x	in	vector	float, int	any
y	in	vector	float, int	same as input x
ret	out	scalar	float, int	1

Description

This function will compute the dot product between the two input vectors x and y. The dot product between two vectors is defined as the sum of the product of the corresponding components of both inputs

```
Dot = x.x*y.x + x.y*y.y + ...
```

Special Considerations

The hardware supports this operation directly through the use of the dp3 and dp4 instructions.

ret exp(x)

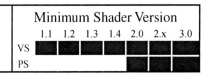

Minimum Shader Version
1.1 1.2 1.3 1.4 2.0 2.x 3.0
VS
PS

Parameters

Name	In/Out	Template Type	Component Type	Size
x	in	scalar, vector or matrix	float	any
ret	out	same as input x	float	same as input x

Description

This function returns base-e exponential of the input value x. For example, the following code

```
float4 main(float4 inPos:POSITION) : POSITION
{
  return exp(float4(-1.0, 0, 0.5, 2.0));
}
```

will yield the following result: 0.36787945, 1, 1.64872122, 7.38905621

Special Considerations

The shader hardware does not have support for a base-e exponential but can achieve similar results through the use of the base-2 exp instruction and adjusting the results. In addition, the exp instruction can only perform an exponential on a single component, requiring multiple executions to process complex types such as vectors and matrices. For example, the following code

```
float4 main(float4 inPos:POSITION) : POSITION
{
  return exp(inPos);
}
```

will generate the following assembly code under vs_1_1:

```
def c0, 1.44269502, 0, 0, 0
mul r0, v0, c0.x
exp oPos.x, r0.x
exp oPos.y, r0.y
exp oPos.z, r0.z
exp oPos.w, r0.w
```

Keep in mind that under vs_1_x, the exp instruction takes multiple clock cycles and will need around 41 instruction slots to execute versus five slots on vs_2_0 and vs_3_0.

ret exp2(x)

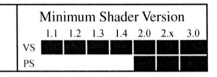

	Minimum Shader Version						
	1.1	1.2	1.3	1.4	2.0	2.x	3.0
VS							
PS							

Parameters

Name	In/Out	Template Type	Component Type	Size
x	in	scalar, vector or matrix	float	any
ret	out	same as input x	float	same as input x

Description

This function returns base-2 exponential of the input value x. For example, the following code

```
float4 main(float4 inPos:POSITION) : POSITION
{
   return exp2(float4(-1.0, 0, 0.5, 2.0));
}
```

will yield the following result: 0.5, 1, 1.41421354, 4

Special Considerations

The shader hardware supports a base-2 by using the *exp* instruction; however, the *exp* instruction can only perform an exponential on a single component, requiring multiple executions to process complex types such as vectors and matrices. For example, the following code

```
float4 main(float4 inPos:POSITION) : POSITION
{
   return exp2(inPos);
}
```

will generate the following assembly code under *vs_1_1*:

```
exp oPos.x, v0.x
exp oPos.y, v0.y
exp oPos.z, v0.z
exp oPos.w, v0.w
```

Keep in mind that under *vs_1_x*, the exp instruction takes multiple clock cycles and will require approximately 40 instruction slots to execute versus four slots on *vs_2_0* and *vs_3_0*.

ret faceforward(n, i, ng)

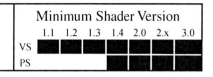

Parameters

Name	In/Out	Template Type	Component Type	Size
n	in	vector	float	any
i	in	vector	float	same as input n
ng	in	vector	float	same as input n
ret	out	vector	float	same as input n

Description

This function tests whether a face is visible. This is accomplished by using the following equation:

```
ret = -n * sign( dot( i, ng ) );
```

Special Considerations

This function does not native hardware support, however it can easily be implemented with the above equation. For example, the following code:

```
float4 main(float4 inPos:POSITION,
            float3 inVector:TEXCOORD0,
            float3 inVector2:TEXCOORD1,
            float3 inVector3:TEXCOORD2) : POSITION
{
   return float4( faceforward(inVector3, inVector2, inVector), 1);
}
```

will produce the following six instructions

```
def c0, 0, -2, 1, 0
mov r0.xyz, v1
dp3 r0.x, r0, v0
sge r0.w, r0.x, c0.x
mul r0.xyz, r0.w, v2
mad oPos.xyz, r0, c0.y, v2
mov oPos.w, c0.z
```

ret floor(x)

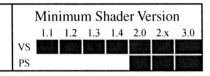

Name	In/Out	Template Type	Component Type	Size
x	in	scalar, vector or matrix	float	any
ret	out	same as input *x*	float	same as input *x*

Description

This function returns the largest integer lesser than input x. This function will operate per-component on vector and matrix inputs. For example, the following code

```
float4 main(float4 inPos:POSITION) : POSITION
{
   return floor(float4(1.0, -1.1, 2.2, 10.001));
}
```

will yield the following result: 1, -2, 2, 10

Special Considerations

The `floor` function does not have direct native hardware support. The task, however, can easily be accomplished by taking the fractional part of the input using the `frc` instruction and subtracting it from the initial input. For example, the following code

```
float4 main(float4 inPos:POSITION) : POSITION
{
   return floor(inPos);
}
```

will generate the following shader assembly under `vs_2_0`:

```
frc r0, v0
add oPos, -r0, v0
```

Under `vs_1_1`, because of instruction scheduling considerations and limitations on the `frc` instruction, the code will generally take four instructions and give the following

```
frc r1.xy, v0.zwzw
mov r0.zw, r1.xyxy
frc r0.xy, v0
add oPos, -r0, v0
```

ret fmod(x,y)

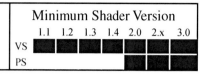

Name	In/Out	Template Type	Component Type	Size
x	in	scalar, vector or matrix	float, int	any
y	in	same as input x	same as input x	same as input x
ret	out	same as input x	same as input x	same as input x

Parameters

Description

This function returns the floating-point reminder f of x/y. This equivalent to saying that $x=i*y+f$, where i is an integer, f has the same sign as x and the absolute value of f is less than the absolute value of y. This function will also operate per-component on inputs of type vector and matrix. For example, the following code

```
float4 main(float4 inPos:POSITION) : POSITION
{
   return fmod( float4(1.0, -1.1, 2.2, 10.00),
                float4(0.5, 10.0, -0.2, 1.1));
}
```

will yield the following result: `-1.10000002, 5.55111512e-017, 0.100000001`

Special Considerations

This function has no direct hardware support and must be emulated through a complex set of operations mimicking the equation above. For example, the following code

```
float4 main(float4 inPos:POSITION,
            float3 inVector:TEXCOORD0,
            float3 inVector2:TEXCOORD1) : POSITION
{
   return float4(fmod(inVector2, inVector),1);
}
```

will yield the following 15 instructions under `vs_1_1`:

```
def c0, 1, 0, 0, 0
rcp r0.x, v0.x
rcp r0.y, v0.y
rcp r0.z, v0.z
mul r0.xyz, r0, v1
max r1.xyz, -r0, r0
```

```
expp r3.y, r1.z
mov r2.z, r3.y
frc r2.xy, r1
sge r0.xyz, r0, -r0
add r1.xyz, r2, r2
mad r0.xyz, r0, r1, -r2
mul oPos.xyz, r0, v0
mov oPos.w, c0.x
```

On 2.0 and 3.0 hardware, the compiler can take advantage of a few special instructions such as lrp to reduce the instruction count to 11, yielding the following:

```
def c0, 1, 0, 0, 0
rcp r0.x, v0.x
rcp r0.y, v0.y
rcp r0.z, v0.z
mul r1.xyz, r0, v1
abs r0.xyz, r1
sge r1.xyz, r1, -r1
frc r2.xyz, r0
lrp r0.xyz, r1, r2, -r2
mul oPos.xyz, r0, v0
mov oPos.w, c0.x
```

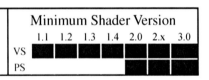

ret frac(x)

	Minimum Shader Version
	1.1 1.2 1.3 1.4 2.0 2.x 3.0
VS	
PS	

Parameters

Name	In/Out	Template Type	Component Type	Size
x	in	scalar, vector or matrix	float	any
ret	out	same as input x	float	same as input x

Description

This function returns the fractional part of the input x such that the result will be between zero and one. This function will operate per-component on inputs of type vector and matrix. For example, the following code

```
float4 main(float4 inPos:POSITION) : POSITION
{
    return frac(float4(1.0, 2.2, 0.76, 10.01));
}
```

will yield the following result: 0, 0.200000003, 0.75999999, 0.00999999978

Special Considerations

This operation is directly supported on the hardware and can be implemented using the `frc` instruction. Under 1.x vertex shaders, the `frc` instruction can only operate on two components at the time and takes more than a single cycle to execute. For example, the following code

```
float4 main(float4 inPos:POSITION) : POSITION
{
   return frac(inPos);
}
```

will yield the following under `vs_1_1`:

```
frc r0.xy, v0.zwzw
mov oPos.zw, r0.xyxy
frc oPos.xy, v0
```

ret frexp(x, out exp)

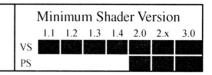

Minimum Shader Version

	1.1	1.2	1.3	1.4	2.0	2.x	3.0
VS							
PS							

Parameters

Name	In/Out	Template Type	Component Type	Size
x	in	scalar, vector or matrix	float	any
exp	out	same as input *x*	float	same as input *x*
ret	out	same as input *x*	float	same as input *x*

Description

This function takes input *x* and separates into mantissa and exponent components. The return value to the function will contain the mantissa where as the `exp` parameter will be filled with the exponent part. If the input is zero, both the mantissa and exponents will be filled with zero. This function is mostly useful to take a high precision floating-point value and decompose it into smaller, more manageable components. For example, the following code

```
float4 main(float4 inPos:POSITION) : POSITION
{
   float4 expret;
   float4 mantissa = frexp(float4(1.0, 2.2, 0.76, 10.01), expret);
   return expret*inPos + mantissa;
}
```

will yield the following result:

```
ret = 0, 2, 4, 0
exp = 1, 0.550000012, 0.75999999, 0.625625014
```

Special Considerations

This function is not natively supported on the hardware and must be emulated through a sequence of *exp*, *log* and *rcp* instructions. For example, the following code

```
float4 main(float4 inPos:POSITION,
            float4 inCol:COLOR0) : POSITION
{
  float4 expret;
  float4 mantissa = frexp(inCol, expret);
  return expret*inPos + mantissa;
}
```

will yield the following instructions:

```
max r1, v1, -v1
sge r0, -r1, r1
add r0, r1, r0
log r0.x, r0.x
log r0.y, r0.y
log r0.z, r0.z
log r0.w, r0.w
frc r2.xy, -r0.zwzw
mov r1.zw, r2.xyxy
frc r1.xy, -r0
add r0, r0, r1
exp r1.x, r0.x
exp r1.y, r0.y
exp r1.z, r0.z
exp r1.w, r0.w
rcp r1.x, r1.x
rcp r1.y, r1.y
rcp r1.z, r1.z
rcp r1.w, r1.w
mul r1, r1, v1
mad oPos, r0, v0, r1
```

Keep in mind that the *exp* instruction is slow on the *vs_1_x* shader model causing stalls. This means that this function will execute in 97 instructions slots on *vs_1_1* hardware versus 19 on *vs_2_0* hardware.

ret fwidth(x)	Minimum Shader Version

	1.1	1.2	1.3	1.4	2.0	2.x	3.0
VS							
PS						■	■

Parameters

Name	In/Out	Template Type	Component Type	Size
x	in	scalar, vector or matrix	float	any
ret	out	same as input *x*	float	same as input *x*

Description

This function is intended as a macro function to compute the value of the partial derivate of the input *x*. This function essentially computes `ret = abs(ddx(x)) + abs(ddy(x))`.

Special Considerations

See the `ddx` and `ddy` functions for information on special considerations related to this function.

ret isfinite(x)	Minimum Shader Version

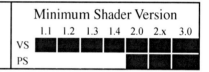

	1.1	1.2	1.3	1.4	2.0	2.x	3.0
VS	■	■	■	■			
PS					■	■	■

Parameters

Name	In/Out	Template Type	Component Type	Size
x	in	scalar, vector or matrix	float	any
ret	out	scalar	bool	1

Description

This function will return *true* if the input *x* is finite, *false* otherwise. This function can be used to verify the validity of some math operations such as the case of a division by zero.

Special Considerations

Although this function is not natively supported on shader hardware, it can easily be evaluated in a few instructions. For example, the following code

```
float4 main(float4 inPos:POSITION) : POSITION
{
   return isfinite(inPos);
}
```

will yield the following three instructions under `vs_1_1`:

```
add r0, -v0, v0
mul r0, r0, r0
sge oPos, -r0, r0
```

ret isinf(x)

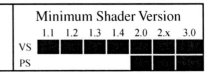

Minimum Shader Version

Parameters

Name	In/Out	Template Type	Component Type	Size
x	in	scalar, vector or matrix	float	any
ret	out	scalar	bool	1

Description

This function will return *true* if the input *x* is not finite, *false* otherwise. This function is essentially the negated version of the *isfinite* function.

Special Considerations

See the *isfinite* function.

ret isnan(x)

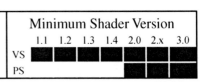

Minimum Shader Version

Parameters

Name	In/Out	Template Type	Component Type	Size
x	in	scalar, vector or matrix	float	any
ret	out	scalar	bool	1

Description

This function will return *true* if the input *x* is either *NAN* or *QNAN*, *false* otherwise. This function can be used to verify the validity of some math operations such as a division by zero.

Special Considerations

Although this function is not natively supported on shader hardware, it can easily be evaluated in a few instructions. For example, the following code

```
float4 main(float4 inPos:POSITION) : POSITION
{
  return isnan(inPos);
}
```

will yield the following three instructions under *vs_1_1*:

```
mul r0, v0, v0
sge r0, r0, -r0
sge oPos, -r0, r0
```

ret ldexp(x, exp)

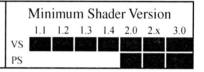

	Minimum Shader Version						
	1.1	1.2	1.3	1.4	2.0	2.x	3.0
VS	■	■	■	■	■	■	■
PS					■	■	■

Parameters

Name	In/Out	Template Type	Component Type	Size
x	in	scalar, vector or matrix	float	any
exp	in	scalar, vector or matrix	float	any
ret	out	same as input *x*	float	same as input *x*

Description

This function in essence does the reverse operation of *frexp* and will return $x*2^{exp}$. The function will also operate per-component on vector and matrix inputs. For example, the following code

```
float4 main(float4 inPos:POSITION) : POSITION
{
  float4 expret = ;
  float4 x = 0, 2, 4, 0
  float4 exp = 1, 0.550000012, 0.75999999, 0.625625014
  return frexp(x, exp);
  return expret*inPos + mantissa;
}
```

will yield the following result: ret = 1.0, 2.2, 0.76, 10.01

Special Considerations

The shader hardware does not have native support for this instruction but can easily be computed with the *exp* instruction. For example, the following code:

```
float4 main(float4 inPos:POSITION,
            float3 inVector:TEXCOORD0,
            float3 inVector2:TEXCOORD1) : POSITION
{
   return float4(ldexp(inVector2, inVector),1);
}
```

will yield the following under *vs_1_1*:

```
exp r0.x, v0.x
exp r0.y, v0.y
exp r0.z, v0.z
mul oPos.xyz, r0, v1
```

Take note that on *vs_1_x* hardware, because of the cost involved with the *exp* instruction, the code will execute in 31 instruction slots versus four on *vs_2_x* hardware and above.

ret length(x)

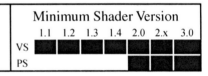

Name	In/Out	Template Type	Component Type	Size
x	in	vector	float	any
ret	out	scalar	float	1

Parameters

Description

This function returns the length of the input vector *x*. The length of a vector is defined as the square root of the sum of the square of each component of the vector. In mathematical terms, this means: $length = sqrt(x.x * x.x + x.y*x.y \ldots)$.

Special Considerations

Although the *length* function does not have direct hardware support, it can easily be accomplished by using the *dp4*, *rsq* and *rcp* instructions. For example, the following code

```
float4 main(float4 inPos:POSITION) : POSITION
{
   return length(inPos);
}
```

will result in the following three instructions:

```
dp4 r0.w, v0, v0
rsq r0.w, r0.w
rcp oPos, r0.w
```

ret lerp(x, y, s)

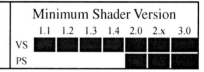

Minimum Shader Version

Parameters

Name	In/Out	Template Type	Component Type	Size
x	in	scalar, vector or matrix	float	any
y	in	scalar, vector or matrix	float	same as input x
s	in	scalar, vector or matrix	float	same as input x
ret	out	same as input x	same as input x	same as input x

Description

This function returns the linear interpolation between the inputs x and y with s being the interpolation factor in the range [0, 1]. The function will return $x+s*(y-x)$ such that the return value is x when s is zero and y when s is one.

Special Considerations

This function is not natively supported on 1.x shader hardware but can be easily implemented using the above equation. For example the following code:

```
float4 main(float4 inPos:POSITION,
            float4 inVector:TEXCOORD0,
            float4 inVector2:TEXCOORD1) : POSITION
{
   return lerp(inVector2, inVector, inPos.x);
}
```

will yield the following under `vs_1_1`:

```
mov r0, v1
```

```
add  r0,  r0,  -v2
mov  r1.w,  v0.x
mad  oPos,  r1.w,  r0,  v2
```

ret lit(n dot l, n dot h, m)

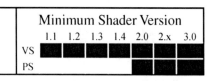

Parameters

Name	In/Out	Template Type	Component Type	Size
l	in	scalar	float	1
h	in	scalar	float	1
m	in	scalar	float	1
ret	out	vector	float	4

Description

This function serves as a macro to calculate a lighting vector containing the ambient, diffuse and specular lighting components from various inputs. The inputs to this function are defined as the dot product of the surface normal and light vector, the dot product of the half-vector and the surface normal and finally a specular lighting factor. The output of the function is defined as follows.

```
ambient = 1.
diffuse = ((n • l) < 0) ? 0 : n • l.
specular = ((n • l) < 0) || ((n • h) < 0) ? 0 : ((n • h) * m).
```

Special Considerations

This function is not natively supported on 1.x shader hardware but can be easily implemented using the above equation. For example the following code

```
float4 main(float4 inPos:POSITION,
            float4 inVector:TEXCOORD0,
            float4 inVector2:TEXCOORD1) : POSITION
{
   return lit(inVector2.x, inVector.x, inPos.x);
}
```

will yield the following under vs_1_1:

```
mov  r0.x, v2.x
mov  r0.y, v1.x
mov  r0.zw, v0.x
```

```
lit oPos, r0
slt r0.w, -v2.x, v2.x
mul o0.y, r0.w, v2.x
slt r0.z, -v1.x, v1.x
mul r0.w, r0.w, r0.z
mov r1.w, v1.x
pow r0.z, r1.w, v0.x
mul o0.z, r0.w, r0.z
mov o0.xw, c0.x
```

ret log(x)

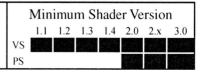

Name	In/Out	Template Type	Component Type	Size
x	in	scalar, vector or matrix	float	any
ret	out	same as input x	float	same as input x

Parameters

Description

This function returns the base-e logarithm of the input x. If the input value is negative, the result will be indefinite. If the input value is zero, the result will be *INF*. This function will operate per-component on vector and matrix inputs. For example, the following code

```
float4 main(float4 inPos:POSITION) : POSITION
{
   return log(float4(0.01, 0.5, 1.0, 2.0));
}
```

will yield the following result:

```
-4.60517025, -0.693147182, 0, 0.693147182
```

Special Considerations

This function is natively supported on shader hardware with the *log* instruction. This instruction, however, can only operate on a scalar value and is for base-2 calculations requiring a correction factor. For example, the following code

```
float4 main(float4 inPos:POSITION) : POSITION
{
   return log(inPos);
}
```

will give the following instructions:

```
def c0, 0.693147182, 0, 0, 0
log r0.x, v0.x
log r0.y, v0.y
log r0.z, v0.z
log r0.w, v0.w
mul oPos, r0, c0.x
```

One thing to note, as with the *exp* instruction, the *log* implementation is slow on 1.x shader hardware causing the above code to execute in 41 instruction slots compared to five slots on 2.0 and above hardware.

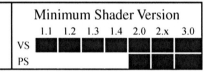

ret log2(x)

Name	In/Out	Template Type	Component Type	Size
x	in	scalar, vector or matrix	float	any
ret	out	same as input *x*	float	same as input *x*

Description

This function returns the base-2 logarithm of the input *x*. If the input value is negative, the result will be indefinite. If the input value is zero, the result will be *INF*. This function will operate per-component on vector and matrix inputs. For example, the following code

```
float4 main(float4 inPos:POSITION) : POSITION
{
   return log(float4(0.01, 0.5, 1.0, 2.0));
}
```

will yield the following result:

```
-6.64385605, -1, 0, 1
```

Special Considerations

This function is natively supported on shader hardware through the use of the *log* instruction; however, this instruction can only operate on a scalar value requiring multiple iterations. For example, the following code

```
float4 main(float4 inPos:POSITION) : POSITION
{
   return log2(inPos);
}
```

will give the following instructions:

```
log oPos.x, v0.x
log oPos.y, v0.y
log oPos.z, v0.z
log oPos.w, v0.w
```

Also note that as with the *exp* instruction, the *log* implementation is slow on 1.x shader hardware causing the above code to execute in 40 instruction slots compared to four instruction slots on 2.0 and above hardware.

ret log10(x)

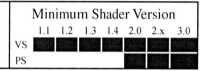

	Minimum Shader Version
	1.1 1.2 1.3 1.4 2.0 2.x 3.0

Parameters

Name	In/Out	Template Type	Component Type	Size
x	in	scalar, vector or matrix	float	any
ret	out	same as input x	float	same as input x

Description

This function returns the base-10 logarithm of the input x. If the input value is negative, the result will be indefinite. If the input value is zero, the result will be *INF*. This function will operate per-component on vector and matrix inputs. For example, the following code

```
float4 main(float4 inPos:POSITION) : POSITION
{
   return log(float4(0.01, 0.5, 1.0, 2.0));
}
```

will yield the following result: -2, -0.30103001, 0, 0.30103001

Special Considerations

This function is natively supported on shader hardware through the use of the *log* instruction. This instruction can only operate on a scalar value and is for base-2 calculations requiring a correction factor. For example, the following code

```
float4 main(float4 inPos:POSITION) : POSITION
{
   return log10(inPos);
}
```

will give the following instructions:

```
def c0, 0.30103001, 0, 0, 0
log r0.x, v0.x
log r0.y, v0.y
log r0.z, v0.z
log r0.w, v0.w
mul oPos, r0, c0.x
```

One thing to note, as with the *exp* instruction, its implementation is slow on 1.x shader hardware causing the above code to execute in 41 instruction slots compared to five 2.0 and above hardware.

ret max(x, y)

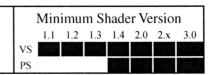

	Minimum Shader Version						
	1.1	1.2	1.3	1.4	2.0	2.x	3.0
VS	■	■	■	■	■	■	■
PS				■	■	■	■

Parameters

Name	In/Out	Template Type	Component Type	Size
x	in	scalar, vector or matrix	float, int	any
y	in	same as input x	same as input x	same as input x
ret	out	same as input x	same as input x	same as input x

Description

This function returns the maximum of both inputs x and y. This function will operate per-component for vector and matrix inputs.

Special Considerations

This function is supported natively on shader hardware.

ret min(x, y)

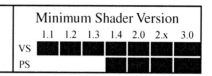

Parameters

Name	In/Out	Template Type	Component Type	Size
x	in	scalar, vector or matrix	float, int	any
y	in	same as input *x*	same as input *x*	same as input *x*
ret	out	same as input *x*	same as input *x*	same as input *x*

Description

This function returns the minimum of both inputs *x* and *y*. This function will operate per-component for vector and matrix inputs.

Special Considerations

This function is supported natively on shader hardware.

ret modf(x, out ip)

Parameters

Name	In/Out	Template Type	Component Type	Size
x	in	scalar, vector or matrix	float, int	any
ip	out	same as input *x*	same as input *x*	same as input *x*
ret	out	same as input *x*	same as input *x*	same as input *x*

Description

This function separates the input *x* into its fractional and integer part, each having the same sign as *x*. The return value to the function is the fractional part and the integer part is supplied in the `ip` output parameter. This function will operate per-component for vector and matrix inputs. For example, the following code

```
float4 main(float4 inPos:POSITION) : POSITION
{
  float4 ip;
  return log(float4(0.01, 0.5, 1.0, 2.0));
}
```

will yield the following results:

```
ret = 0.01, 0.5, 0.0, 0.0
ip = 0.0, 0.0, 1.0, 2.0
```

Special Considerations

This function is not directly supported on shader hardware but can easily be implemented by using the `frc` instruction. On 1.x shaders, the `frc` instruction can only operate on two scalar components at a time. For example, the following code

```
float4 main(float4 inPos:POSITION,
            float4 inCol:COLOR0) : POSITION
{
  float4 ipret;
  float4 fract = modf(inCol, ipret);
  return ipret*inPos + fract;
}
```

will yield the following 13 instructions on *vs_1_1*:

```
slt r0, v1, -v1
frc r3.xy, v1.zwzw
mov r1.zw, r3.xyxy
frc r1.xy, v1
add r2, -r1, v1
slt r1, -r1, r1
mad r0, r0, r1, r2
add r1, -r0, v1
mad oPos, r0, v0, r1
```

but will only result into seven instructions on *vs_2_0*:

```
slt r0, v1, -v1
frc r1, v1
add r2, -r1, v1
slt r1, -r1, r1
mad r0, r0, r1, r2
add r1, -r0, v1
mad oPos, r0, v0, r1
```

ret mul(x, y)

Minimum Shader Version						
	1.1	1.2	1.3	1.4	2.0	2.x	3.0
VS	■	■	■	■	■	■	■
PS	■	■	■	■	■	■	■

Parameters

Name	In/Out	Template Type	Component Type	Size
x	in	scalar	float, int	1
y	in	scalar	same as input x	1
ret	out	scalar	same as input x	1
x	in	scalar	float, int	1
y	in	vector	float, int	any
ret	out	vector	float, int	same as input y
x	in	scalar	float, int	1
y	in	matrix	float, int	any
ret	out	matrix	float, int	same as input y
x	in	vector	float, int	any
y	in	scalar	float, int	1
ret	out	vector	float, int	same as input x
x	in	vector	float, int	any
y	in	vector	float, int	same as input x
ret	out	scalar	float, int	1
x	in	vector	float, int	any
y	in	matrix	float, int	same as x rows
ret	out	vector	float, int	same as y columns
x	in	matrix	float, int	any
y	in	scalar	float, int	1
ret	out	matrix	float, int	same as input x
x	in	matrix	float, int	any
y	in	vector	float, int	same as x columns
ret	out	vector	float, int	same as x rows
x	in	matrix	float, int	any
y	in	matrix	float, int	rows = x columns, columns = x rows
ret	out	matrix	float, int	rows = x rows, columns = y columns

Description

As you can see from the above parameters, this function has nine overridden versions to suit different cases. This function will perform a matrix multiplication between the x and y inputs. If x is a vector, it is treated as a row vector. If y is a vector, it is treated as a column vector. The inner dimension x-columns and y-rows must be equal. The result has the dimension x-rows x y-columns.

Special Considerations

Although matrix multiplications are not directly supported on the shader hardware, they can easily be implemented with the *dp4* and *mad* instructions. For example, the following code

```
float4 main(float4 inPos:POSITION,
            float3 inVector:TEXCOORD0,
            float3 inVector2:TEXCOORD1) : POSITION
{
   return mul(inVector2, inVector);
}
```

will give the following under *vs_1_1*:

```
mov r0.xyz, v1
dp3 oPos, r0, v0
```

The following code

```
float4 main(float4 inPos:POSITION,
            float3 inVector:TEXCOORD0,
            float3 inVector2:TEXCOORD1,
            float3 inVector3:TEXCOORD2,
            float3 inVector4:TEXCOORD3,
            float3 inVector5:TEXCOORD4,
            float3 inVector6:TEXCOORD5,
             ) : POSITION
{
   float3x3 m1 = {inVector, InVector2, inVector3};
   float3x3 m2 = {inVector4, inVector5, inVector6};
   return mul(m1, m2);
}
```

will give the following instructions:

```
mov r0.xyz, v0
mul r1.xyz, r0.y, v3
mov r0.w, v3.x
mul r1.w, r0.w, v1.y
mad r1.xyz, r0.x, v2, r1
mov r0.w, v2.x
mad r1.w, v1.x, r0.w, r1.w
mad oPos.xyz, r0.z, v4, r1
mov r0.w, v4.x
mad oPos.w, v1.z, r0.w, r1.w
```

ret noise(x)	Minimum Shader Version

	1.1 1.2 1.3 1.4 2.0 2.x 3.0
VS	
PS	

Parameters

Name	In/Out	Template Type	Component Type	Size
x	in	vector	float	any
ret	out	scalar	float	1

Description

This function generates Perlin noise values based on the input vector *x*. The values produced by this function change smoothly as you move from one point to another over a space, which means you can use a texture coordinate or another special value to generate random noise.

Special Considerations

Take note that this function will only operate for texture shaders. Texture shaders are a special type of shader used within DirectX to procedurally create textures without having to fill in pixels manually. For more information on texture shaders, please refer to your DirectX SDK documentation.

ret normalize(x)	Minimum Shader Version

	1.1 1.2 1.3 1.4 2.0 2.x 3.0
VS	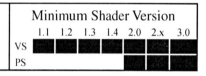
PS	

Parameters

Name	In/Out	Template Type	Component Type	Size
x	in	vector	float	any
ret	out	same as input *x*	float	same as input *x*

Description

This function takes the input vector *x* and returns a normalized version of the input. The process for normalizing a vector is $ret = {}^x/_{length(x)}$. For example, the following code

```
float4 main(float4 inPos:POSITION) : POSITION
{
  return normalize(float4(0.5,1.0,2.0,0.1));
}
```

will yield the following result: 0.218010366, 0.436020732, 0.872041464, 0.0436020717

Special Considerations

The *normalize* function is not directly supported on the shader hardware but can easily be accomplished in a similar way to the *length* function by using the *dp4* and *rsq* instruction. For example, the following code

```
float4 main(float4 inPos:POSITION) : POSITION
{
   return normalize(inPos);
}
```

will yield the following three instructions:

```
dp4 r0.w, v0, v0
rsq r0.w, r0.w
mul oPos, r0.w, v0
```

ret pow(x, y)

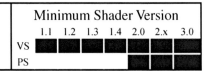

Minimum Shader Version

	1.1	1.2	1.3	1.4	2.0	2.x	3.0
VS	■	■	■	■	■	■	■
PS					■	■	■

Parameters

Name	In/Out	Template Type	Component Type	Size
x	in	scalar, vector or matrix	float	any
y	in	same as input *x*	float	same as input *x*
ret	out	same as input *x*	float	same as input *x*

Description

This function returns the value of *x* to the power of *y*. This function will operate per-component for vector and matrix inputs. For example, the following code

```
float4 main(float4 inPos:POSITION) : POSITION
{
   return pow(float4(0.5,1.0,2.0,0.1),
            float4(0.5,1.0,2.0,3.0));
}
```

will give the following result: 0.707106769, 1, 4, 0.00100000005

Special Considerations

The *pow* function is not directly supported on shader hardware and is implemented through the use of the *log* and *exp* instructions. For example, the following code

```
float4 main(float4 inPos:POSITION,
             float4 inVector:TEXCOORD0,
             float4 inVector2:TEXCOORD1) : POSITION
{
   return pow(inVector2, inVector);
}
```

will generate the following instructions:

```
log r0.x, v1.x
log r0.y, v1.y
log r0.z, v1.z
log r0.w, v1.w
mul r0, r0, v0
exp oPos.x, r0.x
exp oPos.y, r0.y
exp oPos.z, r0.z
exp oPos.w, r0.w
```

Because of the performance restriction of the *log* and *exp* instructions under *vs_1_x*, this code will execute in 81 instruction slots versus nine on *vs_2_0* hardware.

ret radians(x)

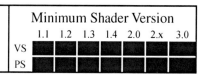

	Minimum Shader Version						
	1.1	1.2	1.3	1.4	2.0	2.x	3.0
VS							
PS							

Parameters

Name	In/Out	Template Type	Component Type	Size
x	in	scalar, vector or matrix	float	any
ret	out	same as input *x*	float	same as input *x*

Description

This function will convert the input *x* from degrees to radians. This is done by taking the input and multiplying it by a constant of $\pi/180$. For example, the following code

```
float4 main(float4 inPos:POSITION) : POSITION
{
    return radians(float4(0.0, 45.0, 60.0, 90.0));
}
```

will yield the following result:

```
0, 0.785398185, 1.04719758, 1.57079637
```

Special Considerations

There is no native support for this function, but, it can easily be computed in a single instruction with the `mul` instruction.

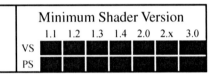

ret reflect(i, n)

			Minimum Shader Version					
			1.1	1.2	1.3	1.4	2.0	2.x	3.0

Parameters

Name	In/Out	Template Type	Component Type	Size
i	in	vector	float	any
n	out	vector	float	same as input x
ret	out	vector	float	same as input x

Description

This function will compute a reflected vector given the incident vector i and a reflection surface normal n. This is computed by using the following equation:

```
ret = i - 2 * dot( i, n) * n
```

Special Considerations

The calculation of a reflection is not directly supported on most shader hardware. The exception to this rule is under certain circumstances under the 1.x pixel shader model where a reflection calculation may get translated into the proper texture fetch operation. In most other circumstances, the function will get implemented through the above function. For example, the following code

```
float4 main(float4 inPos:POSITION,
            float4 inVector:TEXCOORD0,
            float4 inVector2:TEXCOORD1) : POSITION
{
   return reflect(inVector2, inVector);
}
```

will generate the following shader assembly instructions:

```
mov r0, v1
dp4 r1.w, r0, v0
add r1.w, r1.w, r1.w
mad oPos, v0, -r1.w, r0
```

ret refract(i, n, ri)

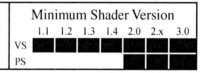

Parameters

Name	In/Out	Template Type	Component Type	Size
i	in	vector	float	any
n	out	vector	float	same as input x
ri	in	scalar	float	1
ret	out	vector	float	same as input x

Description

This function will compute a refracted vector given an incident vector i, a refraction surface normal n and a refraction index ri. The refraction is computed using Snell's law, and if the incident angle is too great for the given index of refraction the result will be (0,0,0).

Special Considerations

The calculation of refraction is not directly supported on most shader hardware. The function will get implemented through the above function. For example, the following code

```
float4 main(float4 inPos:POSITION,
            float4 inVector:TEXCOORD0,
            float4 inVector2:TEXCOORD1) : POSITION
{
   return refract(inVector2, inVector, inPos.x);
}
```

will generate the following shader assembly instructions:

```
mov r0, v2
dp4 r0.w, r0, v1
mul r1.w, v0.x, v0.x
mad r2.w, r0.w, -r0.w, c0.x
mad r2.w, r1.w, -r2.w, c0.x
sge r1.w, r2.w, c0.y
mul r2.w, r2.w, r1.w
rsq r2.w, r2.w
mul r1.w, r1.w, v0.x
rcp r2.w, r2.w
mad r0.w, r1.w, r0.w, r2.w
mul r0, r0.w, v1
mad oPos, r1.w, v2, -r0
```

ret round(x)

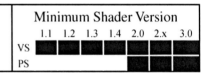

Parameters

Name	In/Out	Template Type	Component Type	Size
x	in	scalar, vector or matrix	float	any
ret	out	same as input x	float	same as input x

Description

This function rounds the input x to its nearest integer. This function will operate per-component on inputs of type vector or matrix. For example, the following code

```
float4 main(float4 inPos:POSITION) : POSITION
{
    return round(float4(1.1, 1.5, 1.6, 1.9));
}
```

will yield the following result: 1, 2, 2, 2

Special Considerations

There is no direct hardware support for this operation, but it can be achieved easily by taking the number, adding 0.5 to it and then removing its fractional component. Since this requires the use of the `frc` instruction, you will need to keep in mind that on 1.x shaders, this instruction can only operate on two scalars at a time. For example, the following code

```
float4 main(float4 inPos:POSITION) : POSITION
{
    return round(inPos);
}
```

will generate the following instructions under *vs_1_1*:

```
add r0, v0, c0.x
frc r2.xy, r0.zwzw
mov r1.zw, r2.xyxy
frc r1.xy, r0
add oPos, r0, -r1
```

ret rsqrt(x)

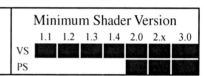

Parameters

Name	In/Out	Template Type	Component Type	Size
x	in	scalar, vector or matrix	float	any
ret	out	same as input x	float	same as input x

Description

This function returns the reciprocal square root of the input x, that is $ret = {}^1/sqrt(x)$. This function will operate per-component on inputs of type vector or matrix. For example, the following code

```
float4 main(float4 inPos:POSITION) : POSITION
{
    return rsqrt(float4(1.1, 1.5, 1.6, 1.9));
}
```

will yield the following result:

```
0.953462601, 0.816496611, 0.790569425, 0.725476265
```

Special Considerations

None of this function is supported on the shader hardware through the *rsq* instruction.

ret saturate(x)

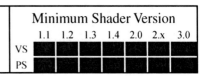

Minimum Shader Version

	1.1	1.2	1.3	1.4	2.0	2.x	3.0
VS							
PS							

Parameters

Name	In/Out	Template Type	Component Type	Size
x	in	scalar, vector or matrix	float	any
ret	out	same as input x	float	same as input x

Description

This function returns the absolute input x clamped to the range [0, 1]. This function will operate per-component for vertex and matrix inputs.

Special Considerations

Since this function is essentially a special case of the `clamp` function, you can see the special considerations there. Take note that some shader implementations allow you to apply a modifier to certain instructions to cause saturation.

ret sign(x)

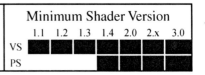

Minimum Shader Version

	1.1	1.2	1.3	1.4	2.0	2.x	3.0
VS							
PS							

Parameters

Name	In/Out	Template Type	Component Type	Size
x	in	scalar, vector or matrix	float, int	any
ret	out	same as input x	int	same as input x

Description

This function returns the sign of its inputs. The function will return -1 if the input is negative and 1 if the input is positive. This function will operate per-component for inputs of type vector and matrix.

Special Considerations

This function is not directly supported on the shader hardware. It can easily be implemented in a few instructions by using the `slt` comparison instruction. For example, the following code

```
float4 main(float4 inPos:POSITION) : POSITION
{
   return sign(inPos);
}
```

will yield the following three instructions:

```
slt r0, -v0, v0
slt r1, v0, -v0
add oPos, r0, -r1
```

		Minimum Shader Version

ret sin(x)

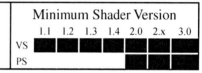

Parameters

Name	In/Out	Template Type	Component Type	Size
x	in	scalar, vector or matrix	float	any
ret	out	same as input x	float	same as input x

Description

This function returns the sine of x. It will operate per-component for vector and matrix inputs. For example, the following code

```
float4 main(float4 inPos:POSITION) : POSITION
{
   return sin(float4(-1.0,- 0.25, 0.5, 0.75));
}
```

will return the following: -0.841470957, -0.247403964, 0.47942555, 0.681638777

Special Considerations

There is no native support for this function and will generaly be evaluated using an approximation such as a Taylor series. For example, the following code

```
float4 main(float4 inPos:POSITION) : POSITION
{
   return sin(inPos);
}
```

will compile to the following 15 instructions under *vs_1_1*:

```
def c0, -0.5, 1, 0, 0
def c1, 0.159154937, 0.25, 6.28318548, -3.14159274
def c2, -2.52398507e-007, 2.47609005e-005, -0.00138883968, 0.0416666418
mad r1, v0, c1.x, c1.y
frc r2.xy, r1.zwzw
mov r0.zw, r2.xyxy
frc r0.xy, r1
mad r0, r0, c1.z, c1.w
mul r0, r0, r0
mad r1, r0, c2.x, c2.y
mad r1, r0, r1, c2.z
mad r1, r0, r1, c2.w
mad r1, r0, r1, c0.x
mad oPos, r0, r1, c0.y
```

ret sincos(x, out s, out c)

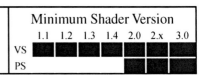

Parameters

Name	In/Out	Template Type	Component Type	Size
x	in	scalar, vector or matrix	float	any
s	out	same as input x	float	same as input x
c	out	same as input x	float	same as input x

Description

This function returns both the sine and cosine of x. The sine of the input will be store in the output parameter s and the cosine in the output parameter c. This function will operate per-component for vector and matrix inputs. For example, the following code

```
float4 main(float4 inPos:POSITION) : POSITION
{
  float4 s,c;
  sincos(float4(-1.0,- 0.25, 0.5, 0.75), s, c);
  return inPosition * s + c;
}
```

will return the following:

```
s = -0.841411114, -0.24740082, 0.47942552, 0.681638718
c = 0.540302336, 0.968912423, 0.87758255, 0.731688857
```

Special Considerations

This function is implemented using a Taylor series approximation. The following code

```
float4 main(float4 inPos:POSITION,
            float4 inTxr:TEXCOORD0) : POSITION
{
  float4 s,c;
  sincos(inTxr, s, c);
  return inPos * s + c;
}
```

will compile to the following 15 instructions under *vs_1_1*:

```
def c0, 0.0416666418, -0.5, 1, 0
def c1, 0.159154937, 0.25, 0.5, -0.00138883968
def c2, 6.28318548, -3.14159274, -2.52398507e-007, 2.47609005e-005
mad r1, v1, c1.x, c1.y
mad r2, v1, c1.x, c1.z
frc r4.xy, r1.zwzw
mov r0.zw, r4.xyxy
frc r0.xy, r1
frc r4.xy, r2.zwzw
mov r1.zw, r4.xyxy
frc r1.xy, r2
mad r0, r0, c2.x, c2.y
mad r1, r1, c2.x, c2.y
mul r0, r0, r0
mul r1, r1, r1
mad r3, r0, c2.z, c2.w
mad r2, r1, c2.z, c2.w
mad r3, r0, r3, c1.w
mad r2, r1, r2, c1.w
mad r3, r0, r3, c0.x
mad r2, r1, r2, c0.x
mad r3, r0, r3, c0.y
mad r2, r1, r2, c0.y
mad r0, r0, r3, c0.z
mad r1, r1, r2, c0.z
mad oPos, v0, r0, r1
```

ret sinh(x)

	Minimum Shader Version
	1.1 1.2 1.3 1.4 2.0 2.x 3.0
VS	
PS	

Parameters

Name	In/Out	Template Type	Component Type	Size
x	in	scalar, vector or matrix	float	any
ret	out	same as input *x*	float	same as input *x*

Description

This function returns the hyperbolic sine of *x*. It will operate per-component for vector and matrix inputs. For example, the following code

```
float4 main(float4 inPos:POSITION) : POSITION
{
    return sinh(float4(-1.0,- 0.25, 0.5, 0.75));
}
```

will return the following: 1.54308069, 1.03141308, 1.12762594, 1.29468334

Special Considerations

The `sinh` function does not have native support on current shader hardware. The compiler will emulate the functionality through the use of a numerical estimation. For example, the following code

```
float4 main(float4 inPos:POSITION) : POSITION
{
    return sinh(inPos);
}
```

will compile to the following under *vs_1_1*:

```
def c0, 1.44269502, 0.5, 0, 0
mul r1, v0, c0.x
exp r0.x, r1.x
exp r0.y, r1.y
exp r0.z, r1.z
exp r0.w, r1.w
exp r1.x, -r1.x
exp r1.y, -r1.y
exp r1.z, -r1.z
exp r1.w, -r1.w
```

```
add r0, r0, r1
mul oPos, r0, c0.y
```

The *exp* instruction is more expensive on *vs_1_x* and will cause stalls, generally leading to an execution of about 83 instruction slots versus 11 instruction slots on *vs_2_x* and *vs_3_x* hardware.

ret smoothstep (min, max, x)

Parameters

Name	In/Out	Template Type	Component Type	Size
x	in	scalar, vector or matrix	float	any
min	in	same as input *x*	float	same as input *x*
max	in	same as input *x*	float	same as input *x*
ret	out	same as input *x*	float	same as input *x*

Description

This function returns a smooth Hermite interpolation between 0 and 1 if the input *x* is in the range of [*min*, *max*]. Thefunction will return 0 if *(x < min)* and 1 if *(x > max)*. This function will also operate per-component on inputs of type vector or matrix. For example, the following code

```
float4 main(float4 inPos:POSITION) : POSITION
{
  return smoothstep(float4(0.2, -0.1, 2.2, 0.75),
                    float4(1.0, 0.0, 4.0, 1.0),
                    float4(0.5, -0.2, 3.5, 1.0));
}
```

will give the following result: 0.31640625, 0, 0.811385453, 1

Special Considerations

Hermite spline interpolation is not directly supported on shader hardware and must be fully implemented by the hardware with the Hermite equations.

Because of the complexity of this functionality, you have to be aware of its performance implications. For example, the following code

```
float4 main(float4 inPos:POSITION,
            float4 inTxr1:TEXCOORD0,
            float4 inTxr2:TEXCOORD1) : POSITION
{
   return smoothstep(inPos, inTxr1, inTxr2);
}
```

will yield the following instructions under *vs_1_1*:

```
mov r0, v1
add r0, r0, -v0
rcp r1.x, r0.x
rcp r1.y, r0.y
rcp r1.z, r0.z
rcp r1.w, r0.w
mov r0, v2
add r0, r0, -v0
mul r0, r1, r0
max r0, r0, c0.x
min r1, r0, c0.y
mad r0, r1, c0.z, c0.w
mul r1, r1, r1
mul oPos, r0, r1
```

ret sqrt(x)

Minimum Shader Version
1.1 1.2 1.3 1.4 2.0 2.x 3.0

Parameters

Name	In/Out	Template Type	Component Type	Size
x	in	scalar, vector or matrix	float	any
ret	out	same as input *x*	float	same as input *x*

Description

This function returns the square root of its input *x*. This function will operate per-component on inputs of type vector and matrix. For example, the following code

```
float4 main(float4 inPos:POSITION) : POSITION
{
   return sqrt(float4(1.1, 1.5, 1.6, 1.9));
}
```

will yield the following result: 1.04880881, 1.22474492, 1.26491106, 1.37840486

Special Considerations

Although this function is not directly supported on shader hardware, it can easily be implemented through the use of a reciprocal square root (rsq) and a reciprocal (rcp).

ret step(y, x)

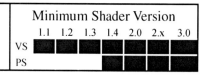

	Minimum Shader Version						
	1.1	1.2	1.3	1.4	2.0	2.x	3.0

Parameters

Name	In/Out	Template Type	Component Type	Size
x	in	scalar, vector or matrix	float	any
y	in	same as input x	float	same as input x
ret	out	same as input x	float	same as input x

Description

This function returns $(x>=y)?1:0$. It will operate per-component on inputs of type vector or matrix.

Special Considerations

This function is supported on the shader hardware through the use of the sge instruction.

ret tan(x)

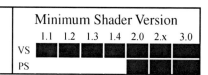

	Minimum Shader Version						
	1.1	1.2	1.3	1.4	2.0	2.x	3.0

Parameters

Name	In/Out	Template Type	Component Type	Size
x	in	scalar, vector or matrix	float	any
ret	out	same as input x	float	same as input x

Description

This function returns the tangent of x. It will operate per-component for vector and matrix inputs. For example, the following code

```
float4 main(float4 inPos:POSITION) : POSITION
{
   return tan(float4(-1.0,- 0.25, 0.5, 0.75));
}
```

will return the following: -1.55740774, -0.255341917, 0.546302497, 0.931596458

Special Considerations

Tangents aren't directly supported on shader hardware and must be emulated by using Taylor series. For example, the following code

```
float4 main(float4 inPos:POSITION) : POSITION
{
   return tan(inPos);
}
```

will compile to the following 35 instructions under *vs_1_1*:

```
mad r1, v0, c1.x, c1.z
frc r4.xy, r1.zwzw
mov r0.zw, r4.xyxy
frc r0.xy, r1
mad r2, v0, c1.x, c1.y
mad r1, r0, c2.x, c2.y
frc r4.xy, r2.zwzw
mov r0.zw, r4.xyxy
frc r0.xy, r2
mul r1, r1, r1
mad r0, r0, c2.x, c2.y
mad r2, r1, c2.z, c2.w
mul r0, r0, r0
mad r3, r1, r2, c1.w
mad r2, r0, c2.z, c2.w
mad r3, r1, r3, c0.x
mad r2, r0, r2, c1.w
mad r3, r1, r3, c0.y
mad r2, r0, r2, c0.x
mad r1, r1, r3, c0.z
mad r2, r0, r2, c0.y
rcp r1.x, r1.x
rcp r1.y, r1.y
rcp r1.z, r1.z
rcp r1.w, r1.w
mad r0, r0, r2, c0.z
mul oPos, r1, r0
```

Note that the same code will only use 23 instruction slots on 2.x and 3.x shaders.

ret tanh(x)

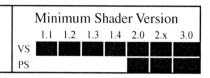

Minimum Shader Version

Parameters

Name	In/Out	Template Type	Component Type	Size
x	in	scalar, vector or matrix	float	any
ret	out	same as input x	float	same as input x

Description

This function returns the hyperbolic tangent of x. It will operate per-component for vector and matrix inputs. For example, the following code

```
float4 main(float4 inPos:POSITION) : POSITION
{
    return tanh(float4(-1.0,- 0.25, 0.5, 0.75));
}
```

will return the following: -0.761594176, -0.244918659, 0.462117165, 0.635148942

Special Considerations

Tangents aren't directly supported on shader hardware and must be emulated through the use of Taylor series. For example, the following code

```
float4 main(float4 inPos:POSITION) : POSITION
{
    return tanh(inPos);
}
```

will compile to the following 88 instructions under `vs_1_1`:

```
def c0, 1.44269502, 0, 0, 0
mul r1, v0, c0.x
exp r0.x, r1.x
exp r0.y, r1.y
exp r0.z, r1.z
exp r0.w, r1.w
exp r2.x, -r1.x
exp r2.y, -r1.y
exp r2.z, -r1.z
exp r2.w, -r1.w
add r1, r0, r2
add r0, r0, -r2
rcp r1.x, r1.x
```

```
rcp r1.y, r1.y
rcp r1.z, r1.z
rcp r1.w, r1.w
mul oPos, r0, r1
```

Because of the cost of the *frc* instruction on 1.x shaders, the same code will only use 16 instruction slots on 2.x and 3.x shaders.

ret transpose(x)

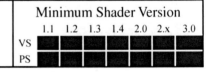

	Minimum Shader Version						
	1.1	1.2	1.3	1.4	2.0	2.x	3.0
VS							
PS							

Parameters

Name	In/Out	Template Type	Component Type	Size
x	in	matrix	float, int, bool	any
ret	out	matrix	float, int, bool	rows = x columns, columns = x rows

Description

This function returns the transpose of the input matrix x.

Special Considerations

This function is not directly supported on shader hardware but can easily be accomplished through a sequence of *mov* instructions to copy the data where needed. In addition, the compiler can pre-transpose the data into constant registers as needed.

Texture Access

There are several flavors of texture access functions serving different purposes. Each of theses flavors exists for several types of textures. For the following sections, I will cover all varieties of texture access functions, and they will be presented in the form *texXX*, where *XX* can be one of the following:

- **1D**: Texture access to a 1-D texture. The input texture coordinates will be a scalar.
- **2D**: Texture access to a 2-D texture. The input texture coordinates will be a two entry vector.
- **3D**: Texture access to a 3-D texture, also known as a volume texture. The input texture coordinates will be a three entry vector.
- **CUBE**: Texture access to a cubemap texture. The input texture coordinate will be a three entry vector.

ret texXX(s,t)	Minimum Shader Version

	1.1	1.2	1.3	1.4	2.0	2.x	3.0
VS							
PS	■	■	■	■	■	■	■

Parameters

Name	In/Out	Template Type	Component Type	Size
s	in	object	sampler	1
t	in	vector	float	depends on texture type
ret	out	vector	float	4

Description

This function performs a simple texture lookup.

Special Considerations

None.

ret texXX(s, t, ddx, ddy)

Minimum Shader Version

1.1   1.2   1.3   1.4   2.0   2.x   3.0

VS

PS

Parameters

Name	In/Out	Template Type	Component Type	Size
s	in	object	sampler	1
t	in	vector	float	depends on texture type
ddx	in	scalar	float	1
ddy	in	scalar	float	1
ret	out	vector	float	4

Description

This function performs a simple texture lookup but uses the partial derivates *ddx* and *ddy* to pick the proper texture mipmap.

Special Considerations

None.

ret texXXbias(s, t)

Minimum Shader Version

1.1   1.2   1.3   1.4   2.0   2.x   3.0

VS

PS

Parameters

Name	In/Out	Template Type	Component Type	Size
s	in	object	sampler	1
t	in	scalar, vector	float	depends on texture type
ret	out	vector	float	4

Description

This function performs a texture lookup where the *w* component is the texture mipmap bias.

Special Considerations

None.

ret texXXlod(s, t)

	Minimum Shader Version
	1.1 1.2 1.3 1.4 2.0 2.x 3.0
VS	
PS	

Parameters

Name	In/Out	Template Type	Component Type	Size
s	in	object	sampler	1
t	in	scalar, vector	float	depends on texture type
ret	out	vector	float	4

Description

This function performs a texture lookup where the *w* component texture mipmap bias.

Special Considerations

None.

ret texXXgrad (s, t, ddx, ddy)

	Minimum Shader Version
	1.1 1.2 1.3 1.4 2.0 2.x 3.0
VS	
PS	

Parameters

Name	In/Out	Template Type	Component Type	Size
s	in	object	sampler	1
t	in	vector	float	depends on texture type
ddx	in	scalar	float	1
ddy	in	scalar	float	1
ret	out	vector	float	4

Description

This function performs a simple texture lookup but uses the partial derivates `ddx` and `ddy` to pick the proper texture mipmap.

Special Considerations

N/A

ret texXXproj(s, t)

	Minimum Shader Version
	1.1 1.2 1.3 1.4 2.0 2.x 3.0
VS	
PS	

Parameters

Name	In/Out	Template Type	Component Type	Size
s	in	object	sampler	1
t	in	scalar, vector	float	depends on texture type
ret	out	vector	float	4

Description

This function performs a projective texture lookup. The texture component is divided by the *w* component before the texture is sampled.

Special Considerations

None.

Appendix C

Standard Semantics and Annotations

Semantics and annotations are the key to adding information to your effects and shaders so the application can have some understanding of the intent behind specific effect parameters. This happens because the use of a standardized set of annotations and semantics allows you to add additional usage information to a parameter for which the application can take advantage.

Keep in mind that the use of standard annotations and semantics is optional but serves to create a common language which can be used by varying applications to understand an effect in the same way. Because of this need, Microsoft has created a set of optional standard semantics and annotations, which can be attached to effect parameters. Any effect implementing these standard semantics and annotations can be read by any application that understands those annotations. In this chapter I will go over the standard semantics and annotations in a simple, reference style. For a more complete usage guide to semantics and annotations, please refer to Chapter 6.

Keep in mind that this reference is loosely inspired by the DirectX 9.0 documentation. For a more complete, up to date reference, I suggest reading the full reference included as part of the DirectX 9.0 SDK's documentation.

Standard Semantics

A standard semantic serves as a hint to an application describing the intended usage of a parameter within an effect file. Standardized semantics make it possible for an application to understand the intention behind an effect parameter and thus makes it possible for developers to create effect files understood by a wide range of applications.

The Table C-1 below goes over all the standard semantics used to augment effect parameters along with the type of data that should be associated with the semantic and its description.

Table C-1 Standard Semantics

Semantics	Type	Description
Ambient	float4	Ambient color.
Attenuation	float3/float4	Attenuation value, whose value can be one of the following: Distance(4 components), Spot(3 components), BoxX(3 components), BoxY(3 components).
BoundingBoxMax	float3	Bounding box maximum for x, y, z.
BoundingBoxMin	float3	Bounding box minimum for x, y, z.
BoundingBoxSize	float3	Bounding box size for x, y, z.
BoundingCenter	foat3	Bounding box center.
BoundingSphereSize	float1	Median bounding sphere radius.
BoundingSphereMin	float1	Minimum bounding sphere radius.
BoundingSphereMax	float1	Maximum bounding sphere radius.
Diffuse	float4	Diffuse color.
ElapsedTime	float1	Elapsed time.
Emissive	float4	Emissive color.
EnvironmentNormal	texture	Environment normal map.
Height	scalar/texture	Height value in a bump map.
Joint	float4	Object space to Frame-Joint space
JointWorld	float4×4	Joint world matrix.
JointWorldInverse	float4×4	Joint inverse world matrix.
JointWorldInverseTranspose	float4×4	Joint transposed, inverse world matrix.
JointWorldView	float4×4	Joint world-view matrix.
JointWorldViewInverse	float4×4	Joint inverse world-view matrix.
JointWorldViewInverseTranspose	float4×4	Joint transposed, inverse world-view matrix.
JointWorldViewProjection	float4×4	Joint world-view-projection matrix.
JointWorldViewProjectionInverse	float4×4	Joint inverse world-view-projection matrix.
JointWorldViewProjectionInverseTranspose	float4×4	Joint transposed, inverse world-view-projection matrix.

Table C-1 Standard Semantics

Semantics	Type	Description
LastTime	float1	Last simulation time.
Normal	float3/float4/ texture	Surface normal vector.
Opacity	float1/float2/ float3/float4/ texture	Object opacity.
Position	float4	XYZW position.
Projection	float4×4	Projection matrix.
ProjectionInverse	float4×4	Inverse projection matrix.
ProjectionInverseTranspose	float4×4	Transposed, inverse projection matrix.
Random	scalar	Random numbers.
Refraction	float1/float2/ float3/float4/ texture	Refraction value for an environment map.
RenderColorTarget	texture	Render target surface.
RenderDepthStencilTarget	texture	Depth/stencil surface.
RenderTargetClipping	float4	Clipping parameters which include: near distance, far distance, width angle (radians), and height angle(radians).
RenderTargetDimensions	float2	Render target width and height in pixels.
Specular	float4	Specular color.
SpecularPower	float1/float2/ float3/float4	Specular power exponent.
StandardsGlobal	float1	Standard annotation version number. Default value is 0.80.
TextureMatrix	float4×4	Texture coordinate transform matrix.
Time	float1	Simulation time.
UnitsScale	float1	Model scale value.
View	float4×4	View matrix.
ViewInverse	float4×4	Inverse view matrix.
ViewInverseTranspose	float4×4	Transposed, inverse view matrix.

Table C-1 Standard Semantics

Semantics	Type	Description
ViewProjection	float4×4	View-projection matrix.
ViewProjectionInverse	float4×4	Inverse view-projection matrix.
ViewProjectionInverseTranspose	float4×4	Transposed, inverse view-projection matrix.
World	float4×4	World matrix.
WorldInverse	float4×4	Inverse world matrix.
WorldInverseTranspose	float4×4	Transposed, inverse world matrix.
WorldView	float4×4	World-view matrix.
WorldViewInverse	float4×4	Inverse world-view matrix.
WorldViewInverseTranspose	float4×4	Transposed, inverse world-view matrix.
WorldViewProjection	float4×4	World-view-projection matrix.
WorldViewProjectionInverse	float4×4	Inverse world-view-projection matrix.
WorldViewProjectionInverseTranspose	float4×4	Transposed, inverse world-view-projection matrix.

Annotations

Annotations are metadata attached to a parameter that can be used by an effect to get additional information about a parameter's intended usage. One example being user-interface annotations that give the necessary information to applications so they can display an appropriate user interface to allow the interactive editing the effect parameter values.

Generic annotations give general information about the purpose of a parameter. A detailed list of the standard general annotations has been included in Table C-2.

Table C-2 Standard Generic Annotations

Name	Type	Description
Normalize	bool	The data in this parameter should be normalized.
Object	string	This annotation indicates the type of object contained by the parameter, which is one of the following values: Geometry, Camera, Frame, Light, RenderTarget.
Semantic	string	Reserved for future use.
SemanticType	string	If Semantic = RenderColorTarget, then this annotation is one of the following values: Color, Normal, Depth, Stencil. If Semantic = Attenuation, then this annotation is one of the following values: Distance, Spot, BoxX, BoxY.
Space	string	Coordinate space used.
Units	string	Unit scale for the parameter, which is one of the following values: Ms, sec, min, hour, Mm, cm, m, km, inch, feet, yard, mile, Rad, deg, RGB, HIS, YUV, IA, Quaternion.
Usage	string	Hint to the application as to what the parameter means.

Texture annotations give more information about the purpose of a texture parameter. A detailed list of the standard texture annotations has been included in Table C-3.

Table C-3 Standard Texture Annotations

Name	Type	Description
Dimensions	float1/ float2/ float3	Suggested dimension for a texture.
Discardable	bool	Indicates that the texture is discardable.
Format	string	Texture format. The valid values for this come from *D3DFORMAT*.
Function	string	Function name to be used to generate the texture. This is also for procedural generation of values for a variable.
MIPLevels	int	Number of mipmap levels requested. Specifying zero indicates to automatically generate miplevels.
ResourceName	string	Resource name for objects, such as a filename for a texture.
ResourceType	string	Texture resource type, which can be one of the following: 1D, 2D, 3D, cube.

Table C-3 Standard Texture Annotations

Name	Type	Description
TargetPS	string	Pixel shader compile target.
TargetVS	string	Vertex shader compile target.
ViewportRatio	float	Suggested ratio for a texture width and height as compared to a viewport width and height.

User-interface annotations give more information about how a parameter can be edited. A detailed list of the standard UI annotations has been included in Table C-4.

Table C-4 Standard User-Interface Annotations

Name	Type	Description
UIHelp	string	Help string to be displayed to the user.
UIMax	float	Maximum control value.
UIMin	float	Minimum control value.
UIName	string	Control name.
UIObject	object	Link to an object in an external application used to tell the application where to extract its data from.
UIStep	float	Incremental step value when incrementing or decrementing a parameter.
UIStepPower	float	Specular reflection power.
UIWidget	string	Usage type of a variable. This provides more specific usage information than the usage specified by a semantic and how the value should be edited. This value is a string value that can be, but is not limited to, one of the following values: Slider, Spinner, Color, Grayscale, Numeric, String, Texture, Direction, Object, None.

Scripting Annotations

To further extend the capabilities of annotations, a special set of scripting annotations were added to specify a list of render tasks for the application to perform. These annotation must be attached to a variable of StandardsGlobal semantics and will serve to control the global execution of an effect.

Annotation scripts are declared with the following syntax:

```
String scriptType = "[ScriptCommand]";
```

Where *scriptType* is one of the following:

- *ScriptExecute*: An entry point for scripts. It can only be placed on techniques and the parameter marked with the *StandardsGlobal* semantic superset of *ScriptFunction*.
- *ScriptFunction:* The script or partial script describing operation of this file.
- *ScriptSetup*: An entry-point script used for setup of existing state.

ScriptCommand is the actual script command to be executed. The script command follows the same syntax:

```
[ScriptCommand]   = [Command];
                    [Command]; [ScriptCommand]
                    [Command]=[Argument];
                    [Command]=[Argument]; [ScriptCommand]

[Command] = command (see the table of commands below)

[Argument] = [Value]
             [Value]![Hint]

[Value] = [Option:string]
          [Option: variable]

[Option:string] = string
                  string,[Option:string]

[Option: parameter] = parameter_name
                      parameter_name,[Option: parameter]

[Hint] = parameter_name
         string
```

where the following elements are:

- *Command*: One of the Script Commands.
- *Argument*: An argument.
- *Value*: A default value.
- *Hint*: A user supplied hint.

In addition, a period (.) can be used to reference a structure member, a pound sign (#) can be used to reference an array element and the "at" sign (@) is used to reference an annotation. The complete set of standard commands supported is listed below in Table C-5.

Table C-5 Standard User-Interface Annotations

Command	Description
ClearSetColor	Clears the render target to this color.
ClearSetDepth	Clears the render target depth buffer to this value.
ClearSetStencil	Clears the render target stencil buffer to this value.
Draw	Indicates what portion of a scene needs to be drawn **Scene**: draw all geometry. **Geometry**: draw inside of a geometry loop. **Buffer**: draw a full screen quad **Arbitrary**: string of draw instructions that a specialized program would understand.
GeometryList	Draw order hint, which can be one of the following: `ZFrontToBack`, `ZBackToFront`, `Scene`, `Arbitrary`.
Hint	Callback hint to the application.
LoopByType	Controls the draw loop when parameter changes are expected or multiple passes are required which can be one of the following. `Passes`(draw all passes), `Lights`(draw with each light enabled), `Geometry`(draw all geometry that uses a particular material), `RenderTargets`(draw all render targets), `Arbitrary`.
LoopByCount	Override `LoopByType`. `LoopByCount` must precede `LoopByType`.
LoopEnd	End of a loop.
LoopGetCount	Loop iteration count.
LoopGetIndex	Loop index count.
Pass	Pass name or number.
RenderColorTarget	Color render target, whose value is one of the following: `Texture` name, `Blank` to reset to default.
RenderDepthStencilTarget	Depth/stencil render target, whose value is one of the following: texture name, `Blank` to reset to default.
Technique	Technique name or number.

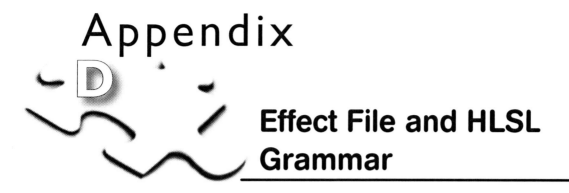

Appendix D

Effect File and HLSL Grammar

In the early chapters of this book, I discussed the details of the HLSL and Effect file grammar and syntax. In this Appendix, I've included a complete listing of the grammar used by DirectX to represent its HLSL and effect files.

Note that this grammar is taken as-is from the DirectX SDK documentation, and you should refer to it for more complete details.

Grammar and Syntax

```
Program :
Program : Decls

Decls : Decl
Decls : Decls Decl
Decl : ';'
Decl : TypeDecl
Decl : VariableDecl
Decl : VarStructDecl
Decl : FunctionDecl
Decl : TechniqueDecl

Usages : Usage
Usages : Usages Usage
Usage : T_KW_STATIC
Usage : T_KW_UNIFORM
Usage : T_KW_EXTERN
Usage : T_KW_VOLATILE
Usage : T_KW_INLINE
Usage : T_KW_SHARED
Usage : ConstUsage
Usage : Target

ConstUsages : ConstUsage
ConstUsages : ConstUsages ConstUsage
ConstUsage : T_KW_CONST
ConstUsage : T_KW_ROW_MAJOR
```

```
ConstUsage : T_KW_COLUMN_MAJOR

UsageType : Type
UsageType : Usages Type

UsageStructDecl : StructDecl
UsageStructDecl : Usages StructDecl

TypeDecl : T_KW_TYPEDEF ConstType TypeDefs ,;'
TypeDecl : T_KW_TYPEDEF ConstStructDecl TypeDefs ,;'
TypeDecl : StructDecl ,;'
TypeDefs : VariableDim
TypeDefs : VariableDim ,,' TypeDefs

Type : BaseType
Type : Struct
Type : TypeId
Type : T_KW_STRUCT TypeId

ConstType : Type
ConstType : ConstUsages Type
ConstTypeDim : ConstType
ConstTypeDim : ConstTypeDim '[' ConstantExpr ']'

BaseType : T_KW_VOID
BaseType : ScalarType
BaseType : VectorType
BaseType : MatrixType
BaseType : ObjectType

ScalarType : T_KW_BOOL
ScalarType : T_KW_INT
ScalarType : T_KW_HALF
ScalarType : T_KW_FLOAT
ScalarType : T_KW_DOUBLE

VectorType : T_KW_VECTOR
VectorType : T_KW_VECTOR '<' ScalarType ',' AddExpr '>'

MatrixType : T_KW_MATRIX
MatrixType : T_KW_MATRIX '<' ScalarType ',' ConstantExpr ',' AddExpr '>'

ObjectType : T_KW_STRING
ObjectType : T_KW_TEXTURE
ObjectType : T_KW_TEXTURE1D
ObjectType : T_KW_TEXTURE2D
ObjectType : T_KW_TEXTURE3D
ObjectType : T_KW_TEXTURECUBE
ObjectType : T_KW_SAMPLER
ObjectType : T_KW_SAMPLER1D
ObjectType : T_KW_SAMPLER2D
```

```
ObjectType : T_KW_SAMPLER3D
ObjectType : T_KW_SAMPLERCUBE
ObjectType : T_KW_PIXELSHADER
ObjectType : T_KW_VERTEXSHADER
ObjectType : T_KW_PIXELFRAGMENT
ObjectType : T_KW_VERTEXFRAGMENT
ObjectType : T_KW_STATEBLOCK

Struct : T_KW_STRUCT StructBegin StructEnd
Struct : T_KW_STRUCT StructBegin StructDecls StructEnd
StructDecl : T_KW_STRUCT Id StructBegin StructEnd
StructDecl : T_KW_STRUCT Id StructBegin StructDecls StructEnd

ConstStructDecl : StructDecl
ConstStructDecl : ConstUsages StructDecl

StructBegin : ,{,
StructDecls : VariableDecl
StructDecls : VariableDecl StructDecls
StructEnd : ,}'

Semantic : ,:' Id
Semantic : ,:' T_KW_REGISTER ,(, Register ,)'
Semantics : Semantic
Semantics : Semantics Semantic
SemanticsOpt :
SemanticsOpt : Semantics

Register : Id
Register : Target ,,' Id

Annotation : AnnotationBegin AnnotationEnd
Annotation : AnnotationBegin AnnotationDecls AnnotationEnd
AnnotationOpt :
AnnotationOpt : Annotation
AnnotationBegin : ,<'
AnnotationDecls : VariableDecl
AnnotationDecls : VariableDecl AnnotationDecls
AnnotationEnd : ,>'

Initializer : ,=' AssignmentExpr
Initializer : ,=' ,{, InitExprs ,}'
Initializer : ,=' ,{, InitExprs ,,' ,}'
InitializerOpt :
InitializerOpt : Initializer

VariableDecl : UsageType Variables ,;'
VarStructDecl : UsageStructDecl Variables ,;'
Variables : Variable
Variables : Variables ',' Variable
Variable : VariableDim SemanticsOpt AnnotationOpt InitializerOpt
```

```
VariableDim : Id
VariableDim : VariableDim '[' ']'
VariableDim : VariableDim '[' ConstantExpr ']'

FunctionDecl : FunctionDef ';'
FunctionDecl : FunctionDef AnnotationOpt StmtBlock
FunctionDef : UsageType Id ParamList SemanticsOpt

ParamList : ParamListBegin ParamListEnd
ParamList : ParamListBegin T_KW_VOID ParamListEnd
ParamList : ParamListBegin ParameterDecls ParamListEnd
ParamListBegin : '('
ParamListEnd : ')'

ParameterDecls : ParameterDecl
ParameterDecls : ParameterDecls ',' ParameterDecl
ParameterDecl : ParamUsageType Variable

ParamUsageType : Type
ParamUsageType : ParamUsages Type

ParamUsages : ParamUsage
ParamUsages : ParamUsages ParamUsage
ParamUsage : T_KW_IN
ParamUsage : T_KW_OUT
ParamUsage : T_KW_INOUT
ParamUsage : T_KW_UNIFORM
ParamUsage : ConstUsage

TechniqueDecl : T_KW_TECHNIQUE IdOpt AnnotationOpt TechniqueBody
TechniqueBody : TechniqueBegin TechniqueEnd
TechniqueBody : TechniqueBegin PassDecls TechniqueEnd
TechniqueBegin : '{'
TechniqueEnd : '}'

PassDecls : PassDecl
PassDecls : PassDecls PassDecl
PassDecl : T_KW_PASS IdOpt AnnotationOpt StateBlock

StateBlock : StateBlockBegin StateBlockEnd
StateBlock : StateBlockBegin States StateBlockEnd
StateBlockBegin : '{'
StateBlockEnd : '}'

States : State
States : States State
State : Id StateIndex StateExprBegin StateExpr StateExprEnd

StateIndex :
StateIndex : '[' Uint ']'
StateExprBegin : ,='
```

```
StateExprEnd : ,;'

StmtBlock : StmtBlockBegin StmtBlockEnd
StmtBlock : StmtBlockBegin Stmts StmtBlockEnd
StmtBlockBegin : '{'
StmtBlockEnd : '}'
Stmts : Stmt
Stmts : Stmts Stmt
SimpleStmt : ,;'
SimpleStmt : Expr ,;'
SimpleStmt : T_KW_RETURN ,;'
SimpleStmt : T_KW_RETURN Expr ,;'
SimpleStmt : T_KW_DO Stmt T_KW_WHILE ,(, Expr ,)' ,;'
SimpleStmt : StmtBlock
SimpleStmt : T_KW_DISCARD ,;'
SimpleStmt : TypeDecl
SimpleStmt : VariableDecl
SimpleStmt : VarStructDecl

NonIfStmt : SimpleStmt
NonIfStmt : T_KW_WHILE ,(, Expr ,)' NonIfStmt
NonIfStmt : For ,(, ForInit ForCond ForStep ,)' NonIfStmt

Stmt : SimpleStmt
Stmt : T_KW_WHILE ,(, Expr ,)' Stmt
Stmt : For ,(, ForInit ForCond ForStep ,)' Stmt
Stmt : T_KW_IF ,(, Expr ,)' Stmt
Stmt : T_KW_IF ,(, Expr ,)' NonIfStmt T_KW_ELSE Stmt

For : T_KW_FOR
ForInit : ,;'
ForInit : Expr ,;'
ForInit : VariableDecl
ForCond : ,;'
ForCond : Expr ,;'
ForStep :
ForStep : Expr

DwordExpr : Dword
DwordExpr : Dword ,|' DwordExpr

StateExpr : DwordExpr
StateExpr : ComplexExpr
StateExpr : ,{, InitExprs ,}'
StateExpr : ,{, InitExprs ,,' ,}'
StateExpr : ,<' RelationalExpr ,>'

SimpleExpr : T_KW_TRUE
SimpleExpr : T_KW_FALSE
SimpleExpr : Uint
SimpleExpr : Float
```

```
SimpleExpr : Strings
SimpleExpr : NonTypeId

ComplexExpr : ‚(‚ Expr ‚)‘
ComplexExpr : TypeId ‚(‚ ArgumentsOpt ‚)‘
ComplexExpr : BaseType ‚(‚ ArgumentsOpt ‚)‘
ComplexExpr : NonTypeId ‚(‚ ArgumentsOpt ‚)‘
ComplexExpr : ObjectExpr

ObjectExpr : AsmDecl
ObjectExpr : AsmDecl Asm
ObjectExpr : Asm
ObjectExpr : AsmFragment
ObjectExpr : T_KW_COMPILE Target NonTypeId ‘(‘ ArgumentsOpt ‘)’
ObjectExpr : T_KW_SAMPLER_STATE StateBlock
ObjectExpr : T_KW_COMPILE_FRAGMENT Target NonTypeId ‘(‘ ArgumentsOpt ‘)’
ObjectExpr : T_KW_STATEBLOCK_STATE StateBlock

PrimaryExpr : SimpleExpr
PrimaryExpr : ComplexExpr
PostfixExpr : PrimaryExpr
PostfixExpr : PostfixExpr ‘[‘ Expr ‘]’
PostfixExpr : PostfixExpr ‘.’ Id
PostfixExpr : PostfixExpr T_OP_INC
PostfixExpr : PostfixExpr T_OP_DEC

UnaryExpr : PostfixExpr
UnaryExpr : T_OP_INC UnaryExpr
UnaryExpr : T_OP_DEC UnaryExpr
UnaryExpr : ‘!’ CastExpr
UnaryExpr : ‘-’ CastExpr
UnaryExpr : ‘+’ CastExpr

CastExpr : UnaryExpr
CastExpr : ‘(‘ ConstTypeDim ‘)’ CastExpr

MulExpr : CastExpr
MulExpr : MulExpr ‘*’ CastExpr
MulExpr : MulExpr ‘/’ CastExpr
MulExpr : MulExpr ‘%’ CastExpr

AddExpr : MulExpr
AddExpr : AddExpr ‘+’ MulExpr
AddExpr : AddExpr ‘-’ MulExpr

RelationalExpr : AddExpr
RelationalExpr : RelationalExpr ‘<’ AddExpr
RelationalExpr : RelationalExpr ‘>’ AddExpr
RelationalExpr : RelationalExpr T_OP_LE AddExpr
RelationalExpr : RelationalExpr T_OP_GE AddExpr
```

```
EqualityExpr : RelationalExpr
EqualityExpr : EqualityExpr T_OP_EQ RelationalExpr
EqualityExpr : EqualityExpr T_OP_NE RelationalExpr

AndExpr : EqualityExpr
AndExpr : AndExpr T_OP_AND EqualityExpr
OrExpr : AndExpr
OrExpr : OrExpr T_OP_OR AndExpr
ConditionalExpr : OrExpr
ConditionalExpr : OrExpr '?' AssignmentExpr ':' ConditionalExpr

AssignmentExpr : ConditionalExpr
AssignmentExpr : CastExpr '=' AssignmentExpr
AssignmentExpr : CastExpr T_OP_ME AssignmentExpr
AssignmentExpr : CastExpr T_OP_DE AssignmentExpr
AssignmentExpr : CastExpr T_OP_RE AssignmentExpr
AssignmentExpr : CastExpr T_OP_AE AssignmentExpr
AssignmentExpr : CastExpr T_OP_SE AssignmentExpr

Arguments : AssignmentExpr
Arguments : Arguments ',' AssignmentExpr
ArgumentsOpt :
ArgumentsOpt : Arguments

InitExpr : AssignmentExpr
InitExpr : '{' InitExprs '}'
InitExpr : '{' InitExprs ',' '}'
InitExprs : InitExpr
InitExprs : InitExprs ',' InitExpr

ConstantExpr : AssignmentExpr
Expr : AssignmentExpr
Expr : Expr ',' AssignmentExpr

Dword : Uint
Dword : '-' Uint
Dword : Float
Dword : '-' Float
Dword : DwordId
Dword : Uint DwordId
DwordId : Id
DwordId : T_KW_TRUE
DwordId : T_KW_FALSE
DwordId : T_KW_TEXTURE

Id : TypeId
Id : NonTypeId
IdOpt :
IdOpt : Id

Target : NonTypeId
```

```
Uint : T_UINT
Uint : T_INT32
Uint : T_UINT32

Float : T_FLOAT
Float : T_FLOAT16
Float : T_FLOAT32
Float : T_FLOAT64

Strings : String
Strings : Strings String
String : T_STRING

TypeId : T_TYPE_ID
NonTypeId : T_NON_TYPE_ID

AsmDecl : T_KW_DECL ,{,
Asm : T_KW_ASM ,{,
AsmFragment : T_KW_ASM_FRAGMENT '{'
```

Index

T

Lightning Source UK Ltd.
Milton Keynes UK
UKOW041907140212

187305UK00006B/94/A